MEASURING GENUINE PROGRESS: AN APPLICATION OF THE GENUINE PROGRESS INDICATOR

MEASURING GENUINE PROGRESS:
AN APPLICATION OF THE GENUINE PROGRESS INDICATOR

PHILIP LAWN
AND
MATTHEW CLARKE

Nova Science Publishers, Inc.
New York

For permission to use material from this book please contact us:
Telephone 631-231-7269; Fax 631-231-8175
Web Site: http://www.novapublishers.com

NOTICE TO THE READER

The Publisher has taken reasonable care in the preparation of this book, but makes no expressed or implied warranty of any kind and assumes no responsibility for any errors or omissions. No liability is assumed for incidental or consequential damages in connection with or arising out of information contained in this book. The Publisher shall not be liable for any special, consequential, or exemplary damages resulting, in whole or in part, from the readers' use of, or reliance upon, this material.

This publication is designed to provide accurate and authoritative information with regard to the subject matter covered herein. It is sold with the clear understanding that the Publisher is not engaged in rendering legal or any other professional services. If legal or any other expert assistance is required, the services of a competent person should be sought. FROM A DECLARATION OF PARTICIPANTS JOINTLY ADOPTED BY A COMMITTEE OF THE AMERICAN BAR ASSOCIATION AND A COMMITTEE OF PUBLISHERS.

LIBRARY OF CONGRESS CATALOGING-IN-PUBLICATION DATA
Lawn, Philip A.
Measuring genuine progress : an application of the genuine progress indicator / Philip Lawn, Matthew Clarke.
    p. cm.
Includes index.
ISBN 1-60021-087-2
1. Gross domestic product--Australia--Victoria. 2. Gross state product--Australia--Victoria. 3. Sustainable development--Australia--Victoria. I. Clarke, Matthew. II. Title.
HC607.V53L39   2006
339.3--dc22   2006006510

Published by Nova Science Publishers, Inc. ✦ *New York*

CONTENTS

LIST OF FIGURES

LIST OF TABLES

PREFACE

This book has been written with the intention of taking the reader through the process of preparing a Genuine Progress Indicator (GPI). The book's presentation reflects the natural progression of identifying the deficiencies commonly found in widely used income-based measures of sustainable well-being; putting forward an alternative measure of sustainable well-being, such as the GPI; explaining how the GPI has been constructed and calculated; presenting and analysing the results of our study; drawing policy conclusions; acknowledging some of the criticisms directed towards the GPI (and defending it in the process); and, finally, concluding with a brief summary.

For those readers those seeking a deeper understanding of the book, Chapters 3-6 will be of most interest. Chapter 3 explains the GPI and the choice of the benefit and cost items used in its construction and calculation. While Chapter 4 involves an assessment of Victoria's GPI performance, Chapter 5 compares the Victorian GPI to that of the Rest-of-Australia. Chapter 6 presents the policy implications of the findings revealed in Chapters 4 and 5 and outlines various initiatives that we believe would increase the sustainable well-being of Victorians and, if implemented nationally, the sustainable well-being of all Australians generally.

Those with an interest in the motivation behind this study and why Gross Domestic Product (GDP) and Gross State Product (GSP) are inadequate indicators of sustainable well-being are directed towards Chapters 1 and 2 of the book.

Chapter 7 is important for those readers sceptical of the GPI methodology. Since the GPI is still a relatively new indicator of sustainable well-being, it would be churlish of us to ignore the criticisms directed towards it by its detractors. We have, therefore, outlined the main criticisms of the GPI in Chapter 7 and defended it where appropriate. Despite its weakness, we are convinced that the GPI is both theoretically and empirically valid.

As will become evident to the reader, the GPI involves a large number of calculations. To present the results in a meaningful manner, it is necessary to include a large number of tables and figures. To increase the ease of reading, we have incorporated the data sources and an explanation as to how each item is estimated (including the tables) in Chapter 9. In this sense, Chapter 9 serves as an appendix to the book.

Regardless of how the book is read, we hope that serious attention is given to the findings of our study and consideration is extended to the policy measures we have recommended.

Philip Lawn, Adelaide
Matthew Clarke, Melbourne
April 2006

ABOUT THE AUTHORS

Philip Lawn
    Faculty of Social Sciences
    Flinders University
    GPO Box 2100, Adelaide, SA, 5001
    Tel: (08) 8201 2838
    Fax: (08) 8201 5071
    E-mail: phil.lawn@flinders.edu.au

Matthew Clarke
    Social Sciences and Planning
    RMIT University
    GPO Box 2476V, Melbourne, Victoria, 3001
    Tel: (03) 9925 2960
    Fax: (03) 9925 1010
    E-mail: matthew.clarke@rmit.edu.au

DISCLAIMER

This book is a reworked version of a report prepared by the authors for the Victorian Department of Premier and Cabinet. The views expressed in this book do not necessarily reflect the policy of the Victorian Department of Premier and Cabinet.

Chapter 1

INTRODUCTION

1.1. THE AIMS AND MOTIVATION OF THE STUDY

It is more than twenty years since the Victorian Government first acknowledged that sustainable well-being does not rest solely on the rate of economic growth. In recognition of the important role played by non-economic goods and services in achieving a more prosperous, equitable, and fulfilling life for Victorians, the following was declared:

> "The principal aim of the Victorian Government is to develop in Victoria a community which possesses prosperity and a high standard of living. The prosperity should be based not only on the acquisition of goods but also on participation in a vigorous intellectual, social, and cultural life within the community. The government also seeks to facilitate an equitable access to this prosperity and to the quality of life which makes it possible, for all sections of the community, so that each member of the Victorian community can achieve both economic security and personal fulfilment" (Department of Budget and Management, 1984, p. 1).

While the social and environmental dimensions of sustainable well-being were somewhat overshadowed during the 1990s, they are again receiving the attention they deserve. Indeed, it is the re-emphasis on non-economic goods and services that has led to the calculation in this book of a Genuine Progress Indicator (GPI) for Australia, Victoria, and the Rest-of-Australia (Australia minus Victoria).

From the results of our research, we aim to reveal the extent to which the sustainable well-being of the average Victorian has advanced over the study period (1986-2003).[1] Second, we wish to show how well Victoria has performed relative to the Rest-of-Australia. Third, by comprehending the factors behind the trend movement in Victoria's GPI (including the link between the GPI and the growth rate of the Victorian economy), we believe a range of policy recommendations can be identified to advance the sustainable well-being of Victoria. We also believe that these policy recommendations are equally applicable to the remainder of Australia and other developed nations.

Four motivating factors have led us to conduct this study. The first is our concern that conventional macroeconomic indicators, such as Gross Domestic Product (GDP) and Gross State Product (GSP), fail to expose the full impact of economic growth on the well-being of the average citizen. Second, we are also fearful that GDP and GSP do not reveal the potential impact that economic growth has on the capacity of the natural environment to sustain economic welfare into the future.

Third, we believe that an absolute reliance on conventional macroeconomic indicators as a means to designing current and future policies may prove perilous. Without indicators to properly account for the full impact of economic growth on sustainable well-being, future policy measures are likely to lead a nation or state down an undesirable pathway where extrication will be both difficult and costly.

Our fourth motivating factor is the plethora of conflicting information relating to the economic, social, and environmental well-being of all Australians. For example, consider the following statistics that many commentators believe are Australia's most impressive macroeconomic fundamentals since the 1960s:

- The rate of growth in Australia's real GDP over the last 8 years has averaged 3.7% per annum (ABS, Catalogue No. 5204.0).
- With the variable home loan interest rate averaging 6.95% between December 1998 and December 2003, interest rates are at their lowest levels for over thirty years (www.infochoice.com.au/banking/news/ratewatch/historical.asp). As a way of comparison, the variable home loan interest rate averaged 12.58% between June 1980 and June 1995 (Foster, 1996, Table 3.21b).
- Barring the financial year following the introduction of the goods and services tax, the annual inflation rate has not exceeded 3.1% since 1996 (ABS, Catalogue No. 6401.0). In the year to September 2004, the Consumer Price Index rose by just 2.3% (RBA, Quarterly Statistical Release, 2004).
- The official unemployment rate as at December 2004 stood at 5.2% which, in today's labour market environment, is considered by some observers to be very close to full employment (ABS, Catalogue No. 6202.0).

Without seeking to downplay the significance of these numbers, it is worth acknowledging a comment made by the Deputy Prime Minister, John Anderson. In noting that not all Australians had benefited from the recent period of 'economic prosperity', John Anderson suggested that the social and moral dimension of economic growth was often neglected at great cost. At the same time, the South Australian Premier's Round Table on Sustainability recognised the potential environmental cost of economic growth by emphasising the need to operate within the absolute limits imposed by the natural environment (Premier's Round Table on Sustainability, 2004).

Given these two plus the earlier high-profiled reminder of the social and environmental dimensions of economic growth, it is therefore worth noting the following statistics that appear to conflict sharply with the macroeconomic 'good news' presented above:

- Based on conservative poverty estimates, one to two million Australians (i.e., 5-10% of the Australian population) live in a state of 'chronic poverty' (Senate Community Affairs Reference Committee, 2004).
- As at February 2003, an estimated 243,700 Australians had been unemployed for 52 weeks or more. Despite the official unemployment rate falling from 8.3% to 6.3% between October 1996 and February 2003, the number of long-term unemployed

people increased by 16,400 over the same period (ABS, Catalogue No. 6203.0). Furthermore, while the average duration of unemployment for people seeking full-time work fell by 9.5 weeks between December 1997 and February 2003, it was still an unacceptably high 51.2 weeks (ABS, Catalogue No. 6203.0).

- As at September 2003, 567,400 Australians were underemployed — i.e., people engaged in employment who wanted to work more hours. Of the 527,700 underemployed part-time workers, 72% of them wanted to work an additional ten or more hours per week (ABS, Catalogue No. 6265.0).

- Around one-quarter of Australian adults consider themselves overworked and, if it were practicable, would work fewer hours even if it resulted in a lower income (Breakspear and Hamilton, 2004).

- Measured in 2002-03 prices, Australia's foreign debt increased from $206.1 billion in 1994 to $357.2 billion in 2003. On a per capita basis, this constitutes a rise over the same period from $11,541 to $17,974 per Australian (ABS, Catalogue No. 5302.0).

- As at June 2004, Australia's total household debt stood at $796.5 billion or around $39,600 per person. This not only amounts to a 67.8% rise in real household debt since June 1999, it equates to 155% of household disposable income.

- The Commonwealth Bank's household affordability index (HIA) fell from around 165.0 in September 2000 to 105.7 in September 2004 (note: a fall in the HIA represents a decline in household affordability). As for Melbourne and the remainder of Victoria, the HIA was 98.8 and 139.1 respectively as at September 2004. The HIA for Melbourne fell by over 45 points from its September 2000 value of around 145.0 (CBA, 2004).

- Approximately two out of five Australian marriages currently end in divorce of which a little more than half of them involve children under 18 years of age (ABS, Catalogue No. 3307.0.55.001; Report of the House of Representatives Standing Committee on Legal and Constitutional Affairs, 1998). This imposes huge psychological costs on the people immediately affected as well as large financial costs on those directly concerned and society at large.

- Almost 60% of the Australian adult population is overweight or obese (Cameron et al., 2003). At current rates of increase, 70% of Australians will be above their healthy weight range by 2010 (ASSO, 2004).

- Approximately 18% of adult Australians suffered a mental disorder at some stage during 1996 (ABS, Catalogue No. 4326.0). Given that the main determinants of mental disorder have remained unchanged or have increased over the last seven years, it is reasonable to believe that around two to three million Australian adults are currently afflicted with a mental disorder of some description.

- According to the Intergovernmental Panel on Climate Change (IPCC), the 31% increase in carbon dioxide and 151% increase in methane levels in the earth's atmosphere over the last two centuries has already led to average global temperatures rising by between 0.4°C and 0.8°C (IPCC, 2001a). Should the world's consumption of energy continue to grow at its present rate, the IPCC predicts that global temperatures will rise between 1.4°C and 5.8°C by 2100. This is likely to result in the loss of 15-35% of the world's biodiversity and, in doing so, greatly reduce the life-support services provided by the natural environment (IPCC, 2001b). As for Australia, it is predicted that climate change will dramatically increase the frequency and magnitude of droughts, thereby placing enormous pressure on a country already stressed by water supply shortages.

- Land clearance in Australia averaged 400,000 hectares per year between 1993 and 2003. In Victoria, however, it averaged just 2,450 hectares per year over the same decade (Graetz et al., 1995; Biodiversity Unit, 1995; ABS, Catalogue No. 1370.0; ABS, Catalogue No. 4613.0). Land clearance greatly reduces the integrity of remaining ecological systems, contributes to greenhouse gas emissions (i.e., by releasing carbon dioxide sequestered in native vegetation), and promotes dryland salinity in Australia's high salinity-prone areas.

- Australia's per capita energy consumption — a major contributor to air pollution and greenhouse gas emissions — increased from 231.1 Petajoules per person in 1993 to 270.0 Petajoules per person in 2004 (ABS, Catalogue No. 4604.0 and 1301.0 (various)). This constitutes a 16.8% increase. In Victoria, per capita energy consumption rose over the same period from 247.1 to 295.4 Petajoules per person — an increase of 19.6%.

In view of this latter suite of alarming statistics, we believe it is reasonable to ask whether the sustainable well-being of the average Australian and Victorian has been rising and, if so, to what extent has it advanced in recent times? In considering these questions, we believe two further questions need to be posed and adequately answered:

- To what extent do GDP and GSP reveal the sustainable progress of Australia and Victoria?
- Why is that GDP, GSP, the inflation rate, interest rates, and official rates of unemployment are included in the category of statistical 'fundamentals' but not the social and environmental impacts of economic growth?

Similar questions to these have already been raised in the past. Efforts undertaken to answer them have led to various GPI studies around the world. Almost all such studies involve the calculation of the GPI at the national level.[2] Examples include GPI estimates of the USA, Canada, the UK, most European and Scandinavian countries, Japan, Thailand, and Chile. Figure 1.1 compares the GPI and GDP of six individual countries. As the figure indicates, there is a tendency, at first, for the GPI to closely follow the upward trend of GDP. However, once GDP reaches an apparent 'threshold' level, the GPI ceases to rise and, in some cases, begins to decline. For virtually all developed countries, this countermoving trend occurred in the 1970s or early 1980s.[3]

We would like to point out that the GPI has also been calculated for Australia (see, for example, Hamilton, 1999). The methodology used in this book differs slightly to previous Australian GPI studies largely because of the incomparability of some national and state-based data. Unavoidably, this has demanded a slightly improvised approach on our part.

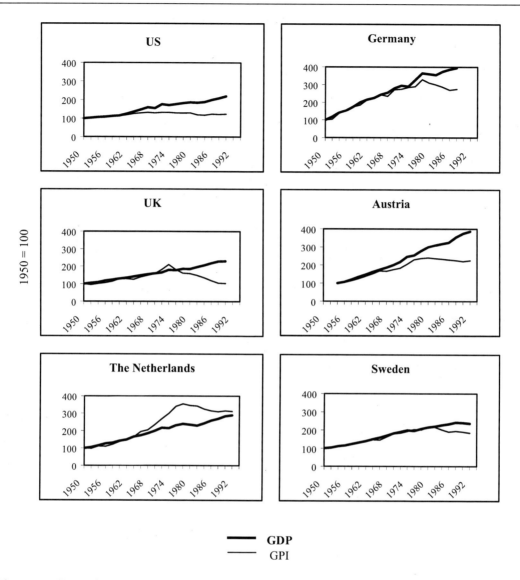

Figure 1.1. Comparison of the GPI and GDP for the USA, Germany, UK, Austria, The Netherlands, and Sweden (Jackson and Stymne, 1996)

Returning back to Figure 1.1, the message it conveys is quite clear — indiscriminate economic growth or economic growth beyond a certain level may be detrimental to sustainable well-being. We believe it is vital to know whether a similar trend movement of the GPI exists for both Australia and Victoria. If it indeed does, it may be necessary for the Victorian and the larger Australian economy to begin a transition to a lower rate of economic growth. In addition, advancing the GPI will require a greater policy focus on qualitative improvement (including greater resource use efficiency), distributional equity, and natural capital maintenance.

1.2. The Structure of the Book

To achieve our aims, this book is structured as follows. In Chapter 2, we explain why the commonly used economic statistics of GDP and GSP are inadequate indicators of sustainable well-being. Following this, in Chapter 3, we explain why the GPI is a far superior indicator of sustainable well-being. In this particular chapter, we fully outline both the rationale for the GPI and the methodology used in its calculation.

The results of the GPI study of Victoria and the Rest-of-Australia (Australia minus Victoria) are presented and analysed in Chapters 4 and 5. By showing why the per capita GPI of Victoria differs to both Victoria's per capita GSP and the per capita GPI of the Rest-of-Australia, we identify and propose a range of policy initiatives in Chapter 6 to raise the sustainable well-being of the average Victorian. Should such policies be implemented, we believe the performance of Victoria *vis-a-vis* the Rest-of-Australia would be further strengthened.

Of course, some degree of caution should always be adopted when a study relies so heavily on one particular indicator. With this in mind, we point out some of the weaknesses of the GPI in Chapter 7. Nonetheless, we are quick to stress that the calculation of GDP and GSP is not without its own methodological and valuation frailties. Since much of the GPI weakness lies in the lack of comprehensive data sources, we put forward some suggestions to facilitate the establishment of a more informative indicator framework. It is our belief that such a framework would greatly improve the reliability of future GPI studies.

In Chapter 8, we summarise our findings, conclusions, and policy recommendations. Finally, in Chapter 9, we reveal the valuation methods and data sources used in the calculation of the nineteen items that make up the GPI. Also included in this final chapter is a series of tables showing how the final value of each item was derived. In this way, the book doubles as a 'manual' to assist other researchers wanting to calculate the GPI at the state/provincial or national level.

Notes

[1] Since the study is based on financial rather than calendar years, all values revealed for a particular year are the values as they stood at the end of June in that year (e.g., June 2003 in the case of 2003).

[2] To our knowledge, the GPI has only been calculated at the state or provincial level in two separate cases — for the American State of Vermont (Costanza et. al, 2004) and the Canadian province of Alberta (Anielski, 2001).

[3] See Clarke and Islam (forthcoming) for a GPI study of a developing country — namely, Thailand.

Chapter 2

WHY ARE GROSS DOMESTIC PRODUCT (GDP) AND GROSS STATE PRODUCT (GSP) INADEQUATE INDICATORS OF SUSTAINABLE WELL-BEING?

2.1. WHAT IS GDP AND GSP?

GDP is a monetary measure of the goods and services annually produced by domestically *located* factors of production (i.e., by the natural and human-made capital located in a particular country). By natural capital, we mean forests, sub-soil assets, fisheries, water resources, and critical ecosystems. Human-made capital, on the other hand, includes the stock of producer goods (e.g., plant, machinery, and equipment) that is used to produce consumer goods and replacement producer goods.

GDP can be measured in *nominal* or *real* values. If GDP is measured in nominal values, it is measured in terms of the prices at the time of production. On the other hand, if GDP is measured in real values, it is measured in terms of the prices of all goods and services in a particular year — often referred to as the base year.

In order to clarify the difference between real and nominal GDP, consider the following basic identity to describe a nation's nominal GDP in 2001-02:

$$\text{nominal GDP}_{2001\text{-}02} = P_{2001\text{-}02} \times Q_{2001\text{-}02} \tag{2.1}$$

where:

- P = the price index of goods and services as at June 2002;
- Q = quantity of goods and services produced during the 2001-02 financial year.

As can be seen from (2.1), the nominal GDP in 2001-02 involves the quantity of goods and services produced during the 2001-02 financial year being multiplied by their prices at the time of production. Assume, now, that the 2003-2004 financial year was chosen as the base year to calculate the real GDP in any particular financial year. The real GDP of 2001-02 would subsequently be measured in terms of the prices of all goods and services as at June 2004. It would thus be:

$$\text{real GDP}_{2001\text{-}02} = P_{2003\text{-}04} \times Q_{2001\text{-}02} \tag{2.2}$$

where:

- P = the price index of goods and services as at June 2004;
- Q = quantity of goods and services produced during the 2001-02 financial year.

Now imagine that we wish to compare the real GDP for each year over a three-year period from 2001-02 to 2003-04. The real GDP for each year would be:

$$\text{real GDP}_{2001\text{-}02} = P_{2003\text{-}04} \times Q_{2001\text{-}02} \tag{2.3}$$

$$\text{real GDP}_{2002\text{-}03} = P_{2003\text{-}04} \times Q_{2002\text{-}03} \tag{2.4}$$

$$\text{real GDP}_{2003\text{-}04} = P_{2003\text{-}04} \times Q_{2003\text{-}04} \tag{2.5}$$

Note that the only 'flexible' variable in each case is the quantity of goods and services produced during the financial year (Q). The prices used to value the goods and services (P) remain constant at $P_{2003\text{-}04}$. By keeping all prices fixed in terms of a base year, annual changes in real GDP reflect differences in the quantity of goods and services produced from year to year. It is for this reason that real GDP is often preferred to nominal GDP in discussions relating to national well-being. It should also be noted that real GDP and nominal GDP are only the same in the base year since, unlike any other year, both are measured in terms of the prices of goods and services during that year.

Why is important to make a distinction between real and nominal values? In simplistic terms, imagine that the price index for the 2003-04 financial year was $10.00 (i.e., $P_{2003\text{-}04}$ = $10.00) and the quantity of goods and services produced during the 2003-04 financial year numbered ten million (i.e., $Q_{2003\text{-}04}$ = 10 million). The nominal GDP for the 2003-04 financial year would be:

$$\text{nominal GDP}_{2003\text{-}04} = P_{2003\text{-}04} \times Q_{2003\text{-}04} \tag{2.6}$$

$$\text{nominal GDP}_{2003\text{-}04} = \$10.00 \times 10 \text{ million} \tag{2.7}$$

$$\text{nominal GDP}_{2003\text{-}04} = \$100 \text{ million} \tag{2.8}$$

Let's assume that over the next financial year, 2004-05, eleven million goods and services were produced. At the same time, inflation was 5% such that the price index for the 2004-05 financial year was $10.50 (i.e., $P_{2004\text{-}05}$ = $10.50). We shall assume that the 5% inflation rate was caused by monetary policy settings by the Reserve Bank of Australia and had nothing to do with the nature of the goods and services produced during the 2004-05 financial year. The nominal GDP for 2004-05 would be:

$$\text{nominal GDP}_{2004\text{-}05} = P_{2004\text{-}05} \times Q_{2004\text{-}05} \tag{2.9}$$

nominal GDP$_{2004-05}$ = $10.50 × 11 million   (2.10)

nominal GDP$_{2004-05}$ = $115.5 million   (2.11)

By comparing (2.8) and (2.11), it is quite evident that nominal GDP has risen by 15.5% from 2003-04 to 2004-05. If we happened to be using GDP as an indicator of national well-being, could we subsequently claim that the citizens of this fictitious nation were 15.5% better off at the end of the 2004-05 financial year? No we could not because a significant factor underlying the rise in nominal GDP is the 5% rise in prices. Inflation, itself, generates no welfare-related benefit. However, if we were to consider the real GDP for 2004-05 based on 2003-04 prices (i.e., based on a price index of P$_{2003-04}$ = $10.00), we would obtain:

real GDP$_{2004-05}$ = P$_{2003-04}$ × Q$_{2004-05}$ (2.12)

real GDP$_{2004-05}$ = $10.00 × 11 million   (2.13)

real GDP$_{2004-05}$ = $110 million   (2.14)

A comparison of (2.8) and (2.14) reveals that real GDP has increased by 10% — the same percentage rise as the increase in the quantity of goods and services produced from 2003-04 to 2004-05 (note: nominal and real GDP in 2003-04 are the same given 2003-04 is our base year). Thus, if there is any truth in the fact that real GDP is an adequate indicator of a nation's well-being, it is because real GDP is able to reflect the percentage rise in the quantity of goods and services produced from one financial year to the next.

What, then, is GSP? GSP is exactly the same as GDP except that GSP refers to the goods and services annually produced by the factors of production located in a particular state, not country. GSP will therefore be referred to in relation to Victoria and GDP in relation to both Australia and Rest-of-Australia.

For the purposes of this book, real GDP and real GSP are used rather than nominal GDP and nominal GSP. The base year chosen for the calculation of all real values is the 2002-03 financial year. That is, the real values of all the benefits and costs applicable to sustainable well-being are measured in terms of market prices as at June 2003.

One final point of clarification. Most readers would have come across Gross National Product (GNP). GNP is much the same as GDP except that it measures the monetary value of the goods and services annually produced by domestically *owned* rather than domestically located factors of production (i.e., by the natural and human-made capital owned by the citizens of a particular country). Since it is customary to use GDP instead of GNP in relation to national well-being, GNP will not be referred to in this book.

2.2. THE SHORTCOMINGS ASSOCIATED WITH GDP AND GSP AS MEASURES OF SUSTAINABLE WELL-BEING

The best way to embark on an assessment of GDP and GSP is to first consider whether they serve as adequate measures of national and state income. While income is a rather blurry concept, most observers agree that income is best defined in the John Hicks tradition as the maximum amount that can be produced and consumed over a specific period without undermining the capacity to produce and consume the same amount in the future (Hicks, 1946). The key aspect of this definition is the need to keep income-generating capital intact. Failure to do so means essentially two things. First, the ability to sustain the same level of output over time is compromised, and second, the current level of output overstates 'true' income. Indeed, the overstated portion of income effectively equals the amount by which income-generating capital has been drawn upon to augment current output.

To understand the Hicksian concept of income, consider the following simple example of a timber plantation. The plantation consists of 1,000 cubic metres of timber that regenerates at 5% per annum. So long as the maximum quantity of timber harvested each year does not exceed 50 cubic metres (i.e., 1,000 m³ x 0.05), the plantation will generate a sustainable supply of timber into the future. What, however, if 100 cubic metres of timber is extracted each year? At the end of the first year, 950 cubic metres of timber will remain. That is:

Beginning of first year	1,000 m³ of timber
During the first year	
timber regeneration (1,000 m³ x 0.05)	+ 50 m³ of timber
timber extracted	− 100 m³ of timber
End of the first year	950 m³ of timber

At the end of the second year, 897.5 cubic metres of timber will remain. That is:

Beginning of second year	950 m³ of timber
During the second year	
timber regeneration (100 m³ x 0.05)	+ 47.5 m³ of timber
timber extracted	− 100 m³ of timber
End of the second year	897.5 m³ of timber

It is not too difficult to see that, should this harvesting policy continue, the timber plantation will eventually cease to exist. Given the definition of income suggested by Hicks, would it be justifiable to regard the 100 cubic metres of timber harvested each year as income? The answer is no. Assuming that all the timber harvested is consumed and not used to establish a replacement asset, only 50 cubic metres of the timber harvested in the first year can be classified as income. The other 50 cubic metres constitutes the depletion or drawing down of income-generating capital — namely, the timber plantation itself. In the second year, only 47.5 cubic metres of the 100 cubic metres can be classified as income, with 52.5 cubic metres equating to capital depletion.

What does this mean for GDP and GSP? In order to constitute first approximations of national and state income, it is necessary to determine what portion of both GDP and GSP involve the depletion of income-generating capital. This refers not only to natural capital but also human-made capital since some portion of GDP or GSP must be set aside to replace worn out and depreciated producer goods such as plant, machinery, and equipment. Consequently, the portion of a nation's or state's output that is required to maintain income-generating capital intact ought not to be used for current consumption purposes. This portion cannot, therefore, be classed as true income.

In addition to this, there are other elements of a nation's or state's annual output that are used for defensive and rehabilitative purposes that, in turn, assist in sustaining output over time. For example, vehicle accident repairs and some medical procedures take place to restore human beings and their productive instruments to something approximating their previous condition. In doing so, the output generated in both instances is not used directly for consumption purposes — it is produced merely to maintain the productivity of human beings, as labour, and existing human-made capital.

Examples of output produced for defensive purposes include flood mitigation projects and crime prevention measures. Somewhat differently, however, output generated in these circumstances occurs to prevent future economic activity from impacting deleteriously on the existing stock of natural and human-made capital (i.e., to minimise future rehabilitative expenditures).

Not unlike the depreciation of human-made and human-made capital, the value of all output produced for rehabilitative and defensive purposes cannot be directly consumed without undermining the capacity to sustain future output. Nor, then, can it be classed as true income.

In all, it has been suggested that a better measure of national income can be calculated by subtracting from GDP the value of depreciated human-made capital and depleted natural capital as well as all defensive and rehabilitative expenditures. Thus, Hicksian national income can be calculated by adhering to the following formula (Daly, 1996):[1]

Hicksian national income = GDP – DEP – DNC – DRE   (2.15)

where:

- GDP = Gross Domestic Product
- DEP = depreciation of human-made capital (producer goods)
- DNC = depletion of natural capital
- DRE = defensive and rehabilitative expenditures.

To calculate Hicksian state income, the same formula would be used except GDP would be replaced by GSP. In addition, the various items subtracted would be estimated at the state level.

Let's assume that we make an adjustment to GDP and GSP as per equation (2.15). We will now possess better measures of national and state income, but will we possess appropriate indicators of sustainable well-being. An increasing number of observers believe not. Why? Whilst Hicksian income measures the quantity of goods and services that can be sustainably produced and consumed, this alone does not encapsulate the full impact of a growing national or state economy on human well-being. Still overlooked by Hicksian income are the following:

- non-market production such as non-paid household and volunteer work;

- the social costs of economic activity such as the cost of unemployment (both observable and hidden), underemployment, and labour underutilisation; the cost of crime; and the cost of family breakdown;
- the impact of a rising foreign debt;
- and the welfare implications of a change in the distribution of income.

The last point is an interesting one for the following reason. Imagine that Hicksian national income remained unchanged from one financial year to the next. Imagine, also, that the richest family's share of Hicksian income increased by $100 per week at the exact expense of the poorest family's share. We shall assume that the welfare contribution made by Hicksian national income to all other citizens remained unchanged. What would happen to the well-being of the richest and the poorest families? Presumably the well-being of the richest family would, *ceteris paribus*, increase very little since the extra $100 per week would impact negligibly on its spending patterns. However, the $100 per week decline in the income of the nation's poorest family would have dire ramifications for its general well-being. Overall, the aggregate well-being of the nation will have fallen but the constancy of Hicksian national income will not reflect this change. As a consequence, there are a number of commentators calling for an adjustment of sort to reflect the welfare-related impact of a changing distribution of income over time.

While the other overlooked aspects listed above are somewhat self-explanatory, three additional factors are not. The first concerns the very nature of what is being produced and subsequently consumed. If Hicksian income is rising, it implies that the quantity of goods and services that can be sustainably produced and consumed is increasing. But surely the nature of the goods being produced and consumed also matters in relation to human well-being? After all, it is possible to produce and consume more goods that contribute little extra to human well-being, yet also produce the same quantity of superior goods and services and be considerably better off. Because Hicksian income only captures the quantitative element of production and consumption, it fails to capture the qualitative dimension associated with production excellence.

May we just highlight that the qualitative conundrum also besets the GPI. Some experimental work is currently being undertaken to incorporate qualitative factors into the calculation of the GPI. In addition, Clarke and Islam (2004) have integrated normative social choice theory into their study of Thailand to account for the different cultural interpretations of sustainable well-being. This latter approach has the potential to permit qualitative adjustments to some of the items that make up the GPI. The methodologies being adopted in both cases will not, however, be employed in this study. Nevertheless, we will be making some assumptions about the various categories of consumption (e.g., alcoholic beverages, cigarettes, and tobacco products) that will lay the foundation for three separate GPI values. This will be further discussed in Chapters 3 and 9.

The second additional overlooked factor is the timing of welfare-related consumption. Quite a significant proportion of consumption expenditure involves the purchase of consumer durables such as cars, televisions, refrigerators, etc. Consider someone who has just purchased a $2,000 television set. Will he or she receive an immediate $2,000 boost in well-being in the same they would receive an immediate $2.50 benefit from purchasing and consuming a fresh but perishable sandwich? The answer is, of course, no. If the television has been purchased on the assumption that it will endure for ten years — i.e., provide the desired transmission service for a decade — the person in question will effectively receive an annual $200 benefit over the lifetime of the television ($2,000 ÷ 10 years). It is clearly incorrect to count the initial $2,000 purchase as a consumption-related benefit during the financial year in which the television was purchased. Yet Hicksian income, like GDP and GSP, treats the full amount of the initial purchase in this manner. Worse still, it overlooks the consumption-related benefits that the television provides in future years.

It has therefore been suggested that all but expenditure on non-durable goods should be subtracted from a measure of well-being in the year in which the expenditure takes place, and that the service provided by existing durable goods should be added. The latter can be achieved by keeping track of the value of the stock of consumer durables; by assuming that the stock depreciates or is 'consumed' at a particular rate (e.g., 10% per annum for a stock of consumer durables that, on average, endures for ten years); and multiplying the value of the stock by the depreciation or consumption rate. The figure calculated equates to the annual service derived from the existing stock of consumer durables.

The final overlooked factor relates to investment expenditure — that is, the accumulation of producer goods such as plant, machinery, and equipment. It has already been pointed out that, in order to calculate Hicksian national and state income, one must subtract from GDP and GSP the value of the output required to keep human-made capital intact. However, unlike investment in most forms of natural capital, the level of investment in human-made capital invariably exceeds this requisite amount. That is, net capital investment (NCI) — which equals gross investment in human-made capital minus its depreciation — is usually positive.

Since Hicksian income represents the quantity of producer goods as well as consumer goods that can be sustainably produced over time, it is entirely legitimate to include net capital investment in a more appropriate measure of national or state income. But this is not the case with sustainable well-being since what we desire is an indicator that reflects the *welfare* experienced in a specific financial year.

If one considers investment more closely, it effectively amounts to deprived or sacrificed consumption that is undertaken to provide the means required to generate a particular level of future consumption. In a sense, then, current consumption and current net capital investment are the antithesis of each other. The first involves a form of conduct that generates welfare in the present; the second involves a deliberative action in the present that is designed to generate future welfare. To count current net capital investment as welfare-enhancing in the present is logically erroneous.

Does this mean that net capital investment will be overlooked in a measure of sustainable well-being? No, because, to a large extent, the benefit of net capital investment will be felt in future years in terms of future consumption-related welfare. So long as the indicator used to measure sustainable well-being during a particular financial year includes expenditure on non-durable consumption goods during that year, past net capital investment — that is, past sacrificed consumption — will be predominantly captured by the indicator. Better still, it will be captured during the period in which the consumption-related welfare is experienced.

Having said this, not all investment expenditure is directed towards the replacement or accumulation of producer goods. Nor is it ultimately reflected in consumption expenditure over subsequent years. For example, a large percentage of publicly-funded investment expenditure (e.g., capital works) involves the construction of roads, bridges, and highways, of schools and hospitals, and of museums, galleries, and libraries. The benefits of this spending flow to the general public in a similar way that services flow from the possessors of consumer durables — i.e., as publicly-provided service capital depreciates through its use. The benefits are not experienced during the financial year that the expenditure takes place. Yet, once again, Hicksian income: (a) treats the full amount of this form of investment expenditure as if this were the case, and (b) ignores the welfare benefits that publicly-provided service capital provides in future years.

2.3. CONCLUDING COMMENTS

GDP and GSP, which are better measured in real rather than nominal terms, are inadequate indicators of sustainable well-being. To begin with, they are poor measures of national and state income. But even if GDP and GSP are adjusted to ascertain closer approximations of the quantity of goods and services that can be sustainably produced and consumed over time, both indicators fail to encapsulate the full impact of a growing national or state economy on sustainable well-being. GDP and GSP not only ignore non-market production, they overlook many social costs, such as the cost unemployment and family breakdown, and make no allowance for the impact that a change in the distribution of income can have on aggregate welfare.

The deficiencies of GDP and GSP — as well as Hicksian income — are also evident in the fact that they only reflect the quantitative element of production and consumption, not the qualitative dimension. In addition, the calculation of GDP and GSP assumes that all current consumption expenditure is welfare-enhancing in the present when, to the contrary, current expenditure on consumer durables generates welfare benefits in future years. The value of all current expenditure on consumer durables should therefore be dispersed over the period in which consumer durables generate useful service to their possessors. The same erroneous assumption is made with respect to publicly-provided service capital and, as such, should be treated in the same manner as consumer durables.

Finally, not unlike expenditure on consumer durables, the computation of GDP, GSP, and Hicksian income are based on the erroneous assumption that net capital investment constitutes a current welfare benefit. The benefits of net capital investment are, however, experienced in terms of future consumption. Thus, in relation to sustainable well-being, the inclusion of net capital investment in measures of GDP, GSP, and Hicksian income is an example of double-counting. It should therefore be omitted.

While it is true that GDP and GSP were never designed to be indicators of sustainable well-being, they are falsely used as if they are. As a consequence, policy-makers continue to steer national and state economies with the wrong economic compass. It is high time that policy-makers utilise a more appropriate compass when designing welfare-enhancing policies. We believe the solution lies, in part, with the deployment of the Genuine Progress Indicator.

NOTE

[1] See Barkley and Seckler (1972) for a similar approach.

Chapter 3

WHAT IS THE GENUINE PROGRESS INDICATOR (GPI)AND HOW IS IT CALCULATED?

3.1. WHAT IS THE GENUINE PROGRESS INDICATOR (GPI)?

The Genuine Progress Indicator (GPI) is a recently established indicator specifically designed to ascertain the impact of a growing economy on sustainable well-being. Comprised of many individual benefit and cost items (19 items in the case of this book), the GPI integrates the wide-ranging impacts of economic growth into a single monetary-based index. As such, the GPI includes benefits and costs of the social and environmental kind as well as those of the standard economic variety. Whilst the GPI embraces some of the national accounting values used in the computation of GDP and GSP, its calculation accounts for a number of benefits and costs that normally escape market valuation.

If one compares the various GPI studies undertaken over the last decade, it is immediately apparent that the list of items used to arrive at the final index value have varied over time, as have some of the valuation methods (see, for instance, Diefenbacher, 1994; Moffatt and Wilson, 1994; Rosenberg and Oegema, 1995; Jackson and Stymne, 1996; Jackson et al., 1997; Stockhammer et al., 1997; Guenno and Tiezzi, 1998; Castaneda, 1999; Hamilton, 1999; Lawn and Sanders 1999; Lawn, 2000a; and Clarke and Islam, 2004). The reason for these disparities is usually related to the availability of data and the preference researchers have for specific valuation methods. Naturally, the lack of a consistent methodology is a major weakness of the GPI that has evoked criticism from many of its detractors. This issue is further discussed in Chapter 7.

3.2. HOW IS THE GPI RELATED TO THE INDEX OF SUSTAINABLE ECONOMIC WELFARE (ISEW)?

Some readers will be aware of a similar index to the GPI called the Index of Sustainable Economic Welfare (ISEW). The two indexes essentially differ in name only, although, not unlike the GPI itself, there are variations in the items used and the valuation methods employed in their calculation.

The index was initially labelled an ISEW because the original designers believed it would better reflect the *economic welfare* associated with economic activity and, by including resource depletion and pollution costs, incorporate a *sustainability* element similar to that of Hicksian income (see Daly and Cobb, 1989). Thus, 'ISEW' was chosen as a functional name to describe its statistical purpose.

It is becoming increasingly common for updated calculations of the index to be referred to as the GPI. The reason for the name alteration has nothing to do with changes in the rationale or theoretical foundation supporting the two indexes which, it should be added, are identical in every way (Lawn, 2003). The preference for GPI is primarily motivated by a desire to raise the profile of the index and to increase the public appeal for an alternative to GDP and GSP.

3.3. THE SUSTAINABLE NET BENEFIT INDEX (SNBI)

Another less-known variation of the GPI and ISEW is the Sustainable Net Benefit Index (SNBI). Once again, there is little disparity between the SNBI methodology and that of the GPI and ISEW. Where the SNBI does differ is in the explanation of the rationale for an alternative index and the presentation of the items used in its calculation (Lawn and Sanders, 1999; Lawn, 2000a and 2003). Rather than having all the items presented in one table (such as Table 3.1), the SNBI involves their dichotomisation into sperate 'benefit' and 'cost' accounts.

The SNBI is obtained by subtracting the total of the cost account from the benefit account. The potential advantage of this approach over the GPI and ISEW is that it directly compares the benefits and costs of a growing economy. In so doing, it strengthens its own theoretical case as well as that of the GPI and ISEW.

3.4. THE ITEMS USED TO CONSTRUCT AND CALCULATE THE GPI

Since the aim of the GPI is to provide a more appropriate measure of sustainable well-being, its construction is primarily based on overcoming the shortcomings associated with GDP, GSP, and Hicksian income that were discussed in Chapter 2. Table 3.1 lists the items used to construct the GPI. The table also reveals the valuation method used in the estimation of each item and whether the item contributes positively (+) or negatively (–) to sustainable well-being. The rationale for the inclusion of each item will now be given along with the justification for the selected valuation method. A full explanation of the valuation methods and how the value of each item has been calculated is provided in Chapter 9.

3.4.1. Consumption Expenditure (Private and Public) (CON)

Unlike Hicksian income, where the foundation item for its calculation is GDP (see equation (2.15)), the construction of the GPI begins with consumption expenditure. The reason for this contrasting approach is simple. As explained previously, some portion of a

Table 3.1: Items and the valuation methods used to calculate the GPI

Item	Welfare impact	Method of valuation
Consumption expenditure (CON) • CON(1) • CON(2) • CON(3)	+	CON = private + public consumption expenditure • No change to CON • Changes to CON as per Table 3.2 • Changes to CON as per CON(2) plus others described in Table 3.2
Expenditure on consumer durables (ECD)	–	ECD equals the sum of private expenditure on clothing, footwear, furnishings, household equipment, and vehicle purchases
Service from consumer durables (SCD)	+	Service equals the depreciation value of existing consumer durables (depreciation rate of stock assumed to be 10% per annum) • SCD = 0.1 × value of consumer durables
Adjusted consumption • Adjusted CON(1) • Adjusted CON(2) • Adjusted CON(3)		Timing adjustment of consumption benefits • CON(1) – ECD + SCD • CON(2) – ECD + SCD • CON(3) – ECD + SCD
Distribution Index (DI)	+/–	DI based on the change in income distribution over the study period (1986 = 100.0)
Adjusted consumption (weighted) (**) • Adjusted CON(1) (weighted) • Adjusted CON(2) (weighted) • Adjusted CON(3) (weighted)		Adjusted CON(1), CON(2), and CON(3) weighted by the DI • Adjusted CON(1) ÷ DI × 100 • Adjusted CON(2) ÷ DI × 100 • Adjusted CON(3) ÷ DI × 100
Welfare generated by publicly-provided service capital (**)	+	Welfare assumed to equal 75% of public sector consumption of fixed capital
Value of non-paid household labour (**)	+	Non-paid household labour is valued using the net opportunity cost method
Value of volunteer labour (**)	+	Volunteer labour is valued using the net opportunity cost method

Table 3.1. Continued

Item	Welfare impact	Method of valuation
Cost of unemployment, underemployment, and labour underutilisation (**)	–	Calculated by multiplying the CU8 number of underutilised labour by the estimated cost per unemployed person
Cost of crime (**)	–	Calculated by multiplying various crime indexes by the estimated cost of each crime category
Cost of family breakdown (**)	–	Calculated by multiplying the approximate number of dysfunctional families (based on divorce numbers) by the estimated cost per family breakdown
Change in foreign debt position (**)	+/–	Annual cost equal to the change in net foreign liabilities from one financial year to the next
Cost of non-renewable resource depletion (*)	–	Calculated by using the El Serafy (1989) 'user cost' formula to determine the amount to set aside to sustain a flow of income equal to that generated by the exhausted resource
Cost of lost agricultural land (*)	–	Calculated to reflect the amount required to compensate citizens for the cumulative impact of past and present agricultural practices
Cost of irrigation water use (*)	–	Calculated to reflect the amount required to compensate citizens for the cumulative impact of excessive irrigation water use
Cost of timber depletion (*)	–	Calculated by using the El Serafy (1989) formula to determine cost where rate of extraction exceeds the rate of regeneration and plantation establishment
Cost of air pollution (*)	–	Calculated by weighting the estimated 1992 cost of air pollution by an air pollution index
Cost of urban waster-water pollution (*)	–	Calculated by weighting the estimated 1994 cost of urban waster-water pollution by a waste-water pollution technology index
Cost of long-term environmental damage (*)	–	Calculated to reflect the amount required to compensate citizens for the long-term environmental impact of energy consumption

Table 3.1. Continued

Item	Welfare impact	Method of valuation
Lost natural capital services (LNCS)		Sum of (*) items. The LNCS sub-total reflects the cost of sacrificing some of the source, sink, and life-support services provided by natural capital
Ecosystem Health Index (EHI)	+/–	EHI based on the change in remnant vegetation
Weighted LNCS (**)		LNCS weighted by EHI (LNCS ÷ 100 × EHI)
Genuine Progress Indicator (GPI) • GPI(1) • GPI(2) • GPI(3)		Sum of (**) items • Beginning with Adjusted CON(1) (weighted) • Beginning with Adjusted CON(2) (weighted) • Beginning with Adjusted CON(3) (weighted)
Population		Population of study region
Per capita GPI • Per capita GPI(1) • Per capita GPI(2) • Per capita GPI(3)		GPI ÷ population • GPI(1) ÷ population • GPI(2) ÷ population • GPI(3) ÷ population

Understandably, a great number of people question the idea of using consumption expenditure as a base item for a measure of sustainable well-being. After all, consumption is often blamed for most contemporary concerns regarding environmental degradation, social fragmentation, and the inability of many to live a purposeful and more satisfying life (Hamilton, 2003). While we harbour similar concerns about 'consumerism', it should be noted that, firstly, consumption unquestionably yields welfare-related benefits. Just how much is a point of conjecture that we have chosen not to debate in this book. Thus, apart from the impact of a changing distribution of income, we assume that the first dollar of consumption expenditure yields the same welfare benefit as the last.

Second, increased consumption also comes at a welfare cost since, presumably, it demands greater work effort that can lead to ill-health, relationship damage, and family breakdown. Furthermore, unless there is greater efficiency of resource use, an increased amount of consumption results in a higher rate of resource depletion, pollution, and ecosystem destruction. As can be seen from Table 3.1, these costs are captured by many of the items of which the GPI is comprised. The consumption expenditure item merely captures the welfare benefit of consumption that cannot be ignored or denied. While it is true that an increase in consumption will exert a positive influence on the GPI, it is possible for the GPI to fall if the social and environmental costs increase at a more accelerated rate.

We therefore think it best that consumption be classed as a 'necessary evil'. It is necessary in the sense that one must consume and, in a sense, destroy goods to experience the benefit they yield.[1] But if more consumption can be enjoyed without having to place greater strain on families, social relationships, and the natural environment, the evil side-effects of consumption can be contained. In turn, this will cause the GPI to rise. Equivalently, the GPI will also rise if the same level of consumption is enjoyed and the many social and environmental costs that make up the GPI are reduced in magnitude.

Overall, electing to have consumption expenditure as the base item of the GPI does not mean that consumption must increase for the GPI to rise. Nor does it mean that the GPI cannot rise if consumption is falling.

In Chapter 2, we pointed out that defensive and rehabilitative expenditures should not be considered welfare-enhancing for the reason that they merely serve to maintain and restore the productive capacity of the economy. Although a clear benefit emerges from such expenditure, it is not felt in the present but in later years by way of future consumption. To include consumption expenditure along with defensive and rehabilitative spending would therefore amount to double-counting. Since a great deal of consumption expenditure includes spending of a defensive and rehabilitative nature, we believe it is necessary to identify and subtract this form of spending.

In addition to this, we also discussed the qualitative dimension of consumption and our desire to make certain assumptions about the nature of various goods consumed. With this in mind, three separate measures of consumption expenditure are set out in Table 3.2. Each measure forms the basis for three different GPI estimates. The first, CON(1), involves no adjustment to the consumption expenditure values drawn from the system of national and state accounts.

The second, CON(2), involves an adjustment to consumption expenditure based on the assumption that cigarettes, tobacco products, and half of all expenditure on alcoholic beverages do not contribute to sustainable well-being. Also included is a defensive expenditure adjustment relating to rent and other dwelling services, and an adjustment to health expenditure based on the assumption that half of all such spending is defensive or rehabilitative in character. Finally, an adjustment is also made to the government component of final consumption expenditure on the understanding that government spending has a substantial 'public goods' element which, by its very nature, is predominantly of the defensive kind.

CON(3), the third measure of consumption expenditure, involves a more austere array of defensive and rehabilitative expenditure adjustments. While its estimation includes the adjustments made to arrive at CON(2), it is further assumed that a defensive component exists in relation to spending on food; electricity, gas, and fuel; the operation of vehicles; transport services; communications; hotels, cafes, and restaurants; and insurance and other financial services. The assumed defensive component is outlined in the right-hand column of Table 3.2 along with, in some cases, the reason for the adjustment. Also made in the calculation of CON(3) is a rehabilitative expenditure adjustment relating to government final consumption expenditure and the operation of vehicles.

Since CON(3) incorporates what we believe are the adjustments necessary to obtain a more accurate reflection of the welfare contribution of consumption expenditure, it is our preferred consumption estimate.

**Table 3.2. CON(1), CON(2), and CON(3) and
the adjustments involved in their estimation**

Consumption measure	Adjustments made to the consumption category
CON(1)	• No adjustment — all consumption expenditure is assumed to contribute positively to human well-being
CON(2)	• *Cigarettes and tobacco* — assumed to make no positive contribution to human well-being
	• *Alcoholic beverages* — assumed that only half of all such expenditure contributes positively to human well-being
	• *Rent and other dwelling services* — assumed that half of all such expenditure is defensive (i.e., required to ensure necessary shelter from the elements)
	• *Health* — assumed that half of all such expenditure is defensive or rehabilitative in nature
	• *Government final consumption expenditure* — assumed that one-quarter of all such expenditure is defensive
CON(3)	• Same as CON(2) plus:
	• *Food* — assumed that half of all such expenditure is defensive
	• *Electricity, gas, and fuel* — assumed that half of all such expenditure is defensive
	• *Operation of vehicles* (includes vehicle repairs and servicing) — assumed that half of this expenditure is either defensive or rehabilitative in nature
	• *Transport services* — assumed that half of all such expenditure is defensive in the sense that it is conducted for commuting purposes and does not contribute positively to human well-being
	• *Communications* — assumed that half of all such expenditure is defensive
	• *Hotels, cafes, and restaurants* — assumed that one-quarter of all such expenditure is defensive. Although this category is dominated by expenditure on food, much of it is prepared beyond the standard necessary to ensure adequate nourishment. Thus, a greater share of it can be considered welfare-enhancing compared to home-cooked food
	• *Insurance and other financial services* — assumed that half of all such expenditure is defensive
	• *Government final consumption expenditure* — on top of the CON(2) adjustment, it is also assumed that one-quarter of all such expenditure is rehabilitative in nature

3.4.2. Expenditure on Consumer Durables (ECD)

The second item used in the calculation of the GPI relates to the expenditure on consumer durables. Because, as explained in Chapter 2, it is incorrect to count the spending on consumer durables as a consumption-related benefit during the financial year in which the expenditure took place, all such expenditure must be subtracted from the base consumption item.

3.4.3. Service from Consumer Durables (SCD)

The third item is included because the existing stock of consumer durables — i.e., consumer durables accumulated over previous years — provides an annual benefit or service to its possessors. To determine the level of service enjoyed, we have assumed that the stock will, on average, endure for ten years. This implies that the stock of consumer durables depreciates or is 'consumed' at the rate of 10% per annum. The annual service generated by the existing stock of consumer durables equates to the current value of the stock multiplied by the 10% depreciation rate.

3.4.4. Adjusted Consumption (Unweighted)

The next item listed in Table 3.1 is not an individual benefit or cost item but a sub-total to indicate the pre-weighted welfare contribution of all consumption expenditure. Three adjusted consumption values are calculated by applying the following basic formula to CON(1), CON(2), and CON(3):

$$
\begin{aligned}
\text{Adjusted consumption} \quad = \quad & \text{consumption expenditure (CON)} \\
- \quad & \text{expenditure on consumer durables (ECD)} \\
+ \quad & \text{service from consumer durables (SCD)} \qquad (3.1)
\end{aligned}
$$

3.4.5. Distribution Index (DI)

The next item involves the construction of a Distribution Index (DI). In Chapter 2, we discussed the impact that the distribution of income can have on the aggregate welfare contribution of consumption expenditure. In order to incorporate this welfare impact into the GPI, we have constructed a Distribution Index (DI) to weight the three adjusted consumption measures in accordance with the changes in the distribution of income over the study period.

Our DI is constructed on the basis that a fall in the ratio of the median annual income to per capita GDP or GSP represents a growing gap between the income of the rich and the poor. How do we rationalise this? If the ratio of the median annual income to per capita GDP or GSP is declining, it means the latter is rising faster than the former. This can only occur if the distribution of income is becoming increasingly skewed towards the higher income level — that is, the rich are getting richer.

We have constructed our DI by setting the ratio of the median annual income to per capita GDP or GSP so it has an index value of 100.0 in the first year of the study period (i.e., 1986 = 100.0). As the ratio rises/falls over the study period, the DI correspondingly increases/decreases. A rise in the DI signifies a growing disparity between the income of the rich and the poor, while a fall in the DI signifies a more equal distribution of income.

There has been some considerable criticism directed at the distributional indexes used in the calculation of the GPI. It is has been suggested that welfare adjustments other than those involving the celebrated Atkinson (1970) index of distributional inequality are indefensibly subjective and ad hoc (e.g., Neumayer, 2000). It is claimed that the Atkinson index is less subjective because it makes explicit the researcher's assumption regarding a society's aversion to income inequality.

We disagree with this criticism. Furthermore, we believe the subjectivity argument applies to the Atkinson index. By starting with an index value of 100.0 in 1986, our DI involves no subjective assumption about the desirability of the distribution of income at the beginning of the study period. We merely make the assumption that an improvement/deterioration in the distribution of income has a positive/negative impact on the overall welfare of a nation's or state's citizens. This is hardly subjective given that the welfare impact of a changing distribution of income has empirical support (Easterlin, 1974; and Abramowitz, 1979). On the other hand, the Atkinson index approach requires the researcher to make an explicit choice as to what is society's aversion to income inequality is at the beginning of the study period. This seems to be far more open to subjectivity.

3.4.6. Adjusted Consumption (Weighted)

This particular item is calculated by weighting the three adjusted consumption measures in line with changes in the DI over the study period. The adjustment is made as per the following basic formula:

$$\text{Adjusted consumption (weighted)} = \frac{\text{Adjusted CON}}{\text{DI}} \times 100.0 \tag{3.2}$$

3.4.7. Welfare from Publicly-provided Service Capital (WPPSC)

This item is incorporated into the calculation of the GPI because, as previously explained, a large percentage of publicly-funded investment expenditure is not directed towards the accumulation of producer goods (e.g., plant, machinery, and equipment). It is instead directed towards the provision of service goods such as roads, bridges, schools, hospitals, and museums. These infrastructural goods generate a flow of welfare not unlike the way services flow from the stock of consumer durables. Hence, like consumer durables, it is erroneous to count current expenditure on publicly-provided service capital as if it is enhancing current welfare.

Having said this, it is necessary to estimate the welfare flowing from past expenditure on publicly-provided service capital. To do this, we assume that 75% of all government investment spending is on service capital rather than producer goods. The welfare from publicly-provided service capital therefore equals the public sector consumption of fixed capital (depreciation of existing capital goods) multiplied by the 75% share of government investment expenditure allocated to the accumulation of service capital.

3.4.8. Value of Non-paid Household Labour

Despite the enormous benefits provided by market-based economic activity, a great deal of welfare-enhancing activity occurs outside the market domain. One such category of non-market activity is non-paid household labour.

To derive the value of non-paid labour, we adopt the net opportunity cost method and assume that the real value of an hour of non-paid household work remains unchanged over the study period. We have, nonetheless, assumed that labour-reducing technological progress embodied in household consumer durables increased at the rate of 1% per annum over the study period. This equates to an 18.4% reduction in the time required to complete the same amount of housework in 2003 compared to 1986.

3.4.9. Value of Volunteer Labour

The value of volunteer labour is included in the calculation of the GPI for the same reason as non-paid household labour. Once again, we have used the net opportunity cost method to impute the value of volunteer labour. We have also assumed that the real value of an hour of volunteer work is the same as non-paid household work and that it remains unchanged over the study period.

3.4.10. Cost of Unemployment, Underemployment, Labour Underutilisation

Perhaps one of the most significant yet recently tolerated social costs is the cost of unemployment. The modern predilection that national governments have for a low-inflation, low-interest rate economic environment has led to the widespread adoption of a 'fight inflation first' stance to macroeconomic policy. In particular, it has resulted in governments and central banks targeting what is often referred to as the non-accelerating inflation rate of unemployment or NAIRU (Mitchell and Muysken, 2002; Lawn, 2004a).

The unfortunate feature of the NAIRU policy is obvious — its success relies on the existence of an unemployed pool of labour. Thus, the macroeconomic health of a nation seemingly depends on the misfortune of a substantial number of 'sacrificed' citizens (Blinder, 1987; Modigliani, 2000; Mitchell and Mosler, 2001).

There is a further downside to the NAIRU stance and the recent reform of Australia's industrial relations system. Rather than increasing the flexibility of work for people engaged in full-time occupations, it has led to the rapid rise in the number of people employed in part-time and casual work. Furthermore, it has brought about an increase in labour underutilisation

— i.e., wastage of willing labour resources — and a rise in the proportion of all workers considered underemployed (Mitchell and Carlson, 2002).

There have been many attempts at measuring the full cost of unemployment, underemployment, and labour underutilisation and the estimates vary considerably. The factors taken into account to determine the cost of 'unemployment' in the broad sense include (Sen, 1997):

- the loss of current output;
- social exclusion and the loss of personal freedom;
- skill deterioration;
- psychological harm;
- ill-health and reduced life expectancy;
- reduced levels of self-motivation;
- an undermining of human relations and family life;
- racial and gender inequality, particularly with respect to income and wealth differentials;
- a loss of social values and responsibility.

We believe that the cost of some of these factors is already reflected in the items used to calculate the GPI. To incorporate them into a cost estimate of unemployment, underemployment, and labour underutilisation would undeniably amount to double-counting. For example (refer to Table 3.1):

- reduced output results in less goods for consumption purposes. It is therefore evidenced by a relative decline in the three base consumption items of CON(1), CON(2), and CON(3);
- the undermining of human relations and family life is revealed in terms of an increase in the cost of crime and family breakdown;
- a loss of social values and responsibility is also reflected by an increasing cost of crime;
- rising ill-health brings about an increase in health expenditure of which half is automatically excluded as a welfare benefit in the case of CON(2) and CON(3) (refer to Table 3.2). It is therefore reasonable to believe that rising ill-health would reduce the proportion of welfare-enhancing consumption expenditure. If so, it would have a negative impact on the base consumption items of CON(2) and CON(3).

To measure the cost of unemployment, underemployment, and labour underutilisation, we began with the comprehensive hours-based measures of labour underutilisation developed by the Centre of Full Employment and Equity (CofFEE) (Mitchell and Carlson, 2002). These measures show, for example, that despite the official unemployment rate of Australia and Victoria respectively falling to 6.2% and 5.9% in June 2003, the hours-based underutilisation or CU8 rate was 11.9% for the former and 10.7% for the latter (CLMI, 2004). CofFEE has calculated the CU8 rate by summing the official unemployment rate and CofFEE's own estimates of hidden unemployment and underemployment.

Second, the CU8 number of underutilised labour was multiplied by a pecuniary figure reflecting the cost per unemployed person over and above the costs already reflected in other items. The justification for this pecuniary figure is provided in Chapter 9.

3.4.11. Cost of Crime

The cost of crime reflects the degradational impact that economic activity has on human relations, social institutions, and the self-esteem of some individual citizens. Our calculation of the total cost of the crime involved aggregating the cost of homicide, assault, robbery, break and entry, motor vehicle theft, and other theft. We established separate crime indexes for each crime category and employed them to weight various estimates of crime costs conducted during the study period.

3.4.12. Cost of Family Breakdown

The family unit is a social institution that not only provides a secure, stable, and organised environment, it serves a crucial child-rearing function. In more recent times, the family unit has become a major casualty of the drive towards higher rates of economic growth. Using the divorce rate as a proxy for family disunity and dysfunctionality, we have calculated what we believe to be the direct and immediate cost of family breakdown.

3.4.13. Change in Foreign Debt

This item is included in the calculation of the GPI because a nation's or state's long-term capacity to sustain the welfare generated by its economic activity depends very much on whether natural capital and human-made capital is domestically or foreign owned. Evidence clearly indicates that many countries with large foreign debts have difficulty maintaining the investment levels needed to keep their stock of human-made capital intact. Furthermore, they are often forced to deplete natural capital stocks to repay debt (George, 1988).

The value for this item is not represented by the total debt position at the end of each financial year but by the change in the foreign debt position from year to year. This item can be either positive or negative although, in Australia's and Victoria's case, was negative for each financial year over the study period.

3.4.14. Cost of Non-renewable Resource Depletion

The items so far discussed from Table 3.1 relate to the economic and social benefits and costs of economic activity. This next particular item — the cost of non-renewable resource depletion — relates to the first of the environmental costs used to calculate the GPI.

Non-renewable resources differ from their renewable counterparts in the sense that they cannot be sustainably exploited. Since the calculation of the GPI requires incorporation of the

Hicksian sustainability concept, this poses a potential problem. To overcome it, the so-called 'user cost' of non-renewable resource depletion is calculated by determining what proportion of depletion profits should be set aside to establish a renewable resource asset capable of generating a sustainable annual flow of income similar to the annual income previously generated by the exhausted resource (El Serafy, 1989; Lawn, 1998 and 2005).

3.4.15. Cost of Lost Agricultural Land

Unlike many non-renewable resources, there is essentially no substitute for fertile agricultural land. Indeed, agricultural land is not only used to provide the primary sustenance-based commodities for a nation or state, it is required to establish renewable resource assets to replace depleted non-renewable resources.

The unique nature of agricultural land demands that a different approach be taken to calculate its loss compared to non-renewable resource assets. In particular, the cost of lost agricultural land for any given year must reflect the amount required to compensate a nation's or state's citizens — in a sense, a compensatory fund — for the cumulative impact of past and present agricultural endeavours.

3.4.16. Cost of Excessive Irrigation Water Use

Because Australia is a very dry continent, a considerable amount of agricultural production relies on irrigation water from its inland rivers. Although it was common, prior to European settlement, for Australia's inland rivers to experience very low water levels, the gradual modification of water flow regimes for irrigation purposes has significantly impacted on river health and neighbouring ecosystems.

It has been shown that to restore the health of Australia's inland rivers, water needs to be periodically released to maintain sufficient environmental water flows (Hamilton and Saddler, 1997). The cost of failing to do this in the past plus the cost of recent large-scale river diversions is steadily mounting. Indeed, it has been estimated that the repair bill confronting the current generation of Australians to restore the Murray-Darling Basin to adequate health is fast approaching the value of the agricultural output it generates (ACF-NFF, 2000). In view of this and the non-substitutable nature of water, the cost of excessive irrigation water use should be calculated in a similar manner to the cost of lost agricultural land — that is, to reflect the financial endowment that is required to compensate citizens for the cumulative impact of excessive irrigation water use.

3.4.17. Cost of Timber Depletion

As a renewable resource, timber can be sustainably exploited so long as the rate at which it is harvested does not exceed its ability to regenerate. Timber stocks can also be increased through plantation establishment. However, should timber stocks decline, the impact is not unlike the depletion of a non-renewable resource. As such, the cost of timber exhaustion should be calculated by employing the previously explained 'user cost' method.

Of course, even if timber stocks are on the rise, it is possible for environmental damage to occur if timber augmentation involves the replacement of slow-growing native forests with fast-growing exotic species. Since the primary purpose of this item is to capture the change in what is a resource-providing function of natural capital, this item will fail to capture any indirect ecological impact of forestry activities. The ecosystem damage is, however, reflected by a negative impact on the Ecosystem Health Index (EHI). The EHI and its implications for the GPI are discussed shortly.

3.4.18. Cost of Air Pollution

The cost of air pollution is the first of two costs associated with the loss of the natural environment's waste-assimilative or sink capacity. In simple terms, the environment's sink capacity diminishes each time the quantity and the quality of the waste generated by economic activity exceeds the innate capacity of the natural environment to safely absorb it. It is our considered opinion that a decline in the environment's sink capacity occurs whenever the emission of various forms of pollution imposes discernible environmental costs.

To calculate what we believe to be the discernible cost of air pollution, we have weighted a point estimate of the cost of air pollution by an air pollution index. The index combines the changing intensity of economic activity over the study period and an assumed rate of pollution-reducing technological progress.

3.4.19. Cost of Urban Waste-water Pollution

With around 86% of the Australian population living in urban areas, Australia is one of the most urbanised countries in the world. At 87%, Victoria is little different (ABS, Catalogue No. 3105.0.65.001). It naturally follows that urban waste-water pollution should constitute a discernible sink-related cost in both Australia and Victoria.

To calculate this item, we follow a similar process to the previous item. That is, we have weighted a point estimate of the per person cost of urban waste-water pollution by the changing number of people living in urban areas together with an assumed rate of pollution-reducing technological progress.

3.4.20. Cost of long-term Environmental Damage

To account in some way for the loss of the natural environment's life-support function, we have included an item to reflect the long-term environmental impact of increasing energy consumption. Why energy consumption? Energy consumption is a major contributing factor to greenhouse gas emissions and the projected change in global climate patterns. As mentioned in Chapter 1, climate change is likely to result in a significant loss of the world's biodiversity and, in Australia's case, dramatically increase the frequency of droughts as well as the intensity of other extreme weather events, such as tropical cyclones.

It should also be remembered that eons of evolution have resulted in the biosphere being able to deal adequately with a particular rate of energy throughput (Blum, 1962; Daly, 1979; Capra, 1982; Norgaard, 1988). An increasing rate of human-induced energy consumption means, inevitably, the degradation of natural capital and the subsequent diminution of the life-support services it provides.

3.4.21. Cost of Lost Natural Capital Services (LNCS)

This particular sub-total reveals the pre-weighted environmental costs of economic activity. Equal to the sum of the environmental cost items marked in Table 3.1 by a single asterisk (*), this sub-total reflects the sacrificed *source* (resource-providing), *sink* (waste-assimilating) and, to some extent, *life-support* services provided by natural capital.

3.4.22. Ecosystem Health Index (EHI)

While it is a relatively simple exercise to estimate the cost of sacrificed source and sink functions, it is exceedingly more difficult to estimate the various costs associated with losing some of the life-support services provided by critical ecosystems. To assist in this regard, we have chosen to weight the cost of lost natural capital services (LNCS) in line with changes in the health of critical ecosystems.

The rationale for adopting this approach is simple. The impact of many resource extractive and pollutive activities is not confined to the damage inflicted on the natural environment's source and sink functions. Damage also extends to ecosystem degradation. A good example is strip mining — a resource-extraction practice requiring the initial removal of terrestrial fauna and flora. Another is agriculture — again, an activity first requiring the clearance of native vegetation.

With this in mind, an Ecosystem Health Index (EHI) is constructed on the premise that remnant vegetation loss constitutes the "greatest threat to biodiversity" and, therefore, to ecosystem functioning (Biodiversity Unit, 1995). A base index value of 100.0 is assigned to the first year of the study period (i.e., 1986 = 100.0) and is adjusted in line with the annual changes in the area of relatively undisturbed land. As the area of relatively undisturbed land declines/increases over the study period, the EHI correspondingly falls/rises (note: an increase in relatively undisturbed land can occur if the rate of disturbance is exceeded by the rate of regrowth). For obvious reasons, a fall in the EHI signifies a worsening state of ecosystem health.

3.4.23. Weighted LNCS

This item is calculated by weighting the cost of LNCS in accordance with changes in the EHI over the study period. The following basic formula is used to make the necessary adjustment:

$$LNCS \text{ (weighted)} = \frac{LNCS}{100} \times EHI$$

(3.3)

3.4.24. Genuine Progress Indicator (GPI)

The GPI is calculated by summing the double-asterisked (**) items appearing in Table 3.1. In view of the three different values previously estimated for consumption expenditure — namely, CON(1), CON(2), and CON(3) — three separate GPI calculations are obtained (i.e., GPI(1), GPI(2), and GPI(3)). Owing to our preference for CON(3) as a more accurate representation of the welfare contribution of consumption expenditure, GPI(3) constitutes our preferred indicator of sustainable well-being. It will thus form the major focus of our attention in Chapters 4 and 5.

3.4.25. Population

To ascertain the genuine progress of the average person living in a particular study region (i.e., nation or state/province), it is necessary to calculate the GPI on a per capita basis. This requires the population numbers of the study region to be included in Table 3.1.

3.4.26. Per Capita GPI

The per capita GPI of a particular study region is calculated by dividing the final GPI value by the region's population.

3.5. ADDITIONAL STUDY ITEMS

In Chapter 1, it was indicated that one of the aims of this study is to establish a possible link between the Victorian GPI and the growth rate of the Victorian economy. In order to do this, it is necessary to determine the extent to which the scale of the Victorian economy has grown.

Whether one is referring to a population of rabbits or a population of human-made goods, the magnitude of the population will increase if the number of rabbits or goods at the end of a particular period is greater than the number at the beginning. For this to occur in the case of human-made goods, the amount of *durable* goods added to the existing stock (production) must exceed the amount by which the existing stock declines (depreciation).

Strangely, real GDP and real GSP are often used as indicators of economic growth at the national and state levels even though they do little more than indicate, at best, how many goods are being physically added to the economy. Neither indicates the amount by which the number of goods has declined.[2] To better ascertain whether an economy is growing and to assess the impact of Victoria's prevailing growth strategy on sustainable well-being, a number of additional items require estimation. A brief explanation of each additional item and its relevance to the growth assessment in Chapter 4 will now be provided.

3.5.1. Investment Expenditure (Private and Public) (INV)

The first additional item includes the private sector investment in producer goods and, in the case of the government sector, investment in both producer goods and publicly-provided service capital (INV). This particular figure can be drawn straight from the system of national and state accounts.

3.5.2. Investment in All Human-made Capital (INV*)

To determine how much is being added to the total stock of all human-made capital, it is also necessary to include household investment in consumer durables. This latter investment element is equivalent to the expenditure on consumer durables (ECD) and is the same figure used in the calculation of the GPI.

To calculate the investment in *all* human-made capital, one simply employs the following formula:

$$
\begin{aligned}
\text{Investment in all human-made capital (INV*)} \quad &= \quad \text{investment expenditure (INV)} \\
&+ \quad \text{expenditure on consumer durables (ECD)}
\end{aligned}
\tag{3.4}
$$

Some observers would question whether consumer durables ought to be included in the stock of human-made capital since the stock is normally referred to in terms of producer goods only. We, however, believe that consumer durables are no different to producer goods other than the question of ownership. For example, why should a refrigerator in a corner shop be regarded as human-made capital but not the same refrigerator in a house? In our opinion, a distinction should only be made along the lines that some human-made capital constitutes business capital, while the remainder constitutes household capital. As such, our treatment of human-made capital is the same as that recommended long ago by Irving Fisher (1906).

3.5.3. Consumption of Fixed Capital (DEP)

This next item — the consumption of fixed capital — effectively equals the depreciation value of all private and public sector producer goods as well as publicly-provided service capital (DEP). It is included to assist in determining the amount by which the existing stock of all human-made capital has declined. The annual values for the consumption of fixed capital can also be drawn straight from the system of national accounts.

3.5.4. Depreciation of All Human-made Capital (DEP*)

To determine how much of the total stock of all human-made capital is depreciating through its use, it is necessary to include the depreciation of household consumer durables. As previously discussed in relation to the calculation of the GPI, the depreciation of the stock of consumer durables equates to the annual service that the existing stock generates through its use (SCD). To recall, this equals the current value of the stock of consumer durables multiplied by an assumed 10% depreciation rate.

Overall, the depreciation of all human-made capital (DEP*) is calculated as per equation (3.5) below:

Dep. of *all* human-made capital (DEP*) = Consumption of fixed capital (DEP)
                                        + depreciation of household consumer
                                                    durables (SCD)   (3.5)

3.5.5. Net Capital Investment (NCI)

As mentioned above, if the quantity of durable goods being added to the economy exceeds the amount by which the existing stock of durables goods is in decline, the physical scale of the economy expands. Note, therefore, that all *non-durable* goods produced during a particular year do not alter the physical scale of the economy over that year because, presumably, they have either been completely consumed or have perished.

To compare the quantity of durable goods being added and subtracted from the existing stock, it is necessary to calculate what is often referred to as net capital investment (NCI). For the purposes of our study, NCI is equal to the following:

Net capital investment (NCI)	=	investment in all human-made capital (INV*)	
	–	depreciation of all human-made capital (DEP*)	(3.6)

Clearly, if NCI is positive/negative, the economy is physically growing/contracting. On the other hand, if NCI = 0, the economy is effectively in a steady physical state. Although a steady-state economy is non-growing, it is not a static economy. A steady-state economy offers considerable scope for qualitative improvement should all new goods be qualitatively superior to all worn out goods requiring replacement.

3.5.6. NCI/DEP* Ratio

The next additional item is the NCI/DEP* ratio and is included to ascertain the rate at which the net addition of all human-made capital is growing or declining. It serves as a useful ratio to describe a government's prevailing growth strategy.

3.5.7. Growth strategy

For the purposes of this study, the following range of values for the NCI/DEP* ratio will be used to particularise the nature of a government's growth strategy:

- Rapid-growth occurs when NCI/DEP* ≥ 0.5
- High-growth occurs when $0.25 \leq$ NCI/DEP* < 0.5
- Low-growth occurs when $0 <$ NCI/DEP* < 0.25
- A steady-state occurs when NCI/DEP* $= 0$.

What do these values mean? At an NCI/DEP* ratio of 0.5 or more, the net addition of all human-made capital is more than half as much as the quantity of depreciated human-made capital. In such circumstances, a *rapid* rate of growth can be said to be taking place. A *high* rate of growth occurs when the net addition of all human-made capital is between one-quarter and one-half of all depreciated human-made capital, whereas a *low* rate of growth takes place when the net addition of all human-made capital is between zero and one-quarter of depreciated human-made capital. Naturally, when the NCI/DEP* ratio is zero, the economy is in a steady (non-growing) physical state.

The distinction we have drawn here between the various growth strategies is an arbitrary one. However, as we shall see in Chapters 4, 5, and 6, the distinction becomes very useful when making assessments regarding the link between the growth of the Victorian economy and the Victorian GPI. The distinction is also useful when making policy recommendations concerning future rates of growth of the Victorian economy.

NOTES

[1] In actual fact, no goods are truly destroyed or consumed. Because of the *law of conservation of matter and energy*, the matter embodied in goods and services cannot be destroyed. What is destroyed, however, is the use value embodied in goods and services that is initially added to matter-energy during the production phase of the economic process. Also destroyed in both the production and consumption phases of the economic process is the 'usefulness' of matter-energy — a consequence of the *Entropy Law*. This is why there is a constant need to extract virgin resources to fuel the economic process irrespective of the rate of recycling which, in any case, only applies to matter, not energy, and can never be 100% efficient.

[2] Worse still, real GDP and real GSP include the production of non-durable consumption goods that are either immediately consumed or quickly perish. Hence, real GDP and real GSP overstate the number of goods that are physically added to the economy.

AN ASSESSMENT OF
VICTORIA'S GPI PERFORMANCE

4.1. THE GPI OF VICTORIA (1986-2003)

The following four sections of Chapter 4 focus on the Victorian GPI and the factors underlying the performance of the Victorian economy. In the second section, we analyse the component items of the GPI to help explain the trend movement of Victoria's GPI.

To begin our assessment of the Victorian economy, Table 4.1 reveals the values for each of the items outlined and discussed in Chapter 3. The values for GPI(1), GPI(2), and GPI(3) are revealed in their aggregate and per capita forms (columns *ee*, *ff*, *gg*, *jj*, *kk*, and *ll*). These indicators also appear in an indexed form (columns *nn*, *oo*, and *pp*). Indexes are provided to facilitate an easier comparison of the relative change of each indicator over the study period. In order to succinctly reveal the sustainable well-being of the average Victorian over the study period, consider Figure 4.1. Based on the calculations appearing in columns *jj*, *kk*, and *ll* in Table 4.1, Figure 4.1 shows that all three per capita GPI values were higher in 2003 than in 1986.

Because the variation between the three per capita GPI values is due only to the different treatment of consumption-related welfare, the trend movement of the three indicators is largely identical. However, the disparity between each of the three indicators intensified over the study period. For example, in 1986, the difference between per capita GPI(1) and per capita GPI(3) was $8,190 per Victorian, but increased to $9,572 per Victorian by 2003. Despite this, GPI(1) grew by 20.3% over the study period whereas GPI(3) grew by 21.8%.

It was explained in Chapter 3 that GPI(3) is our preferred indicator of sustainable well-being because its calculation involves the most comprehensive adjustments to consumption expenditure. We shall therefore focus on its value and movements for the remainder of section 4.1.

Per capita GPI(3) began the study period at $18,839 per Victorian and increased to $22,951 per Victorian by 2003. This can be considered a very modest rise — indeed, an increase of just 21.8% over the study period or, equivalently, an average rate of growth of 1.46% per annum. Interestingly, per capita GPI(3) fluctuated throughout the study period. After an initial steep rise to $20,879 per Victorian in 1987, per capita GPI(3) varied minimally from year to year to be slightly lower in 1993 at $20,336 per Victorian. However, per capita GPI(3) fluctuated considerably over the next seven years. Rising and falling in each alternate year between 1993 and 2000, per capita GPI(3) was marginally higher in 2000 at $21,677 per Victorian. The per capita GPI(3) then proceeded to rise in both 2001 and 2002, but fell in 2003. The 2003 value of $22,951 per Victorian was slightly lower than its 1999 peak of $23,403.

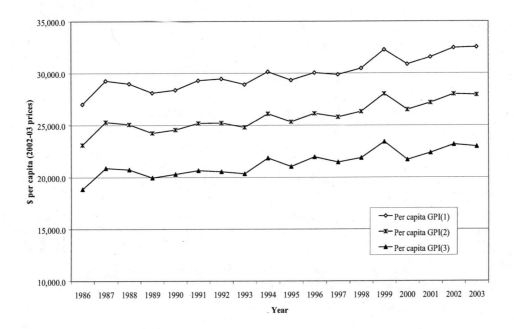

Figure 4.1. Per capita Genuine Progress Indicator (GPI)(1), (2), and (3): Victoria, 1986-2003

Overall, it can be concluded that following a general but small decline in per capita GPI(3) between 1987 and 1993, there was a general rise in per capita GPI(3) between 1993 and 2003. However, in view of the predominantly high rate of economic growth in Victoria between 1993 to 2003, it would appear, even at this early stage, that the sustainable well-being of the average Victorian rose disappointingly over the 1993-2003 period. This suggests that the additional benefits generated by economic growth have been almost entirely matched by the increase in additional social and environmental costs. This will be discussed in greater detail later.

4.2. COMPONENTS OF VICTORIA'S GPI

In this section, we aim to explain the fluctuations in Victoria's per capita GPI; why its general rise did not begin until after 1993; and why the rise in the per capita GPI was disappointing when compared to the rate of economic growth. To do this, we will now examine the component items that make up the GPI to determine which had the greatest impact on its overall trend movement.

Table 4.1: Genuine Progress Indicator (GPI) and real GSP for Victoria, 1986-2003

Year	CON(1) ($) a	CON(2) ($) b	CON(3) ($) c	ECD ($) d	Consumer durables ($) e	SCD ($) f (e x 0.1)	Adjusted CON(1) ($) g (a - d + f)	Adjusted CON(2) ($) h (b - d + f)	Adjusted CON(3) ($) i (c - d + f)	Distribution index j 1986 =100.0	Weighted CON(1) ($) k (g/j) x 100	Weighted CON(2) ($) l (h/j) x 100	Weighted CON(3) ($) m (i/j) x 100
1985					83,957.4								
1986	91,681.0	75,364.8	57,602.8	-10,144.0	85,868.1	8,395.7	89,932.7	73,616.5	55,854.5	100.0	89,932.7	73,616.5	55,854.5
1987	93,310.0	76,744.3	58,397.3	-9,701.0	87,381.0	8,586.8	92,195.8	75,630.1	57,283.1	98.7	93,364.3	76,588.6	58,009.1
1988	95,912.0	78,835.0	59,939.5	-9,728.0	89,154.3	8,738.1	94,922.1	77,845.1	58,949.6	102.1	92,938.0	76,217.9	57,717.4
1989	99,913.0	82,219.3	62,635.0	-10,065.0	91,070.8	8,915.4	98,763.4	81,069.7	61,485.4	105.7	93,456.4	76,713.4	58,181.5
1990	102,677.0	84,568.3	64,413.3	-10,209.0	93,068.8	9,107.1	101,575.1	83,466.3	63,311.3	107.9	94,118.3	77,338.9	58,663.5
1991	101,989.0	83,580.0	63,298.3	-9,289.0	93,669.4	9,306.9	102,006.9	83,597.9	63,316.1	101.1	100,900.7	82,691.3	62,629.5
1992	103,549.0	84,873.8	64,308.3	-9,205.0	93,950.4	9,366.9	103,710.9	85,035.7	64,470.2	98.6	105,172.0	86,233.7	65,378.4
1993	104,551.0	85,651.8	65,256.3	-9,582.0	94,779.7	9,395.0	104,364.0	85,464.8	65,069.3	102.3	102,028.2	83,551.9	63,612.9
1994	105,056.0	86,072.0	65,867.8	-9,436.0	96,212.8	9,478.0	105,098.0	86,114.0	65,909.7	105.2	99,859.2	81,821.5	62,624.4
1995	109,851.0	90,278.0	69,241.5	-9,689.0	97,048.0	9,621.3	109,783.3	90,210.3	69,173.8	108.2	101,469.6	83,378.8	63,935.4
1996	113,335.0	93,146.0	71,464.0	-9,843.0	96,747.0	9,704.8	113,196.8	93,007.8	71,325.8	113.3	99,886.5	82,071.5	62,938.9
1997	116,417.0	95,760.5	73,609.3	-10,418.0	97,464.0	9,674.7	115,673.7	95,017.2	72,866.0	110.5	104,712.5	86,013.4	65,961.2
1998	121,603.0	100,459.5	77,659.5	-11,570.0	99,306.0	9,746.4	119,779.4	98,635.9	75,835.9	110.1	108,755.4	89,557.9	68,856.3
1999	127,435.0	105,413.3	81,419.3	-12,662.0	101,903.0	9,930.6	124,703.6	102,681.9	78,687.9	110.7	112,650.0	92,756.8	71,082.0
2000	132,668.0	110,028.8	84,994.0	-13,374.0	105,068.0	10,190.3	129,484.3	106,845.1	81,810.3	109.5	118,267.7	97,589.6	74,723.5
2001	136,277.0	112,797.5	86,983.0	-13,471.0	109,250.0	10,506.8	133,312.8	109,833.3	84,018.8	111.3	119,759.8	98,667.3	75,477.2
2002	141,293.0	117,099.8	90,836.3	-14,512.0	114,557.0	10,925.0	137,706.0	113,512.8	87,249.3	111.7	123,278.0	101,619.6	78,107.8
2003	146,482.0	121,399.3	94,193.3	-15,378.0	120,353.0	11,455.7	142,559.7	117,477.0	90,271.0	111.2	128,169.3	105,618.5	81,158.7

Note: All values are in millions of 2002-2003 dollars except where indicated

Table 4.1 (Continued): Genuine Progress Indicator (GPI) and real GSP for Victoria, 1986-2003

Year	WPPSC ($) n	H/hold labour ($) o	Volunteer labour ($) p	Cost of u/e ($) q	Cost of crime ($) r	Cost of family b/d ($) s	Vic. share of o/s debt ($) t	Non-ren. res. dep. ($) u	Lost agric. land ($) v	Irrig. water use ($) w	Timber dep. ($) x	Air polln. ($) y	Urban w/w polln. ($) z
1985													
1986	3,486.0	58,397.9	2,222.0	-4,233.9	-3,488.4	-855.6	-11,706.5	-3,018.7	-1,007.2	-3,863.3	28.3	-1,544.9	-1,103.1
1987	3,304.0	58,985.4	2,668.7	-4,505.3	-3,893.7	-866.8	-4,148.7	-2,850.9	-1,015.9	-3,948.5	26.3	-1,565.8	-1,096.3
1988	2,911.9	59,555.6	3,115.4	-3,948.6	-3,904.7	-878.0	-3,387.2	-3,351.3	-1,024.7	-4,090.1	26.3	-1,633.5	-1,098.7
1989	2,731.6	60,108.8	3,562.2	-3,613.1	-3,906.6	-889.1	-6,394.5	-3,519.1	-1,033.9	-4,164.1	32.8	-1,682.4	-1,102.1
1990	3,586.3	60,645.1	4,008.9	-3,421.8	-3,662.3	-900.3	-5,558.7	-3,767.6	-1,043.2	-4,273.3	11.4	-1,757.6	-1,105.3
1991	3,578.9	61,164.9	4,455.6	-6,253.3	-3,885.0	-911.4	-3,865.6	-4,349.6	-1,052.4	-4,418.0	6.8	-1,702.5	-1,105.8
1992	3,877.9	62,491.9	4,902.3	-8,538.4	-3,552.4	-861.4	-6,048.2	-4,362.3	-1,061.5	-4,563.6	35.9	-1,645.6	-1,103.2
1993	2,982.3	63,786.7	5,349.1	-9,263.1	-3,224.8	-895.2	-4,544.1	-4,441.2	-1,070.8	-4,611.7	-3.4	-1,699.2	-1,096.8
1994	3,367.7	65,049.6	5,795.8	-9,353.7	-2,992.1	-919.1	1,790.3	-4,300.2	-1,080.4	-4,708.8	-14.5	-1,741.5	-1,090.4
1995	3,812.2	66,281.3	6,242.5	-8,079.4	-2,887.5	-969.1	-5,688.7	-3,914.6	-1,090.1	-4,876.1	-14.6	-1,784.9	-1,088.5
1996	3,164.4	67,482.3	6,689.3	-7,361.6	-2,840.6	-1,022.5	-862.5	-3,691.2	-1,100.0	-5,014.0	23.1	-1,845.8	-1,089.7
1997	2,052.3	67,945.4	7,136.0	-7,863.0	-3,040.3	-1,020.2	-4,116.0	-3,385.8	-1,110.0	-5,161.8	23.1	-1,879.7	-1,087.5
1998	2,552.5	68,392.7	7,582.7	-7,528.7	-3,191.9	-1,007.5	-5,239.4	-3,257.5	-1,120.1	-5,296.4	102.6	-1,953.0	-1,087.1
1999	3,076.4	68,824.4	8,029.4	-7,129.1	-3,486.8	-1,043.1	-784.7	-2,342.5	-1,130.5	-5,403.7	102.6	-2,070.1	-1,088.4
2000	3,084.4	69,241.0	8,476.2	-6,340.1	-3,751.5	-982.5	-11,205.0	-3,212.7	-1,141.4	-5,468.9	102.5	-2,116.4	-1,091.3
2001	3,002.8	69,642.5	8,922.9	-6,030.6	-4,016.9	-1,089.3	-7,561.9	-2,973.4	-1,152.6	-5,591.7	102.6	-2,157.2	-1,095.7
2002	3,318.2	70,029.3	9,369.6	-6,491.7	-4,262.5	-1,063.1	-5,157.1	-2,521.0	-1,164.1	-5,716.1	59.1	-2,214.8	-1,097.5
2003	3,557.1	70,401.6	9,816.4	-6,203.4	-4,545.8	-1,083.6	-8,251.9	-2,556.1	-1,176.0	-5,826.6	102.6	-2,249.3	-1,100.7

Note: All values are in millions of 2002-2003 dollars except where indicated

Table 4.1 (Continued): Genuine Progress Indicator (GPI) and real GSP for Victoria, 1986-2003

Year	L-T env damage ($)	LNCS ($)	EHI	Weighted LNCS ($)	GPI (1) ($)	GPI (2) ($)	GPI (3) ($)	Real GSP ($)	Vic. Pop. (thousands)	Per capita GPI (1) ($)	Per capita GPI (2) ($)	Per capita GPI (3) ($)	Per capita real GSP ($)
	aa	bb	cc	dd	ee	ff	gg	hh	ii	jj	kk	ll	mm
		u to aa	1986 = 100.0	(bb/cc) x 100						(ee/ii)	(ff/ii)	(gg/ii)	(hh/ii)
1985													
1986	-10,780.9	-21,289.7	100.0	-21,289.7	112,464.5	96,148.3	78,386.3	111,277.3	4,160.9	27,029.2	23,107.8	18,839.0	26,743.9
1987	-11,174.2	-21,625.3	99.9	-21,648.4	123,259.6	106,483.9	87,904.4	113,913.9	4,210.1	29,277.0	25,292.4	20,879.4	27,057.2
1988	-11,579.6	-22,751.6	99.8	-22,808.5	123,594.0	106,873.9	88,373.4	120,027.6	4,262.6	28,995.2	25,072.7	20,732.4	28,158.5
1989	-12,008.4	-23,477.2	99.6	-23,562.8	121,492.7	104,749.7	86,217.8	124,854.1	4,320.2	28,122.2	24,246.7	19,957.1	28,900.3
1990	-12,457.6	-24,393.1	99.6	-24,502.8	124,312.7	107,533.4	88,858.0	131,737.0	4,378.6	28,391.0	24,558.9	20,293.7	30,086.6
1991	-12,897.5	-25,518.9	99.5	-25,642.3	129,542.5	111,333.2	91,271.3	128,882.9	4,420.4	29,305.8	25,186.4	20,647.9	29,156.6
1992	-13,332.0	-26,032.3	99.5	-26,167.0	131,276.9	112,338.6	91,483.3	125,822.0	4,455.0	29,467.3	25,216.3	20,535.0	28,242.9
1993	-13,783.4	-26,706.5	99.5	-26,853.8	129,365.3	110,889.0	90,950.0	131,224.1	4,472.4	28,925.3	24,794.1	20,335.9	29,340.9
1994	-14,234.0	-27,169.8	99.4	-27,328.8	135,268.8	117,231.1	98,034.0	135,835.7	4,487.6	30,143.0	26,123.5	21,845.7	30,269.3
1995	-14,704.6	-27,473.4	99.4	-27,643.6	132,537.4	114,446.6	95,003.2	140,606.5	4,517.4	29,339.4	25,334.7	21,030.6	31,125.6
1996	-15,188.6	-27,906.2	99.4	-28,088.6	137,046.7	119,231.6	100,099.1	146,860.5	4,560.2	30,053.1	26,146.4	21,950.8	32,205.2
1997	-15,680.0	-28,281.8	99.3	-28,476.3	137,330.4	118,631.3	98,579.1	151,056.9	4,597.2	29,872.6	25,805.1	21,443.3	32,858.4
1998	-16,202.9	-28,814.5	99.3	-29,022.4	141,293.3	122,095.8	101,394.2	158,516.3	4,637.8	30,465.5	26,326.1	21,862.5	34,179.1
1999	-16,743.9	-28,676.4	99.3	-28,893.0	151,243.6	131,350.4	109,675.6	169,699.3	4,686.4	32,272.9	28,028.0	23,402.9	36,211.0
2000	-17,300.9	-30,228.9	99.2	-30,467.6	146,322.5	125,644.3	102,778.2	175,225.5	4,741.3	30,861.0	26,499.8	21,677.0	36,957.0
2001	-17,864.9	-30,732.9	99.2	-30,986.0	151,643.4	130,550.9	107,360.7	180,391.3	4,804.7	31,561.3	27,171.3	22,344.8	37,544.6
2002	-18,446.2	-31,100.7	99.1	-31,367.5	157,653.2	135,994.8	112,483.0	187,064.4	4,857.2	32,457.5	27,998.4	23,157.9	38,512.6
2003	-19,038.9	-31,845.0	99.1	-32,129.1	159,730.6	137,179.8	112,720.1	191,875.1	4,911.4	32,522.3	27,930.8	22,950.6	39,067.1

Note: All values are in millions of 2002-2003 dollars except where indicated

Table 4.1 (Continued): Genuine Progress Indicator (GPI) and real GSP for Victoria, 1986-2003

Year	Per capita GPI (1) ($)	Per capita GPI (2) ($)	Per capita GPI (3) ($)	Per capita real GSP	INV ($)	INV* ($)	DEP ($)	DEP* ($)	NCI ($)	NCI/DEP* ($)	Growth rate
	1986 = 100.0	1986 = 100.0	1986 = 100.0	1986 = 100.0							
	mm	oo	pp	qq	rr	ss	tt	uu	vv	ww	xx
						$(rr + d)$		$(tt + n)$	$(ss - zu)$	(vv/uu)	
1985											
1986	100.0	100.0	100.0	100.0	20,786.0	30,930.0	13,441.1	21,836.9	9,093.1	0.42	high
1987	108.3	109.5	110.8	101.2	21,276.0	30,977.0	14,343.9	22,930.7	8,046.3	0.35	high
1988	107.3	108.5	110.1	105.3	22,268.0	31,996.0	14,830.8	23,568.9	8,427.1	0.36	high
1989	104.0	104.9	105.9	108.1	24,872.0	34,937.0	15,776.1	24,691.6	10,245.4	0.41	high
1990	105.0	106.3	107.7	112.5	24,721.0	34,930.0	15,801.6	24,908.7	10,021.3	0.40	high
1991	108.4	109.0	109.6	109.0	20,159.0	29,448.0	15,042.1	24,349.0	5,099.0	0.21	low
1992	109.0	109.1	109.0	105.6	18,760.0	27,965.0	15,336.8	24,703.8	3,261.2	0.13	low
1993	107.0	107.3	107.9	109.7	20,471.0	30,053.0	16,217.5	25,612.5	4,440.5	0.17	low
1994	111.5	113.1	116.0	113.2	22,506.0	31,942.0	17,388.3	26,866.3	5,075.7	0.19	low
1995	108.5	109.6	111.6	116.4	23,889.0	33,578.0	17,067.0	26,688.3	6,889.7	0.26	low/high
1996	111.2	113.1	116.5	120.4	25,857.0	35,700.0	18,729.2	28,434.0	7,266.0	0.26	low/high
1997	110.5	111.7	113.8	122.9	29,883.0	40,301.0	21,201.6	30,876.3	9,424.7	0.31	high
1998	112.7	113.9	116.0	127.8	31,571.0	43,141.0	21,765.4	31,511.8	11,629.2	0.37	high
1999	119.4	121.3	124.2	135.4	36,251.0	48,913.0	24,259.3	34,189.9	14,723.1	0.43	high
2000	114.2	114.7	115.1	138.2	39,483.0	52,857.0	26,357.6	36,547.9	16,309.1	0.45	high
2001	116.8	117.6	118.6	140.4	38,165.0	51,636.0	27,731.0	38,237.8	13,398.2	0.35	high
2002	120.1	121.2	122.9	144.0	42,153.0	56,665.0	29,626.4	40,551.4	16,113.6	0.40	high
2003	120.3	120.9	121.8	146.1	47,856.0	63,234.0	31,119.6	42,575.3	20,658.7	0.49	high/rapid

Note: All values are in millions of 2002-2003 dollars except where indicated

4.2.1. Consumption-related Welfare

As the largest component of the GPI, consumption-related welfare appears on the first page of Table 4.1. This particular page summarises the various adjustments made to consumption expenditure to arrive at the three weighted measures of CON(1), CON(2), and CON(3) in columns *k*, *l*, and *m*.

In order to graphically illustrate the impact of the adjustments, turn to Figure 4.2. It is clear from this figure and Table 4.1 that Victoria's consumption-related welfare rose only marginally between 1986 and 1996. For example, weighted CON(3) was $55,855 million in 1986 and $62,939 million in 1996. This constitutes a 12.7% increase over the 1986-1996 period or an average rise of just 0.81% per annum. However, Victoria's consumption-related welfare grew strongly after 1996. By 2003, weighted CON(3) had risen to $81,159 million. This amounted to an average annual rise between 1996 and 2003 of 3.70% — 4.6 times the rate of increase during the 1986-1996 period.

The stifled increase in consumption-related welfare during the 1986-1996 period can be attributed to the very small rise in Victoria's consumption expenditure (CON) between 1986 and 1994. Although consumption expenditure gathered momentum following 1994, it was not captured by CON(3) until 1997 because a considerable proportion of the upsurge was devoted to the purchase of consumer durables. As previously explained, the welfare benefit of consumer durables is not enjoyed at the time of spending but later as the stock of consumer durables depreciates through use.

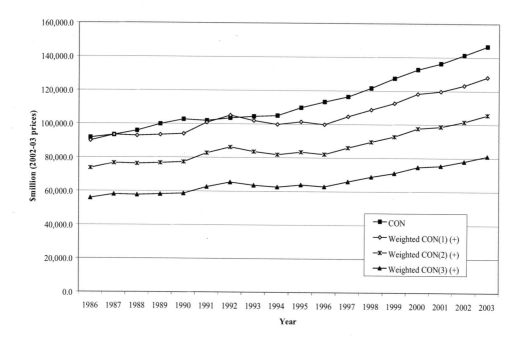

Figure 4.2. Consumption-related welfare – CON and Weighted CON(1), CON(2), CON(3): Victoria, 1986-2003

One of the interesting aspects regarding Victoria's consumption-related welfare is that its impact on per capita GPI(3) appears to have alternated during the study period. This is particularly evident from the comparison between per capita GPI(3) and per capita weighted CON(3) in Figure 4.3. The seemingly positive correlation between the two indicators from 1986 and 1991 gives way to a negative correlation between 1991 and 1997. Following 1997, no clear positive or negative correlation emerges, although, as the respective index values in Figure 4.4 shows, the steady rise in per capita CON(3) after 1997 appears to have had a positive impact on per capita GPI(3) except for 2000 and 2003.

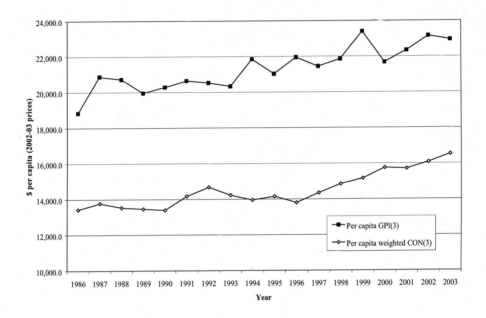

Figure 4.3. Per capita GPI(3) and per capita Weighted CON(3): Victoria, 1986-2003

A concerning observation from Figure 4.4 is the extent to which per capita CON(3) rises much more rapidly than per capita GPI(3) beyond 1996. Indeed, the index value of per capita CON(3) surpasses the index value of GPI(3) by 2003. This again suggests that the extra social and environmental costs associated with a higher level of consumption maybe approaching the value of the additional benefits. This cannot be verified at this point but should become clearer either way once we reveal our analysis of the social and environmental cost items later in this chapter.

4.2.2. Expenditure on Consumer Durables (ECD), Service from Consumer Durables (SCD), and Welfare from Publicly-provided Service Capital (WPPSC)

Two of the next three items — namely, expenditure on consumer durables (ECD) and the service from consumer durables (SCD) — are used in the calculation of consumption-related welfare (columns *d* and *f* in Table 4.1). Figure 4.5 shows that Victoria's expenditure on consumer durables was only fractionally higher in 1997 than at the beginning of the study period ($10,144 million in 1986 and $10,418 million in 1997). Expenditure on consumer durables then rose steeply to be $15,378 million by 2003.

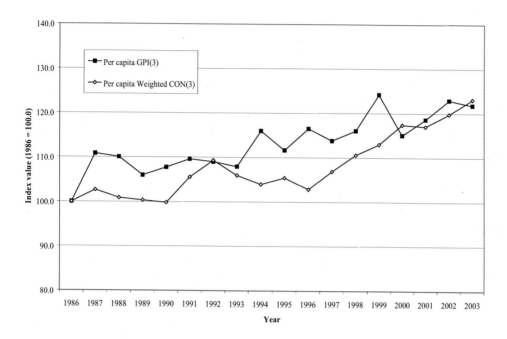

Figure 4.4. Index values of per capita GPI(3) and per capita Weighted CON(3): Victoria, 1986-2003

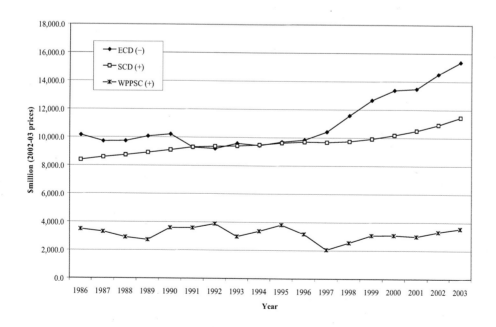

Figure 4.5. Expenditure on consumer durables (ECD), serivce from consumer durables (SCD), and welfare from publicly-provided service capital (WPPSC): Victoria, 1986-2003

As for the service from consumer durables, it increased gradually between 1986 ($8,396 million) and 1999 ($9,931 million) but began to rise more sharply in the final years of the study period ($11,456 million by 2003). Despite the fluctuations in the expenditure on consumer durables, Figure 4.5 shows that the variation in the annual service from consumer durables was considerably more stable. This can be explained by the fact that the service enjoyed in any particular year depends on the depreciation of a ten-year running stock (see sub-section 3.4.3). As a consequence, the service impact of any large annual change in the accumulation of the stock of consumer durables is substantially tempered.

Having said this, the steep rise in the expenditure on consumer durables after 1996 was eventually felt by way of an increase in the service from consumer durables during the latter years of the study period (2000-2003). Barring a steep and sudden decline in expenditure on consumer durables, the escalation of the service from consumer durables should continue for some time into the future.

Also included in Figure 4.5 is the welfare generated by publicly-provided service capital (WPPSC) (column *n* in Table 4.1). Figure 4.5 clearly illustrates an overall and significant decline in the welfare from service capital between 1986 ($3,486 million) and 1997 ($2,052 million). While the welfare level had recovered to $3,557 million by 2003, Figure 4.6 reveals that the ratio of welfare from service capital to Victoria's GPI(3) was a little over 3 per cent. It began at nearly 4.5 per cent in 1986. This indicates a general decline in the contribution made by publicly-provided service capital to the sustainable well-being of the average Victorian. It should be said, nevertheless, that this contribution increased from a low of just over 2 per cent in 1997. However, had the 1986 intensity of contribution existed in 2003, the sustainable well-being of the average Victorian would have been approximately $300 higher.[1]

4.2.3. Distribution Index (DI)

The Distribution Index (DI) used to weight the three measures of adjusted consumption expenditure is revealed in column *j* in Table 4.1. The change in Victoria's DI is illustrated in Figure 4.7.

As can be clearly evidenced from Figure 4.7, Victoria's DI fluctuated throughout the study period. The DI began at 100.0 in 1986 and finished at a value of 111.2 in 2003. The increase in the DI indicates that the income disparity between the rich and the poor was much greater at the end of the study period than in the beginning. Having said this, the steepest rise in the DI occurred between 1992 (DI = 98.6) and 1996 (DI = 113.3). Thus, from 1996 onwards, the DI remained relatively steady, suggesting the problem of distributional inequality stabilised in Victoria over the latter part of the study period.

The negative impact of a rising DI is portrayed in Figure 4.8. This figure reveals two curves — the first curve representing an unweighted per capita CON(3); the second curve representing per capita CON(3) weighted by the DI. Between 1992 and 1996, the rapid escalation of the DI led to the decline in per capita weighted CON(3) even though its unweighted counterpart rose over the same period. While the relatively steady DI value from 1996 to 2003 arrested the widening gap between the unweighted and weighted measures of per capita CON(3), a significant gap between the two remained in 2003. Indeed, the failure to have the distribution of income at the 1986 level meant that the sustainable well-being of the average Victorian was nearly $1,900 lower in 2003 than it would otherwise have been.

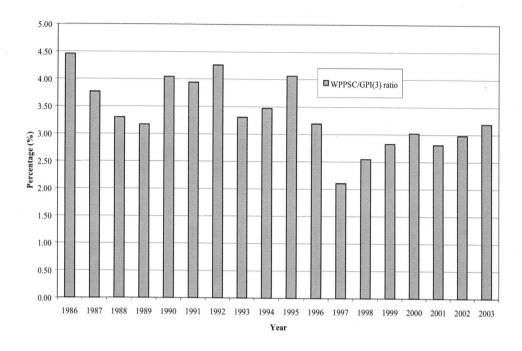

Figure 4.6. Ratio of welfare from publicly-provided service capital (WPPSC) to GPI(3): Victoria, 1986-2003

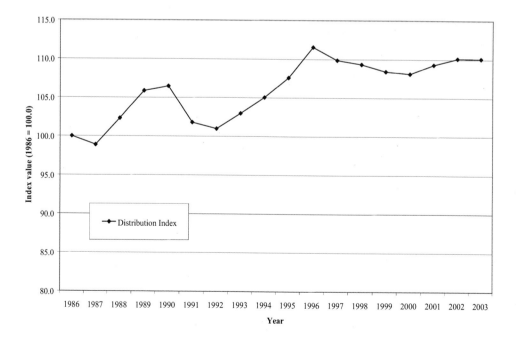

Figure 4.7. Distribution Index (DI): Victoria, 1986-2003

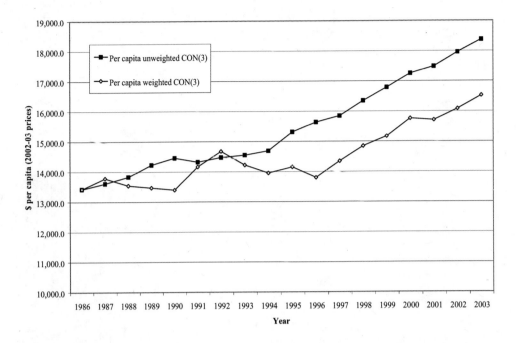

Figure 4.8. Per capita unweighted CON(3) and per capita weighted CON(3): Victoria, 1986-2003

4.2.4. Value of Unpaid Work

The next two items under consideration are the value of non-paid household and volunteer work which, together, constitute the total value of unpaid work (columns *o* and *p* in Table 4.1). Ranging from $58,398 million in 1986 to $70,402 million in 2003, the value of household labour stood as the second largest component of Victoria's GPI. For this reason alone, the value of unpaid work was of great importance to the sustainable well-being of Victorians.

Figure 4.9 reveals the changing value of non-paid household and volunteer work over the study period. The figure also includes a curve to represent the total value of unpaid work. While the sheer magnitude of unpaid work contributed significantly to the value of Victoria's GPI(3), its smooth but gradual rise ensured it played little or no part in the fluctuation of Victoria's GPI(3) over the study period.

4.2.5. Social Costs of Unemployment, Crime, and Family Breakdown

Representing three social afflictions of economic activity, the costs of unemployment, crime, and family breakdown appear in columns *q*, *r*, and *s* in Table 4.1. They are graphically presented in Figure 4.10. While it can be seen that the cost of family breakdown varied trivially in Victoria over the study period, the same cannot be said for the cost of crime. After beginning at $3,488 million in 1986, the cost of crime reached a low of $2,841 million in 1996. It then rose to $4,546 million by 2003. At around 5% of the total value of Victoria's

GPI(3) during most of the study period, it can be concluded that the combined cost of crime and family breakdown played a minor but not insignificant role in the sustainable well-being of Victorians.

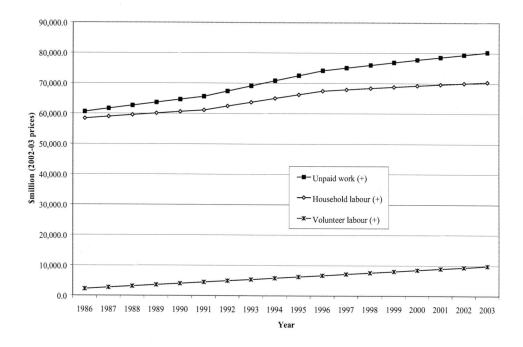

Figure 4.9. Value of non-paid household and volunteer labour: Victoria, 1986-2003

Of the three social costs of economic activity, the greatest influence on Victoria's GPI(3) was undoubtedly the cost of unemployment, underemployment, and labour underutilisation (unemployment broadly defined). Not only was the cost of unemployment substantial in magnitude, it varied greatly over the study period. Following a small decline in the cost of unemployment in Victoria between 1986 ($4,234 million) and 1990 ($3,422 million), it rose sharply to be $9,354 million by 1994. Between 1994 and 2003, the cost of unemployment fell gradually to $6,203 million or, equivalently, to 5.5% of the total value of Victoria's GPI(3).

Although not provided here (see Tables 9.12 and 9.13 in Chapter 9), the cost of unemployment was 46.5% higher in 2003 than it was in 1986 despite Victoria's official unemployment rate being 6.2% in 1986 and 5.9% in 2003. The much larger cost of unemployment was due to the higher rate of underemployment and the steady increase in the proportion of the labour force engaged in part-time and casual work. Unless this recent transformation of the labour market is reversed, the future cost of unemployment is likely to be significantly higher for any official unemployment rate.

To gauge the possible influence of the cost of unemployment on Victoria's GPI(3), consider the respective index values of both in Figure 4.11. Between 1986 and 1994, the initial decline and later steep rise in the cost of unemployment had little impact on Victoria's GPI(3). It would appear, therefore, that since Victoria's GPI(3) remained steady during this period, the fluctuating cost of unemployment mirrored and consequently offset the many benefits reflected in other GPI items.

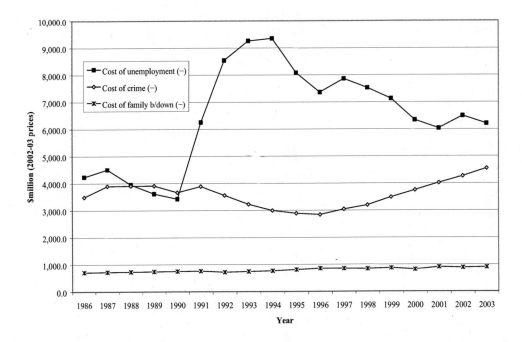

Figure 4.10. Cost of unemployment (CU8), crime, and family breakdown: Victoria, 1986-2003

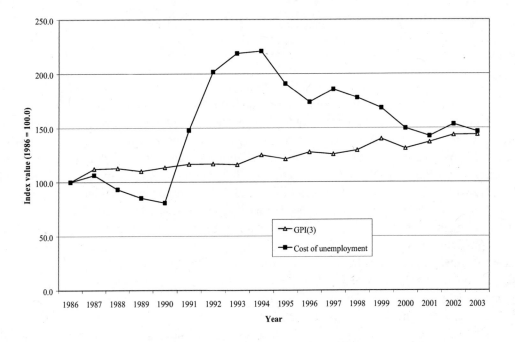

Figure 4.11. Index values of GPI(3) and cost of unemployment: Victoria, 1986-2003

Following 1994, as underemployment and labour underutilisation intensified, Victoria's GPI(3) grew increasingly sensitive to changes in the official unemployment rate. Between 1994 and 1999, Victoria's GPI(3) and the cost of unemployment moved in opposite directions. This was at a time when the cost of unemployment peaked at 9.5% of the total value of Victoria's GPI(3). However, as the cost of unemployment diminished after 1999, its impact on Victoria's GPI(3) significantly waned.

4.2.6. Victoria's Share of the Change in Australia's Foreign Debt

The change in Victoria's share of Australia's foreign debt movements is revealed in column *t* in Table 4.1 and illustrated in Figure 4.12. Figure 4.12 shows that Victoria's share of the change in foreign debt fluctuated wildly throughout the study period. Starting with an increase in net foreign liabilities of $11,707 million in 1986, Victoria's foreign debt position continued to deteriorate — though not as intensely — in every year up to 1993. In 1994, Victoria experienced a decline in net foreign liabilities (i.e., reduction in foreign debt) of $1,790 million.

Unfortunately, the foreign debt position of Victoria again deteriorated from 1995 to 2003. During this period, the largest increase in net foreign liabilities occurred in 2000 ($11,205 million). The increase in Victoria's foreign debt in the last year of the study period amounted to $8,252 million.

Possible explanations for the fluctuation in Victoria's share of Australia's foreign debt position include: (a) exchange rate movements over the study period; (b) the changing relative cost of production *vis-a-vis* the rest of the world; (c) changing real incomes of Australians/Victorians and overseas consumers; and (d) increasing consumer access to credit facilities.

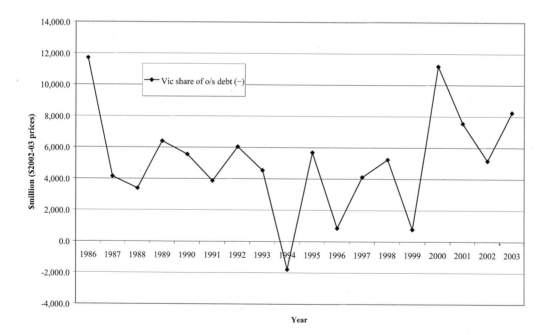

Figure 4.12. Victoria's share of change in foreign (overseas) debt, 1986-2003

Figure 4.13 compares the index values of Victoria's per capita GPI(3) and Victoria's share of the change in Australia's foreign debt. There are two good reasons to believe that Victoria's share of the change in foreign debt had a major influence on the sustainable well-being of the average Victorian. First, at various times during the study period, Victoria's change in net foreign liabilities constituted more than ten percent of the final value of Victoria's GPI(3) (e.g., 1986 and 2000). Second, as Figure 4.13 highlights, Victoria's per capita GPI(3) and its change in net foreign liabilities moved in opposite directions in every year during the study period except 1988, 1993, and 1998. Indeed, the most significant variations in Victoria's foreign debt position corresponded with the most notable changes in its per capital GPI(3) — namely, 1987, 1994-1996, 1999-2001, and 2003.

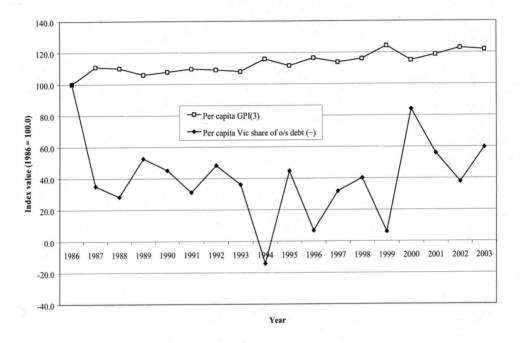

Figure 4.13. Index values of per capita GPI(3) and the per capita share of foreign debt: Victoria, 1986-2003

4.2.7. Cost of Sacrificed Source Function of Natural Capital

Having dealt with the economic and social elements of the GPI, the analysis now shifts to the environmental cost items. Three of Victoria's major source-related environmental costs — i.e., the cost of non-renewable resource depletion, lost agricultural land, and excessive irrigation water use — are disclosed in columns u, v, and w in Table 4.1. All three environmental costs appear in Figure 4.14.

As can be clearly seen from Figure 4.14, the cost of lost agricultural land in Victoria was the smallest of the three environmental costs. While the cost of lost agricultural land rose throughput the study period, the rise was both gradual and minimal ($1,007 million in 1986 to $1,176 million in 2003). The same, however, cannot be said about the cost of excessive irrigation water use in Victoria. Being a state that relies heavily on the Murray-Darling Basin for its agricultural output, Victoria's cost of excessive irrigation water use was both large and continuously on the rise throughput the study period ($3,863 million in 1986 and $5,827 million in 2003).

As for the cost of non-renewable resource depletion (i.e., sub-soil assets), the most glaring difference between it and the agriculture-related costs was its large variation over the study period and its significant decline after 1993. Apart from a rise in 2000, the cost of non-renewable resource depletion fell sharply from a high of $4,441 million in 1993 to just $2,556 million by 2003.

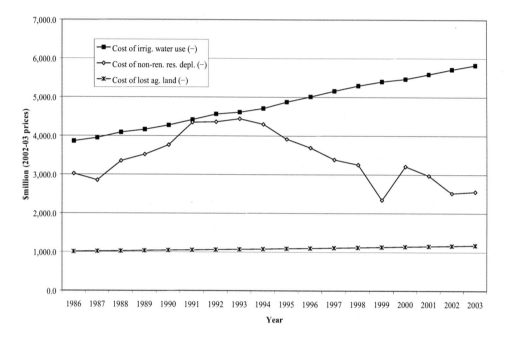

Figure 4.14. Cost of non-renewable resource depletion, lost agricultural land, and excessive irrigation water use: Victoria, 1986-2003

Having said this, the combined cost of non-renewable resource depletion, lost agricultural land, and excessive irrigation water use remained significant throughout the study period. It ranged from a low of 8.1% of Victoria's GPI(3) in 1999 to a high of 11.1% in 1993. By the end of the study period, it was still 8.5% of Victoria's GPI(3). This is little doubt that these three source-related environmental costs played a considerable role in the fluctuation of Victoria's sustainable well-being. Furthermore, there is no reason to doubt why these costs should not do likewise in the future.

4.2.8. Cost of Timber Depletion

The cost of timber depletion appears in column *x* of Table 4.1. Because of its negligible value, no illustrative figure is provided. From Table 4.1, it can be seen that Victoria enjoyed very small gains in timber stocks throughput most of the study period. Only between 1993 and 1995 did Victoria suffer a meagre decline in timber stocks.

Of course, it must be remembered that the values appearing in column x cover all types and forms of timber. It is therefore conceivable that the area of old-growth forests could have declined during the study period only to be offset by increases in plantation timber and forest regrowth. Thus, timber stocks could have increased at the same time forest ecosystems were being destroyed. As explained in sub-section 3.4.22, any ecological impact of forestry activities is captured by the Ecosystem Health Index (EHI).

4.2.9. Cost of Air and Urban Waste-water Pollution

The two major sink-related costs of air and urban waste-water pollution appear in columns y and z in Table 4.1. They are both graphically illustrated in Figure 4.15.

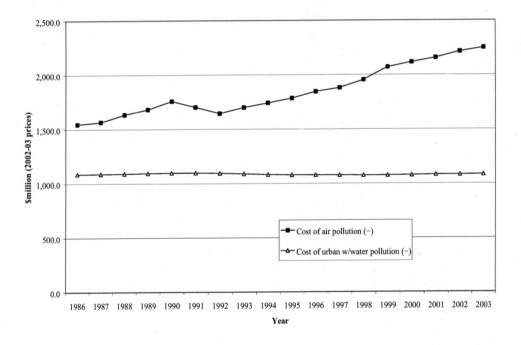

Figure 4.15. Cost of air and urban waste-water pollution: Victoria, 1986-2003

Figure 4.15 reveals that the cost of urban waste-water pollution in Victoria remained quite steady at around $1,100 million over the entire study period. It consequently had very little influence on the trend movement of Victoria's per capita GPI(3).

Conversely, the cost of air pollution in Victoria was both higher and much less stable. Only in 1991 and 1992 did the cost of air pollution fall. Despite technological advances in the area of pollution abatement, the cost of air pollution in Victoria rose from $1,545 million in 1986 to $2,249 million in 2003. At around 2% of the total value of Victoria's GPI(3), air pollution had a minor but not inconsequential impact on the sustainable well-being of Victorians.

4.2.10. Cost of Long-term Environmental Damage

As a consequence of a 55.7% increase in Victoria's energy consumption over the study period, the escalating cost of long-term environmental damage is revealed in column *aa* of Table 4.1 and Figure 4.16.

Starting at $10,781 million in 1986, the cost of long-term environmental damage steadily increased to $19,039 million by 2003. Given both the steepness in the rise and the sheer magnitude of its value, the cost of long-term environmental damage had a major influence on Victoria's per capita GPI(3).

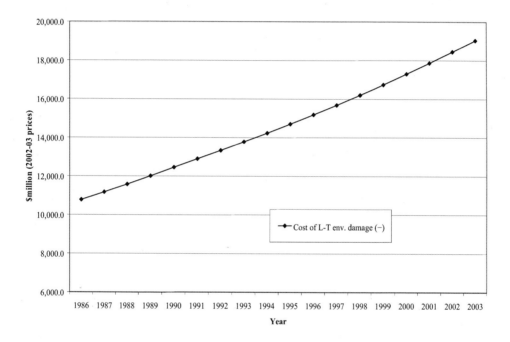

Figure 4.16. Cost of long-term environmental damage: Victoria, 1986-2003

4.2.11. Ecosystem Health Index (EHI) and the Cost of Lost Natural Capital Services (Weighted and Unweighted)

The final items up for consideration are Victoria's Ecosystem Health Index (EHI) and the cost of lost natural capital services (LNCS), both weighted and unweighted (columns *bb*, *cc*, and *dd* in Table 4.1).

Due to the very small rate of natural vegetation clearance over the study period, Victoria's EHI declined marginally from an index value of 100.0 in 1986 to an index value of 99.1 by 2003 (see Figure 4.17). So inconsequential was the change in Victoria's EHI that the difference between the unweighted and weighted cost of lost natural capital services was negligible (approximately $60 per Victorian in 2003). For this reason, it was only worth revealing the weighted cost of lost natural capital services in Figure 4.18.

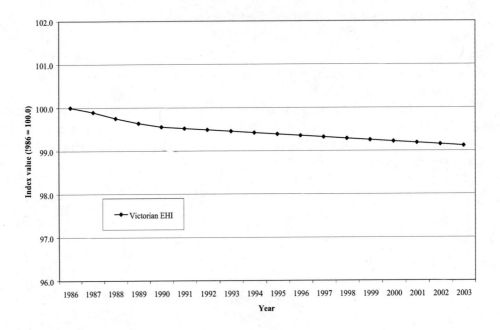

Figure 4.17. Ecosystem Health Index (EHI): Victoria, 1986-2003

It can be easily seen from Figure 4.18 that the environmental cost of Victoria's economic activity (LNCS) increased markedly over the study period. It in fact rose from $21,290 million in 1986 to $32,129 million by 2003. This constituted an increase from $5,117 per Victorian in 1986 to $6,542 per Victorian by 2003.

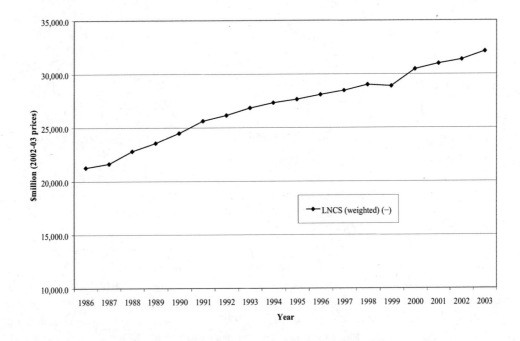

Figure 4.18. Cost of lost natural capital services (LNCS) – weighted: Victoria, 1986-2003

In order to demonstrate the impact of the rise in environmental costs on Victoria's per capita GPI(3), the index values of both are provided in Figure 4.19. The figure clearly shows that the index values of per capita GPI(3) and per capita weighted LNCS moved in opposite directions in most years during the study period. The countermovement of both index values was most notable in the late-1980s, mid-1990s, 1999, 2000, and 2003. Since the cost of lost natural capital services seriously influenced Victoria's per capita GPI(3), there is little doubt that environmental costs almost kept pace with the value of the additional benefits associated with higher consumption levels. As a consequence, the factors underlying the rise in Victoria's environmental costs should constitute a priority concern of policy-makers.

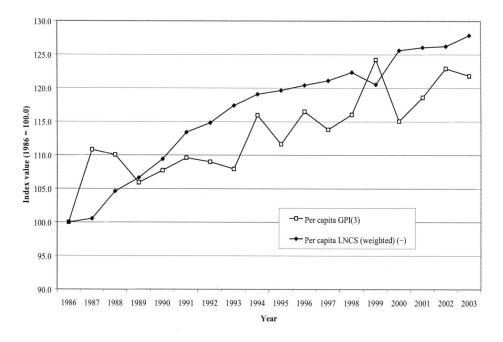

Figure 4.19. Index values of per capita GPI(3) and per capita lost natural capital services (weighted): Victoria, 1986-2003

In particular, policy-makers should endeavour to reduce Victoria's 'ecological footprint' and ensure it does not exceed the state's biocapacity. The ecological footprint is the equivalent area of land *required* to generate the renewable resources and absorb the wastes associated with current and projected levels of economic activity (Wackernagel and Rees, 1996). Biocapacity refers to the amount of *available* land that a state or nation has to generate an on-going supply of renewable resources and absorb its own wastes plus the pollution of other states and nations. Unsustainability occurs if the ecological footprint of a nation or state exceeds its biocapacity.

4.3. VICTORIA'S GPI VERSUS GSP

This particular section of the book focuses on a comparison between Victoria's per capita GPI(3) and its per capita GSP. The value of Victoria's aggregate and per capita GSP is revealed in columns *hh* and *mm* in Table 4.1. Victoria's per capita GSP is also provided in an indexed form in column *qq*. The three different measures of Victoria's per capita GPI — namely, GPI(1), GPI(2), and GPI(3) — and Victoria's per capita GSP are presented in Figure 4.20. In view of our preference for GPI(3) as a more accurate indicator of sustainable well-being, it is evident that Victoria's per capita GSP substantially overstated the genuine progress of the average Victorian throughout the study period. Moreover, the gap between Victoria's per capita GPI(3) and per capita GSP grew between 1986 and 2003. For instance, in 1986, Victoria's per capita GSP was $26,744, while its per capita GPI(3) was $18,839 — a difference of $7,905 per Victorian. By 2003, this disparity had proliferated to $11,136 per Victorian (i.e., Victoria's per capita GSP was $39,067 and its per capita GPI(3) was $27,931).

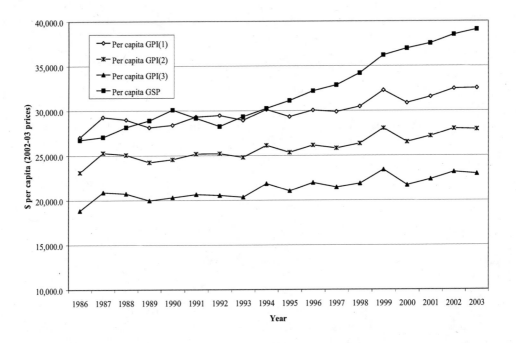

Figure 4.20. Per capita Genuine Progress Indicator (GPI) (1), (2), and (3) and per capita Gross State Product (GSP): Victoria, 1986-2003

Interestingly, the difference between the two indicators changed very little between 1986 and 1993. Although this had a lot to do with the slow rate of growth in Victoria's per capita GSP over this period, a disconcerting aspect of the comparison between the two indicators is that, beyond 1993, per capita GPI(3) did not accelerate in the same manner as per capita GSP. This is best illustrated in Figure 4.21 by the respective index values of per capita GPI(3) and per capita GSP.

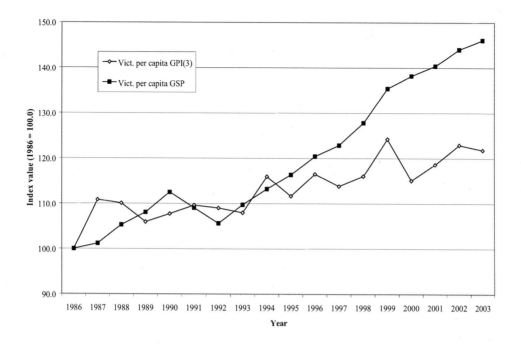

Figure 4.21. Index values of per capita GPI(3) and per capita GSP: Victoria, 1986-2003

Figure 4.21 shows that Victoria's per capita GPI(3) closely followed the trend movement of its per capita GSP until 1996. Beyond 1996, and particularly after 1999, the growth rate of Victoria's GPI(3) was unable to keep pace with the rate of increase in Victoria's per capita GSP. This suggests that the rapid increase in per capita GSP over the past decade did not translate very effectively into a rise in sustainable well-being. Second, and as alluded to earlier, it appears that as much as the rise in per capita GSP yielded significant extra benefits to the average Victorian, it came at the expense of increasing social and environmental costs.

Figures 4.20 and 4.21 lead one to reconsider whether a high rate of GSP growth is desirable for Victoria and, moreover, whether policies specifically aimed at increasing Victoria's GSP may be detrimental to the sustainable well-being of the average Victorian. We believe, for instance, that Victoria's per capita GPI(3) would be much higher if there was a greater policy focus on qualitative improvement, improved efficiency of resource use, distributional equity, and natural capital maintenance.

4.4. VICTORIA'S GPI AND THE
GROWTH OF THE VICTORIAN ECONOMY

While a comparison of GSP and the GPI provides greater insight into the extent to which the aggregate production of goods and services translates into sustainable well-being, it indicates little about the relationship between the GPI and the growth rate of a state's economy. To recall from section 3.5, real GSP cannot be used to determine if the economy has physically grown in scale. This requires the calculation of net capital investment (NCI) which is equal to the investment in all durable goods/human-made capital (INV*) minus its depreciation (DEP*) (see equation 3.5).

Estimates of INV*, DEP*, and NCI for Victoria appear in columns *ss*, *uu*, and *vv* in Table 4.1. Also revealed is Victoria's NCI/DEP* ratio in column *ww*. In the final column, we describe the prevailing growth rate of the Victorian economy based on the growth categorisations outlined in sub-section 3.5.7.

INV*, DEP*, and NCI are graphically illustrated in Figure 4.22. As can be seen from this figure, investment in all human-made capital (INV*) fluctuated throughout the study period. Beginning at $30,930 million in 1986, INV* slowly increased in the first few years but then drastically declined in 1991 and 1992. After falling to a low of $27,965 million in 1992, a rapid rate of investment growth took place that saw INV* eventually reach $63,234 million by 2003.

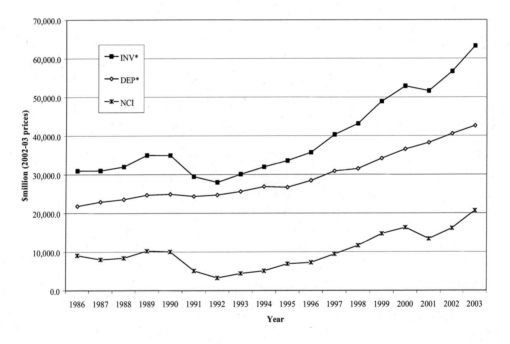

Figure 4.22. Investment (INV*), depreciation of all human-made capital (DEP*), and net capital investment (NCI): Victoria, 1986-2003

Unlike investment, the depreciation value of all human-made capital (DEP*) grew steadily over the entire study period. The only exceptions were 1991 and 1995. However, the decreases in both years were miniscule. Overall, DEP* almost doubled to be $42,575 million in 2003 after starting at $21,837 million in 1986.

Owing to the fluctuation in INV* and the steady but unspectacular rise in DEP*, the increase in the stock of all human-made capital varied considerably between 1986 and 2003. As Figure 4.22 shows, there was no year in which the stock of all human-made capital declined (i.e., when the physical scale of the Victorian economy diminished). Column *xx* in Table 4.1 indicates that the prevailing growth rate of the Victorian economy was *high* between 1986 and 1990. While a *low* rate of growth occurred between 1991 and 1994, the growth rate of the Victorian economy recovered somewhat to be hovering in the *low/high* range in 1995 and 1996. A *high* rate of growth returned in 1997 and continued to 2002 before reaching a near *rapid* rate in 2003.

To gain a greater appreciation of the possible impact that the growth of the Victorian economy had on its per capita GPI(3), consider Figure 4.23. In almost every year between 1986 and 1993, Victoria's per capita GPI(3) moved in the opposite direction to the NCI/DEP* ratio. Of particular note is the fact that Victoria's per capita GPI(3) did not accompany the dramatic decline in the growth rate of the Victorian economy that occurred between 1989 and 1992. Indeed, one of the largest increases in Victoria's per capita GPI(3) occurred in 1994 when the prevailing growth rate of the Victorian economy was low and, moreover, had followed three previous years in the low growth category.

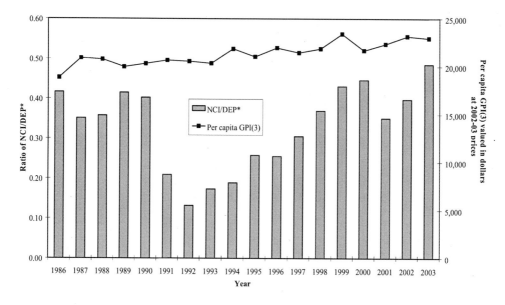

Figure 4.23. Per capita GPI(3) and the ratio of nt capital investment (NCI) to all human-made capital depreciation (DEP*); Victoria, 1986-2003

Contrary to expectation, the increased rate of growth of the Victorian economy between 1995 and 2000 did not significantly increase Victoria's per capita GPI(3). Furthermore, one of the more significant declines in Victoria's per capita GPI(3) occurred in 2000. This particular year happened to be the last in a run of eight straight years of escalating growth. Given the turnaround rise in per capita GPI(3) in 2001 — a year in which the growth rate of the Victorian economy declined — one is compelled to ask whether a continuing high rate of growth eventually has a negative impact on sustainable well-being. The question is by no means definitively answered by Figure 4.22, however, an affirmative answer is further supported by the slight fall in Victoria's per capita GPI(3) in 2003 — a year in which the growth rate of the Victorian economy almost advanced into rapid growth territory.

The message from Figure 4.23 is therefore similar to the one indicated by Figures 4.20 and 4.21 in relation to Victoria's GSP — that is, a high to rapid rate of growth of the

Victorian economy growth may be detrimental to the sustainable well-being of the average Victorian. Further questions raised by Figure 4.23 include the following:

- Would Victoria's per capita GPI(3) have been higher if the Victorian economy was physically smaller in scale but qualitatively better? That is, could a smaller but qualitatively superior economy have yielded greater welfare benefits and reduced the social and environmental costs of economic activity?
- If the answer to both the above questions is yes, is not time for Victoria to make the transition to a lower rate of growth and to discover ways to facilitate qualitative improvement and production excellence?
- Should a high rate of growth continue to be the prime objective of economic policy, can we be certain that the welfare benefits of growth will increase in the future as they have in the past when, on the other side of the ledger, it is clear that the social and environmental costs of growth are on the rise and showing no sign of abating?

The final question may prove to be as important as the previous three insofar as a continuing high/rapid growth policy could eventually result in per capita GPI(3) falling. Based on the evidence presented, there seems to be no guarantee that the sustainable well-being of the average Victorian will continue to rise — even if at a slower rate than in the past — should a high or rapid growth rate remain the principal objective of policy-makers.

4.5. SUMMARY

As a consequence of the analysis conducted in this chapter, a great deal has been established regarding the genuine progress of Victoria over the study period. To clarify matters before moving onto Chapter 5, it is worth recapitulating to summarise the major findings of Chapter 4:

- The sustainable well-being of the average Victorian — as denoted by Victoria's per capita GPI(3) — fluctuated over the study period but, overall, rose moderately from a value of $18,839 per Victorian in 1986 to $22,951 per Victorian by 2003. This constituted a 21.8% rise in sustainable well-being over the study period or an average rate of increase of 1.46% per annum. Having said this, the majority of the increase in Victoria's per capita GPI(3) occurred after 1993.
- Victoria's per capita GSP greatly overstated the sustainable well-being of the average Victorian throughout the study period. The disparity between Victoria's per capita GSP and per capita GPI(3) increased from $7,905 per Victorian in 1986 to $11,136 per Victorian by 2003.
- Victoria's per capita GPI(3) closely followed the trend movement of its per capita GSP between 1986 and 1996 (i.e., the gap between the two indicators remained largely unchanged). Beyond 1996, the growth rate of Victoria's GPI(3) was unable to keep pace with the rate of increase in Victoria's per capita GSP.
- The Victorian economy physically grew in scale in every year between 1986 and 2003. However, the rate of growth varied from:

> High:- 1986 to 1990
> Low:- 1991 to 1994
> Low/high:- 1995 and 1996
> High:- 1997 to 2002
> Rapid/high:- 2003.

- Between 1986 and 1993, Victoria's per capita GPI(3) moved in the apposite direction to the NCI/DEP* ratio (i.e., to the growth rate of Victorian economy).

- Despite a dramatic decline in the growth rate of the Victorian economy between 1989 and 1992, Victoria's per capita GPI(3) did not decline over this period ($19,957 per Victorian in 1989 and $20,535 per Victorian in 1992).

- One of the largest increases in Victoria's per capita GPI(3) occurred in 1994 — a low growth year that followed three previous years of low growth.

- The high rate of growth of the Victorian economy between 1995 and 2000 did not significantly increase Victoria's per capita GPI(3) ($25,335 per Victorian in 1995 and $26,499 per Victorian in 2000). Indeed, Victoria's per capita GPI(3) fell in 2000.

- Victoria's per capita GPI(3) rose in 2001 — a year in which the growth rate of the Victorian economy declined.

- After rising again in 2001 and 2002, Victoria's per capita GPI(3) decreased in 2003 — a year in which the Victorian economy grew at a high/rapid rate.

- The high growth rates of the Victorian economy over the past decade failed to translate effectively into the sustainable well-being of the average Victorian. This suggests that the extra benefits generated by high rates of growth were largely offset by the ever-increasing rise in social and environmental costs. Moreover, it begs the question as to whether Victoria's per capita GPI(3) would have been higher in 2003 if the Victorian economy had been physically smaller but qualitatively better.

- Minor influences on Victoria's per capita GPI(3) were:
  > the rise in the service from consumer durables (SCD) after 1996;
  > the decrease in the welfare from publicly-provided service capital (WPPSC) between 1992 and 1997;
  > the increase in the combined cost of crime and family breakdown after 1996.

- Major influences on Victoria's per capita GPI(3) included:
  > the sheer magnitude of Weighted CON(3) and its increase after 1997;
  > the steep rise in the Distribution Index (DI) between 1992 and 1997;
  > the value of unpaid work (non-paid household work plus volunteer work);
  > the rapid increase in the cost of unemployment (broadly defined) between 1990 and 1994 and the continuing relative high cost of unemployment between 1996 and 2003 despite the significant fall in the official unemployment rate;
  > the wild fluctuations throughout the study period of Victoria's share of the change in Australia's foreign debt;
  > the increasing cost of environmental damage (lost natural capital services or LNCS) — in particular, the rising cost of long-term environmental damage caused by Victoria's excessive rate of energy consumption.

NOTE

₁ This, of course, assumes that all other items that make up Victoria's per capita GPI(3) maintain their same values. This is highly unlikely. Some observers would argue that since a boost in government expenditure 'crowds out' private sector spending, some downward pressure would be exerted on the GPI. Others have shown that the supposed negative impact of government expenditure on private sector spending is a fallacy (Mitchell and Watts, 1997 and 2001). This debate aside, there is a strong likelihood that increased government expenditure on service capital would augment the demand for natural resources and, in so doing, directly increase the values of some environmental cost items. On the other hand, a boost in government expenditure can lower the cost of unemployment. Moreover, if the increase in government expenditure is well directed, it can facilitate the development and uptake of 'green' technologies that could help to reduce the value of some environmental costs associated with all economic activities. In all, we think an increase in well directed government expenditure on service capital can boost the sustainable well-being of a nation's or state's citizens.

Chapter 5

A COMPARISON OF VICTORIA'S PERFORMANCE RELATIVE TO THE REST-OF-AUSTRALIA

5.1. COMPARING THE GPI OF VICTORIA AND THE REST-OF-AUSTRALIA

We have so far conducted a very comprehensive assessment of Victoria's genuine progress performance. Our focus of attention now shifts to the performance of Victoria *vis-a-vis* the Rest-of-Australia. A comparative analysis is potentially valuable in that a great deal can be learned about what Victoria is doing differently to the Rest-of-Australia that could be especially beneficial or detrimental to sustainable well-being. This knowledge can then be used in the formulation of future policies.

Before moving on, it is important to point out that 'Rest-of-Australia' implies Australia minus Victoria. As such, the comparative analysis conducted in Chapter 5 reveals nothing about Victoria's performance relative to a particular Australian state. Indeed, it is simultaneously possible for Victoria to be outperforming the Rest-of-Australia while another state is outperforming Victoria, or vice versa.

To assist in our comparative analysis, Table 5.1 is provided below. The table is identical in structure to Table 4.1 except that the values in each column relate to the Rest-of-Australia. Based on columns *ll* in Tables 4.1 and 5.1, Figure 5.1 reveals the per capita GPI(3) of Victoria and the Rest-of-Australia.

As Figure 5.1 clearly shows, the sustainable well-being of the average Victorian was consistently higher than that of the average person living elsewhere in Australia. Furthermore, the difference between Victoria and the Rest-of-Australia increased over the study period. For example, while the difference in per capita GPI(3) of Victoria and the Rest-of-Australia was $2,105 per person in 1986 ($18,839 for Victoria and $16,734 for the Rest-of-Australia), it had more than doubled by 2003 to $4,331 per person ($22,951 for Victoria and $18,620 for the Rest-of-Australia). Not surprisingly, the percentage rise in per capita GPI(3) over the study period for Victoria was significantly higher than that of the Rest-of-Australia (21.8% versus 11.3%).

Table 5.1: Genuine Progress Indicator (GPI) and real gross product of the Rest-of-Australia (Australia minus Victoria), 1986-2003

Year	CON(1) ($)	CON(2) ($)	CON(3) ($)	ECD ($)	Consumer durables ($)	SCD ($)	Adjusted CON(1) ($)	Adjusted CON(2) ($)	Adjusted CON(3) ($)	Distribution index	Weighted CON(1) ($)	Weighted CON(2) ($)	Weighted CON(3) ($)
	a	b	c	d	e	f (e x 0.1)	g (a - d + f)	h (b - d + f)	i (c - d + f)	j (1986=100.0)	k (g/j) x 100	l (h/j) x 100	m (i/j) x 100
1985					237,917.4								
1986	255,409.0	209,077.0	159,308.8	-26,980.0	242,809.4	23,791.7	252,220.7	205,888.7	156,120.5	100.0	252,220.7	205,888.7	156,120.5
1987	259,239.0	212,071.0	160,827.3	-25,052.0	245,766.8	24,280.9	258,467.9	211,299.9	160,056.2	98.9	261,212.5	213,543.6	161,755.7
1988	268,098.0	219,341.3	166,495.0	-25,765.0	249,924.1	24,576.7	266,909.7	218,152.9	165,306.7	102.4	260,730.3	213,102.4	161,479.6
1989	278,577.0	227,959.8	173,863.3	-27,505.0	255,142.5	24,992.4	276,064.4	225,447.2	171,350.7	105.9	260,606.7	212,823.7	161,756.2
1990	292,375.0	239,397.8	182,711.8	-29,035.0	261,562.8	25,514.2	288,854.2	235,877.0	179,191.0	106.0	272,611.0	222,612.8	169,114.5
1991	298,603.0	244,322.3	186,272.0	-28,419.0	265,820.1	26,156.3	296,340.3	242,059.5	184,009.3	102.0	290,427.4	237,229.7	180,337.7
1992	304,670.0	249,448.5	190,521.0	-28,889.0	269,696.9	26,582.0	302,363.0	247,141.5	188,214.0	101.8	296,933.0	242,703.2	184,834.0
1993	310,834.0	254,655.0	194,637.5	-29,338.0	274,400.9	26,969.7	308,465.7	252,286.7	192,269.2	103.2	298,848.4	244,420.9	186,274.7
1994	319,345.0	262,134.0	201,031.8	-30,277.0	278,564.2	27,440.1	316,508.1	259,297.1	198,194.8	105.0	301,482.5	246,987.5	188,785.9
1995	332,494.0	273,644.5	210,129.5	-32,095.0	283,355.0	27,856.4	328,255.4	269,405.9	205,890.9	107.4	305,570.0	250,787.5	191,662.0
1996	346,890.0	286,029.3	219,842.0	-33,047.0	289,422.0	28,335.5	342,178.5	281,317.8	215,130.5	111.0	308,352.1	253,507.8	193,863.5
1997	355,694.0	293,299.8	225,654.5	-33,702.0	298,072.0	28,942.2	350,934.2	288,540.0	220,894.7	109.7	319,945.3	263,060.7	201,388.8
1998	371,679.0	306,974.3	236,336.3	-35,829.0	308,136.0	29,807.2	365,657.2	300,952.5	230,314.5	109.1	335,166.6	275,857.3	211,109.5
1999	388,408.0	321,299.3	247,384.8	-37,184.0	317,815.0	30,813.6	382,037.6	314,928.9	241,014.4	107.7	354,738.1	292,424.8	223,792.0
2000	403,226.0	333,934.5	256,840.8	-38,442.0	327,222.0	31,781.5	396,565.5	327,274.0	250,180.3	107.7	368,302.8	303,949.6	232,350.2
2001	413,528.0	342,079.0	263,115.5	-38,874.0	337,677.0	32,722.2	407,376.2	335,927.2	256,963.7	108.6	375,009.7	309,237.4	236,547.7
2002	425,260.0	351,300.0	270,237.0	-40,031.0	348,819.0	33,767.7	418,996.7	345,036.7	263,973.7	109.6	382,384.3	314,887.0	240,907.4
2003	442,585.0	365,564.5	282,044.0	-43,105.0	362,586.0	34,881.9	434,361.9	357,341.4	273,820.9	109.7	395,926.2	325,721.0	249,591.1

Note: All values are in millions of 2002-2003 dollars except where indicated

Table 5.1 (Continued): Genuine Progress Indicator (GPI) and real gross product of the Rest-of-Australia (Australia minus Victoria), 1986-2003

Year	WPPSC ($)	H/hold labour ($)	Volunteer labour ($)	Cost of u/e ($)	Cost of crime ($)	Cost of family b/d	ROA share o/s debt ($)	Non-ren. res. dep. ($)	Lost agric. land ($)	Irrig. water use ($)	Timber dep. ($)	Air polln. ($)	Urban w/w polln. ($)
	n	o	p	q	r	s	t	u	v	w	x	y	z
1985													
1986	12,211.4	166,726.3	14,728.8	-16,029.1	-7,294.3	-2,371.1	-31,917.5	-12,320.8	-33,614.9	-9,839.0	113.3	-4,397.0	-3,083.4
1987	13,156.9	169,393.4	15,236.6	-17,180.0	-8,011.1	-2,446.1	-11,249.4	-11,635.8	-33,919.6	-10,055.7	113.0	-4,456.6	-3,089.9
1988	10,585.6	171,991.4	15,744.5	-15,880.0	-7,883.9	-2,521.0	-9,298.0	-13,678.3	-34,229.9	-10,417.4	113.0	-4,649.3	-3,118.7
1989	9,910.7	174,521.3	16,252.4	-13,173.5	-8,071.9	-2,596.0	-17,464.1	-14,363.2	-34,545.6	-10,622.8	111.0	-4,788.4	-3,146.6
1990	11,957.3	176,984.3	16,760.3	-14,943.4	-8,930.9	-2,670.9	-16,203.4	-16,040.8	-34,866.8	-10,882.7	226.1	-4,888.2	-3,163.0
1991	13,732.9	179,381.4	17,268.2	-21,996.1	-9,218.8	-2,745.9	-11,579.5	-16,717.1	-35,193.9	-11,241.2	8.9	-4,871.1	-3,180.3
1992	15,064.3	184,442.2	17,776.1	-25,195.2	-9,957.8	-2,882.0	-17,654.2	-17,734.8	-35,526.8	-11,621.1	87.4	-4,880.4	-3,194.8
1993	14,410.5	189,385.1	18,212.5	-24,589.4	-10,587.7	-3,063.9	-13,653.1	-17,788.0	-35,864.1	-11,763.1	131.4	-4,998.8	-3,204.0
1994	12,638.1	194,212.2	18,683.2	-22,470.2	-10,661.2	-3,035.8	5,595.0	-18,322.6	-36,203.3	-12,001.5	-50.2	-5,148.2	-3,215.7
1995	13,062.0	198,925.0	19,189.7	-20,163.5	-10,915.5	-3,100.4	-17,467.0	-20,265.3	-36,547.0	-12,352.0	-50.5	-5,325.2	-3,234.3
1996	13,013.6	203,525.5	19,733.3	-21,268.6	-11,324.8	-3,272.4	-2,714.6	-22,350.1	-36,896.3	-12,693.2	-51.1	-5,493.1	-3,252.6
1997	12,873.3	204,282.1	20,315.5	-22,268.1	-12,280.8	-3,178.3	-12,762.1	-23,082.8	-37,251.2	-13,082.0	-51.1	-5,659.1	-3,261.2
1998	10,165.9	205,003.7	20,823.4	-21,987.1	-13,044.5	-3,197.8	-16,356.2	-24,084.9	-37,609.4	-13,442.0	361.2	-5,844.0	-3,266.2
1999	12,324.7	205,690.9	21,331.3	-20,563.7	-13,342.7	-3,260.1	-2,489.3	-24,885.1	-37,966.2	-13,768.8	361.2	-6,059.6	-3,275.1
2000	11,586.9	206,344.5	21,839.2	-19,968.3	-14,283.0	-3,102.9	-35,125.1	-25,552.8	-38,328.2	-13,931.8	361.3	-6,235.1	-3,285.0
2001	13,600.1	206,965.0	22,347.1	-21,861.1	-14,725.0	-3,440.2	-23,905.6	-27,934.2	-38,704.7	-14,314.8	361.2	-6,280.6	-3,270.3
2002	13,957.1	207,552.9	22,855.0	-20,797.6	-13,424.9	-3,357.7	-16,005.2	-28,294.5	-39,095.8	-14,645.2	102.8	-6,463.2	-3,310.6
2003	12,522.9	208,108.9	23,362.8	-21,720.5	-14,171.9	-3,422.5	-25,739.1	-28,370.6	-39,501.4	-14,955.8	361.2	-6,581.4	-3,320.9

Note: All values are in millions of 2002-2003 dollars except where indicated

Table 5.1 (Continued): Genuine Progress Indicator (GPI) and real gross product of the Rest-of-Australia (Australia minus Victoria), 1986-2003

Year	L-T env damage ($)	LNCS ($)	EHI	Weighted LNCS ($)	GPI (1) ($)	GPI (2) ($)	GPI (3) ($)	Real GDP (ROA) ($)	ROA Pop. (thousands)	Per capita GPI (1) ($)	Per capita GPI (2) ($)	Per capita GPI (3) ($)	Per capita real GDP ($)
	aa	bb	cc	dd	ee	ff	gg	hh	ii	jj	kk	ll	mm
		u to aa	1986 = 100.0	(bb/cc) x 100						(ee/ii)	(ff/ii)	(gg/ii)	(hh/ii)
1985													
1986	-30,609.2	-93,751.1	100.0	-93,751.1	294,524.0	248,192.0	198,423.8	316,712.4	11,857.5	24,838.6	20,931.2	16,734.0	26,709.9
1987	-31,651.4	-94,696.0	99.8	-94,888.9	325,224.0	277,555.2	225,767.3	324,216.6	12,053.8	26,981.1	23,026.4	18,730.0	26,897.5
1988	-32,725.6	-98,706.1	99.5	-99,190.1	324,278.8	276,650.9	225,028.1	341,617.1	12,269.6	26,429.5	22,547.7	18,340.3	27,842.6
1989	-33,862.1	-101,217.7	99.3	-101,921.9	318,063.7	270,280.7	219,213.2	355,354.0	12,494.3	25,456.8	21,632.4	17,545.1	28,441.4
1990	-35,024.5	-104,639.9	99.0	-105,650.7	329,913.6	279,915.5	226,417.1	366,389.1	12,686.5	26,005.0	22,064.0	17,847.0	28,880.2
1991	-36,196.5	-107,391.2	98.9	-108,580.2	346,689.4	293,491.7	236,599.8	368,761.9	12,863.7	26,951.1	22,815.6	18,392.9	28,666.9
1992	-37,397.2	-110,267.7	98.8	-111,644.6	346,881.7	292,651.9	234,782.7	373,158.8	13,039.7	26,602.0	22,443.2	18,005.3	28,617.2
1993	-38,613.3	-112,099.8	98.6	-113,658.8	355,303.6	300,876.1	242,729.8	386,028.7	13,194.7	26,927.7	22,802.8	18,396.0	29,256.3
1994	-39,871.0	-114,812.5	98.5	-116,572.6	379,871.3	325,376.2	267,174.7	401,544.1	13,367.2	28,418.2	24,341.4	19,987.4	30,039.6
1995	-41,183.9	-118,958.3	98.4	-120,951.8	364,148.5	309,366.1	250,240.5	419,505.3	13,554.4	26,865.8	22,824.1	18,462.0	30,949.8
1996	-42,540.5	-123,277.0	98.2	-125,565.2	380,478.9	325,634.6	265,990.4	437,061.7	13,750.6	27,670.1	23,681.6	19,344.0	31,785.0
1997	-43,932.7	-126,320.0	98.0	-128,893.5	378,033.4	321,148.9	259,477.0	454,766.4	13,920.4	27,156.9	23,070.4	18,640.1	32,669.1
1998	-45,361.6	-129,246.9	97.8	-132,114.9	384,459.1	325,149.8	260,402.1	474,325.6	14,073.5	27,318.0	23,103.8	18,503.1	33,703.6
1999	-46,851.1	-132,444.6	97.7	-135,625.1	418,804.3	356,491.0	287,858.2	496,739.0	14,239.5	29,411.5	25,035.4	20,215.5	34,884.7
2000	-48,377.0	-135,348.7	97.5	-138,832.3	396,761.8	332,408.6	260,809.2	516,241.0	14,412.0	27,529.9	23,064.6	18,096.6	35,820.1
2001	-49,914.3	-140,057.7	97.3	-143,904.7	410,085.2	344,312.9	271,623.1	525,209.4	14,608.5	28,071.7	23,569.3	18,593.5	35,952.3
2002	-51,490.5	-143,197.0	97.2	-147,378.8	425,785.0	358,287.7	284,308.1	545,879.2	14,783.8	28,800.9	24,235.2	19,231.1	36,924.3
2003	-53,089.5	-145,458.4	97.0	-149,959.6	424,907.2	354,702.1	278,572.2	561,423.3	14,961.2	28,400.6	23,708.1	18,619.6	37,525.2

Note: All values are in millions of 2002-2003 dollars except where indicated

Table 5.1 (Continued): Genuine Progress Indicator (GPI) and real gross product of the Rest-of-Australia (Australia minus Victoria), 1986-2003

Year	Per capita GPI (1) ($)	Per capita GPI (2) ($)	Per capita GPI (3) ($)	Per capita real GDP	INV ($)	INV* ($)	DEP ($)	DEP* ($)	NCI ($)	NCI/DEP* ($)	Growth strategy
	mn	oo	pp	qq	rr	ss	tt	uu	vv	ww	xx
	1986 = 100.0	1986 = 100.0	1986 = 100.0	1986 = 100.0		$(rr + d)$		$(tt + n)$	$(ss - uu)$	(vv/uu)	
1985											
1986	100.0	100.0	100.0	100.0	68,079.0	95,059.0	44,022.9	67,814.6	27,244.4	0.40	high
1987	108.6	110.0	111.9	100.7	67,651.0	92,703.0	45,609.1	69,890.0	22,813.0	0.33	high
1988	106.4	107.7	109.6	104.2	73,275.0	99,040.0	48,802.2	73,378.9	25,661.1	0.35	high
1989	102.5	103.3	104.8	106.5	81,407.0	108,912.0	51,635.9	76,628.3	32,283.7	0.42	high
1990	104.7	105.4	106.7	108.1	82,357.0	111,392.0	52,642.4	78,156.6	33,235.4	0.43	high
1991	108.5	109.0	109.9	107.3	75,902.0	104,321.0	56,635.9	82,792.2	21,528.8	0.26	low/high
1992	107.1	107.2	107.6	107.1	72,405.0	101,294.0	59,193.2	85,775.2	15,518.8	0.18	low
1993	108.4	108.9	109.9	109.5	76,486.0	105,824.0	60,593.5	87,563.2	18,260.8	0.21	low
1994	114.4	116.3	119.4	112.5	80,884.0	111,161.0	62,491.7	89,931.8	21,229.2	0.24	low/high
1995	108.2	109.0	110.3	115.9	91,616.0	123,711.0	65,453.0	93,309.5	30,401.5	0.33	high
1996	111.4	113.1	115.6	119.0	91,663.0	124,710.0	66,394.8	94,730.3	29,979.7	0.32	high
1997	109.3	110.2	111.4	122.3	95,489.0	129,191.0	67,748.4	96,690.6	32,500.4	0.34	high
1998	110.0	110.4	110.6	126.2	104,448.0	140,277.0	72,007.6	101,814.8	38,462.2	0.38	high
1999	118.4	119.6	120.8	130.6	110,177.0	147,361.0	73,730.7	104,544.3	42,816.7	0.41	high
2000	110.8	110.2	108.1	134.1	115,998.0	154,440.0	77,436.4	109,217.9	45,222.1	0.41	high
2001	113.0	112.6	111.1	134.6	110,076.0	148,950.0	75,804.1	108,526.3	40,423.7	0.37	high
2002	116.0	115.8	114.9	138.2	120,357.0	160,388.0	84,590.6	118,358.3	42,029.7	0.36	high
2003	114.3	113.3	111.3	140.5	135,769.0	178,874.0	88,287.4	123,169.3	55,704.7	0.45	high

Note: All values are in millions of 2002-2003 dollars except where indicated

What is especially interesting is that the gap between the per capita GPI(3) of Victoria and the Rest-of-Australia grew most intensely between 2000 and 2003. This is particularly obvious from Figure 5.2 which compares the index values of per capita GPI(3) for Victoria and the Rest-of-Australia (see columns *pp* in Tables 4.1 and 5.1). Figure 5.2 reveals that the per capita GPI(3) of the Rest-of-Australia grew at a faster rate than it did for Victoria between 1986 and 1994 (16.0% for Victoria and 19.4% for the Rest-of-Australia). While the trend was subsequently reversed after 1994, the superior growth rate of Victoria's per capita GPI(3) did not emerge until after 2000 when, quite clearly, the gap between the two indexed curves began to noticeably widen.

It is also evident from Figures 5.1 and 5.2 that the trend movement in per capita GPI(3) was much the same for both Victoria and the Rest-of-Australia. Only in 1993 and 1998 did the per capita GPI(3) of Victoria and the Rest-of-Australia move in opposite directions. In many ways, this should be expected given that, firstly, many factors and government policies affecting Australia as a whole also affect Victoria. Second, the Victorian economy constitutes the second largest in Australia and consequently has a significant impact on the broader Australian economy.

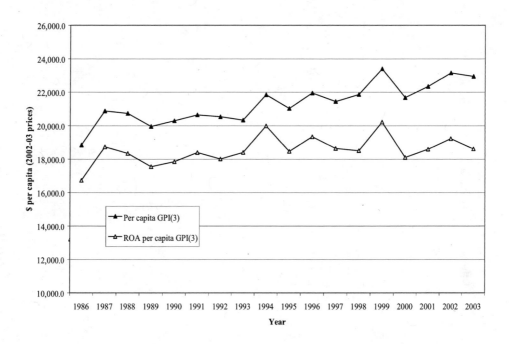

Figure 5.1. Per capita GPI(3) of Victoria versus per capita GPI(3) of the Rest-of-Australia (ROA) (Australia minus Victoria), 1986-2003

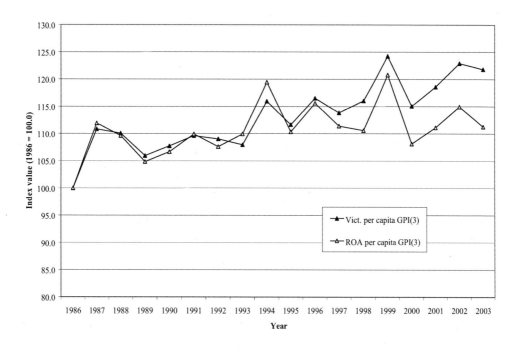

Figure 5.2. Index values of per capita GPI(3) of Victoria versus per capita GPI(3) of the Rest-of-Australia (ROA), 1986-2003

5.2. COMPARING THE GPI COMPONENTS OF VICTORIA AND THE REST-OF-AUSTRALIA

To determine why Victoria outperformed the Rest-of-Australia over the study period it is necessary to compare the items that make up the per capita GPI(3) of Victoria and the Rest-of-Australia. It should be pointed out that the focus of attention in this section is not so much on the aggregate values of the component items because the Victorian values are understandably dwarfed by those of the Rest-of-Australia. The focus is instead on the per capita values. In addition, we aim to direct our attention to the dominant items and/or items where a clear disparity exists between Victoria and the Rest-of-Australia.

5.2.1. Consumption-related Welfare

Figure 5.3 is derived from the values in column *m* of Tables 4.1 and 5.1. It shows that the per capita weighted CON(3) for Victoria and the Rest-of-Australia differed minimally throughput the study period. Having said this, per capita weighted CON(3) was higher in Victoria between 1986 and 1993 but lower from 1994 onwards. This is a significant observation in that the contribution of consumption-related welfare to Victoria's sustainable well-being was less than that of the Rest-of-Australia after 1993 despite Victoria's per capita GPI(3) being much higher. It suggests, even at this earlier stage, that most of Victoria's non-economic cost items were much lower than they were for the Rest-of-Australia.

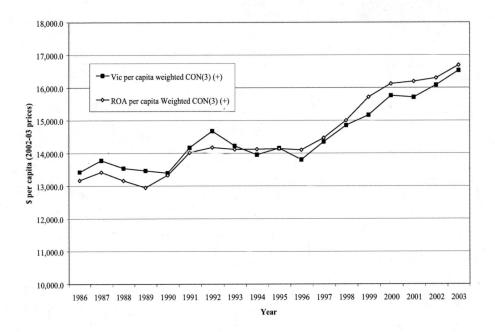

Figure 5.3. Per capita weighted CON(3): Victoria versus Rest-of-Australia, 1986-2003

5.2.2. Distribution Index (DI)

The Distribution Indexes (DI) of both Victoria and the Rest-of-Australia are revealed in column *j* in Tables 4.1 and 5.1. They are both presented in Figure 5.4 below.

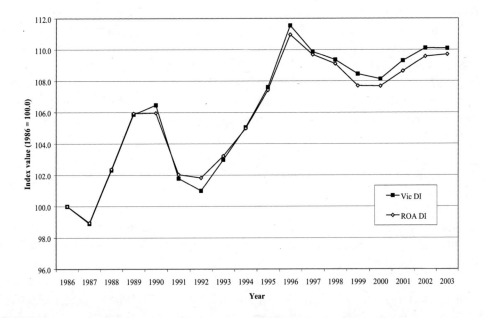

Figure 5.4. Distribution Index (DI): Victoria versus Rest-of-Australia, 1986-2003

Figure 5.4 illustrates that the respective DIs of Victoria and the Rest-of-Australia differed little over the study period. However, between 1992 and 1996, the distribution of income in Victoria changed from being slightly more equal to marginally more unequal than the Rest-of-Australia. The disparity between the two indexes continued in favour of the Rest-of-Australia through to 2003. While the difference in the distribution of income was not enough to explain the variation in the performances of Victoria and the Rest-of-Australia, Figure 5.4 indicates that more needs to be done in Victoria to reduce the widening gap between the rich and the poor.

5.2.3. Cost of Unemployment, Underemployment, Labour Underutilisation

Of the three social cost items which make up the GPI, a disparity between Victoria and the Rest-of-Australia exists most glaringly in the case of the cost of unemployment, underemployment, and labour underutilisation (column q in Tables 4.1 and 5.1). A comparison between the per capita cost of unemployment for Victoria and the Rest-of-Australia is revealed in Figure 5.5.

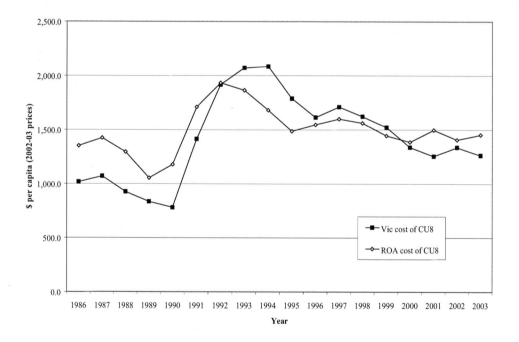

Figure 5.5. Per capita cost of unemployment, underemployment, and labour underutilization (CU8): Victoria versus Rest-of-Australia, 1986-2003

Figure 5.5 demonstrates that the per capita cost of unemployment (broadly defined) was much lower in Victoria than the Rest-of-Australia between 1986 and 1992, but was higher during the period from 1993 to 1999. Following 1999, the per capita cost of unemployment in Victoria fell despite it rising slightly in the Rest-of-Australia. Overall, the per capita cost of unemployment improved by around $600 per person in Victoria relative to the Rest-of-

Australia between 1994 and 2003. This is a notable relative gain that undoubtedly contributed to the widening of the gap between the per capita GPI(3) of Victoria and that of the Rest-of-Australia.

One of the main reasons for Victoria's superior relative performance in terms of the cost of unemployment was its ability to create a healthy number of full-time jobs and minimise the growth in part-time and casual employment. As mentioned in sub-section 4.2.5, Victoria has not escaped the scourge of employment casualisation that has sharply increased the cost of underemployment, but it has managed to limit its growth relative to a number of other states.

5.2.4. Cost of Non-renewable Resource Depletion

The difference between Victoria and the Rest-of-Australia was greatest in relation to the various environmental cost items. The first of these, the cost of non-renewable resource depletion, appears in column u in Tables 4.1 and 5.1. As Figure 5.6 graphically illustrates, the per capita cost of non-renewable resource depletion was much lower in Victoria than it was for the Rest-of-Australia. Furthermore, after a general rise in the per capita cost of non-renewable resource depletion for both Victoria and the Rest-of-Australia between 1987 and 1993, the per capita cost for Victoria steeply declined in all but the year 2000. Conversely, the per capita cost of non-renewable resource depletion for the Rest-of-Australia rose sharply for most years between 1993 and 2003.

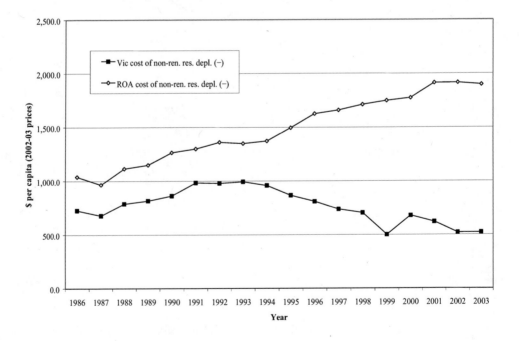

Figure 5.6. Per capita cost of non-renewable resource depletion: Victoria versus Rest-of-Australia, 1986-2003

Again, this is a significant welfare-influencing difference that demonstrates Victoria's much reduced reliance on mining proceeds as a means of financing its consumption of goods and services. It also suggests that Victoria is better able to operate within its biophysical means by generating a significantly larger proportion of genuine money income from value-adding activities compared to Western Australia and Queensland and, to a lesser extent, New South Wales and South Australia.

5.2.5. Cost of Lost Agricultural Land

The respective costs of lost agricultural land for Victoria and the Rest-of-Australia appear in column v in Tables 4.1 and 5.1. The per capita costs for Victoria and the Rest-of-Australia are presented in Figure 5.7. It is plainly clear from Figure 5.7 that the per capita cost of lost agricultural land was much less for Victoria than the Rest-of-Australia. The difference in the per capita cost of lost agricultural land between Victoria and the Rest-of-Australia varied from around $2,600 per person in 1986 to around $2,400 per person by 2003. In view of the magnitude of this variance, the lower per capita cost of lost agricultural land in Victoria was yet another strong factor underlying the disparity between Victoria's per capita GPI(3) and that of the Rest-of-Australia. It also points to Victoria not having to rely as heavily on the depletion of a natural capital asset to finance its consumption endeavours.

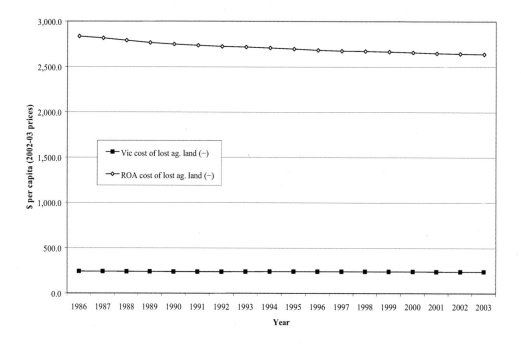

Figure 5.7. Per capita cost of lost agricultural land: Victoria versus Rest-of-Australia, 1986-2003

Although a greater proportion of agricultural activities in Victoria are of the more intensive varieties (i.e., there is only a very small percentage of pastoral ventures in Victoria), a number of factors contribute to Victoria's smaller per capita cost. They include: (a) the much smaller area of land being used in Victoria for agricultural purposes; (b) the higher general fertility of Victoria's agricultural land; (c) the relative abundance of remnant vegetation in most agricultural districts (e.g., compared to the Yorke Peninsula and Lower-North farming districts of South Australia and the grain-growing regions east of Perth); and (d) Victoria's more reliable rainfall which reduces the exposure of agricultural land to erosion-generating conditions. The adoption of more sustainable land management practices and the confinement of human activity to land already significantly modified by agricultural industries is therefore necessary if Victoria is to minimise its cost of land degradation and maintain its edge over the Rest-of-Australia.

5.2.6. Cost of Excessive Irrigation Water Use

Given Victoria's heavy reliance on irrigation water, particularly from the highly stressed Murray-Darling Basin, one would expect Victoria's per capita cost of excessive irrigation water use to be much higher than the Rest-of-Australia. Based on the values appearing in column *w* in Tables 4.1 and 5.1, Figure 5.8 reveals this to be precisely the case but not to the extent anticipated.

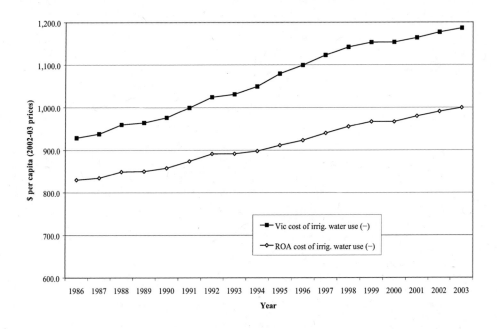

Figure 5.8. Per capita cost of excessive irrigation water use: Victoria versus Rest-of-Australia, 1986-2003

Although the difference in the per capita cost of excessive irrigation water use between Victoria and the Rest-of-Australia increased between 1986 and 1999, the gap closed slightly over the last four years of the study period. From the beginning of the study period to the end, the disparity rose from around $100 to $190 per person. The disparity peaked at around $200 per person in 1999.

The magnitude of the disparity could by no means be singled out as the major reason for the difference between the per capita GPI(3) of Victoria and the Rest-of-Australia, but there is little doubt that a bridging of the gap between the per capita costs would strengthen the relative position of Victoria. If nothing else, Figure 5.8 indicates that Victoria should seek to improve its use and allocation of Australia's inland water resources.

5.2.7. Cost of Long-term Environmental Damage

The per capita cost of long-term environmental damage for Victoria and the Rest-of-Australia is revealed in Figure 5.9. The values are obtained from column *aa* in Tables 4.1 and 5.1. Figure 5.9 shows that Victoria's per capita cost of long-term environmental damage was much the same as it was for the Rest-of-Australia in 1986. However, beyond 1986, the per capita cost for Victoria increased at a much greater rate than the Rest-of-Australia. Indeed, it was approximately $350 per person or 10% higher in Victoria by 2003. The growing gap can be largely attributed to Victoria's rapidly rising per capita energy consumption.

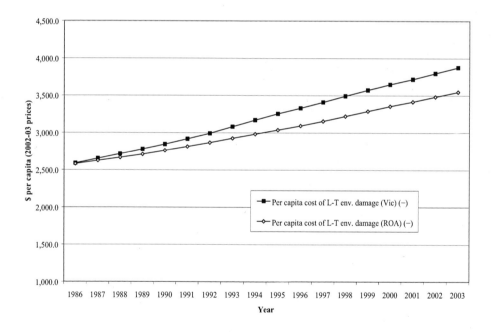

Figure 5.9. Per capita cost of long-term environmental damage: Victoria versus Rest-of-Australia, 1986-2003

The disconcerting aspect of Figure 5.9 is the apparent reduced capacity on the part of Victoria to quell its energy consumption and, more importantly, its failure to find better and cleaner ways of using energy. Increased energy efficiency and the transition towards renewable energy sources clearly requires greater policy emphasis if Victoria is to reduce its per capita energy consumption and bridge the cost gap between itself and the Rest-of-Australia.

5.2.8. Ecosystem Health Index (EHI)

One of the considerable strengths of the Victorian performance over that of the Rest-of-Australia is in relation to the Ecosystem Health Index (EHI). The values for their respective indexes appear in column *cc* in Tables 4.1 and 5.1. Figure 5.10 shows that the Victorian EHI did not fall at anywhere near the same rate as the EHI of the Rest-of-Australia. There are two main reasons for this. First, as explained in sub-section 4.2.11, Victoria's rate of native vegetation clearance was very low over the entire study period. Second, the rate of native vegetation clearance in Queensland and, to some degree, New South Wales was recklessly excessive.

Should Victoria maintain its low rate of vegetation clearance, or better still, confine clearance to significantly disturbed areas and allow for periodic regrowth, it should all but cease the decline of its EHI. In turn, Victoria would position itself in a very strong position relative to the Rest-of-Australia.

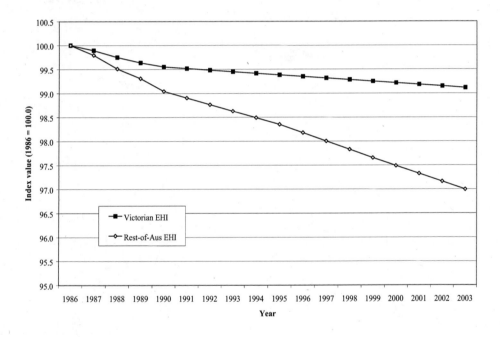

Figure 5.10. Ecosystem Health Index (EHI): Victoria versus Rest-of-Australia, 1986-2003

5.2.9. Lost Natural Capital Services (Weighted)

Figure 5.11 below reveals the superior environmental performance of Victoria compared to the Rest-of-Australia (see columns *bb* and *dd* in Tables 4.1 and 5.1). The dramatic difference between Victoria and the Rest-of-Australia is the product of Victoria's lower unweighted per capita cost of lost natural capital services (LNCS) and its higher EHI.

Interestingly, the difference between the per capita weighted LNCS of Victoria and the Rest-of-Australia narrowed between 1986 and 1993 — from around $2,900 per person in 1986 to $2,600 by 1993. Thereafter, the gap widened to be around $3,500 per person in 2003.

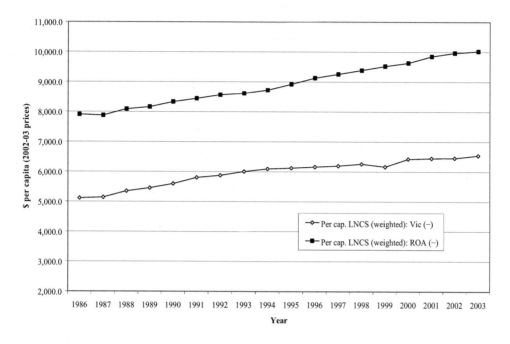

Figure 5.11. Per capita cost of lost natural capital services (LNCS) - weighted: Victoria versus Rest-of-Australia, 1986-2003

Apart from the broadening disparity in the respective EHIs, Victoria's lower per capita cost of non-renewable resource depletion and lost agricultural land were major contributing factors behind the superior environmental performance of Victoria. However, should Victoria be able to reduce its cost of long-term environmental damage and excessive irrigation water use through greater energy and water efficiency, it would be well on the way to further strengthening its relative position. Moreover, it would greater assist in further increasing the gap between the sustainable well-being of the average Victorian and that of the average person living elsewhere in Australia.

5.2.10. Per capita GPI(3) and the Physical Growth Rate of the Economy

In section 4.4, we compared the trend movement of Victoria's per capita GPI(3) with the physical growth rate of the Victorian economy (i.e., the magnitude of the NCI/DEP* ratio). We concluded that high rates of growth had failed to translate effectively into the sustainable well-being of the average Victorian. Indeed, Victoria's per capita GPI(3) often rose in a year of low growth and invariably declined after an extensive period of high growth.

In order to determine whether a similar pattern occurred with the economy of the Rest-of-Australia, consider Figure 5.12 below. Figure 5.12 is constructed from the values appearing in columns *ss*, *uu*, *vv*, and *ww* in Tables 4.1 and 5.1. The figure shows that, in the mid to late-1980s, the higher rate of growth of the Victorian economy narrowed the gap between the per capita GPI(3) of Victoria and that of the Rest-of-Australia. The gap, however, widened during the period from 1993 to 1998 when the Victorian economy grew at a much lower rate than the economy of the Rest-of-Australia. Finally, from 1999 to the end of the study period, the very high rates of growth of both economies in 2000 and 2003 caused the per capita GPI(3) of Victoria and the Rest-of-Australia to decline.

Overall, the message appears to be very transparent — a lower rate of growth is beneficial to sustainable well-being and is a relationship that could be intensified if more was done in both Victoria and Australia generally to narrow the gap between the rich and the poor; increase resource use efficiency; encourage better rather than more production; and endeavour to keep renewable natural capital stocks and critical ecosystems intact.

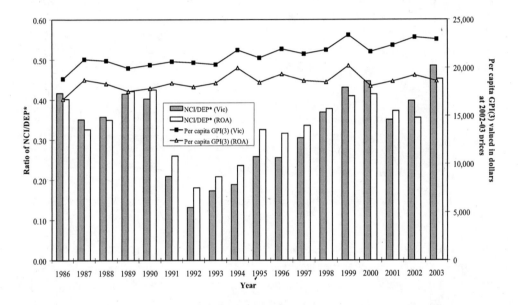

Figure 5.12. Per capita GPI(3) and the ratio of net capital investment (NCI) to human-made capital depreciation (DEP*): Victoria versus Rest-of-Australia, 1986-2003

5.3. SUMMARY

Having compared the per capita GPI(3) of Victoria with that of the Rest-of-Australia and also analysed the items where clear disparities exist, we are well placed to: (a) outline the policies to increase the sustainable well-being of Victoria, and (b) improve the relative performance of Victoria *vis-a-vis* Rest-of-Australia. To assist the policy recommendation process, Chapter 5 can be summarised by way of the following:

- The sustainable well-being of the average Victorian was consistently higher than that of the average person living elsewhere in Australia. Beginning with a difference in per capita GPI(3) of $2,105 per person in 1986, the disparity between Victoria and the Rest-of-Australia increased to $4,331 per person by 2003.

- The percentage rise in per capita GPI(3) over the study period for Victoria was 21.8% but only 11.3% for the Rest-of-Australia. The gap between the per capita GPI(3) of Victoria and the Rest-of-Australia grew most intensely between 2000 and 2003.

- Not unlike the Victorian situation, continuing high growth rates of the Rest-of-Australian economy had a detrimental impact on sustainable well-being. Conversely, the per capita GPI(3) of the Rest-of-Australia often increased during a year of low growth.

- The similar relationship between per capita GPI(3) and the prevailing growth rate of the Victorian and Rest-of-Australian economies reaffirms the possibility that the sustainable well-being of the average Australian might have been higher in 2003 if the policy emphasis had been directed more towards distributional equity, resource use efficiency, and natural capital maintenance.

- Minor factors underlying the difference between the per capita GPI(3) of Victoria and the Rest-of-Australia were:
  - Victoria's lower per capita cost of unemployment (broadly defined) in the latter years of the study period resulting from Victoria's capacity to create a larger number of full-time jobs;
  - Victoria's higher Ecosystem Health Index (EHI) arising from its much smaller rate of native vegetation clearance over the study period.

- Major reasons for Victoria's superior per capita GPI(3) include:
  - Victoria's lower per capita cost of non-renewable resource depletion, particularly after 1993;
  - Victoria's significantly lower per capita cost of lost agricultural land;
  - overall, and given the similar per capita consumption-related welfare of Victoria and the Rest-of-Australia throughout the study period, Victoria's much lower social and environmental costs. Victoria's environmental performance was vastly superior as reflected by its considerably lower per capita cost of lost natural capital services.

- However, Victoria was outperformed by the Rest-of-Australia in terms of:
  - excessive rates of irrigation water use;
  - per capita energy consumption;
  - and, to a lesser extent, air pollution.

Chapter 6

POLICY IMPLICATIONS OF THE GPI RESULTS

6.1. INTRODUCTION

Having completed the analysis of Victoria's genuine progress performance, we now turn to the policy component of the book (Lawn, 2000a; Clarke, 2004; and Clarke, forthcoming). In our endeavour to outline a range of policy initiatives to increase the sustainable well-being of the average Victorian, we will focus our attention on Chapters 4 and 5 and the conclusions drawn and elucidated in sections 4.5 and 5.3.

It is very true that the Victorian Government is limited in its capacity to increase Victoria's GPI if only because many policy instruments and legislative avenues are beyond its means of control. Indeed, a great deal of what impacts on Victoria's economy, society, and natural environment remains the exclusive domain of the Federal Government. Although we will be spending some brief time examining the Victorian Government's approach to policy, on the whole, we will be outlining policies without regard to which government has the greatest or exclusive policy influence. Thus, the recommendations we are about to make are directed as much towards the Federal Government as they are the Victorian Government.

We are also cognisant of the fact that policies are not made in a political vacuum. Policies that may be of great value to a state's citizens cannot always be implemented immediately or at all because of institutional failings, misgivings held by the majority of the population, and concerns that some people could be adversely affected. We believe that any proposed policy that negatively impacts on a small percentage of the population warrants compensation in some form — perhaps in the form of a direct compensation payment or a community level project to offset localised impacts. In this way, the welfare of affected citizens can be maintained so as to allow beneficial policies to be introduced.

Despite the influence of political realities on the types of policies that can be reasonably implemented by governments, we will be recommending policies without this in mind. We want to do this in order to stimulate debate on all the possible means to increase sustainable well-being. Hence, some of our policy recommendations may seem extreme, impractical, and even somewhat polemic. We have, however, endeavoured to remain entirely apolitical in our expressed views and judgments.

6.2. A COMMENT ON THE VICTORIAN GOVERNMENT'S RECENT ECONOMIC STATEMENT (2004)

In April 2004, the Victorian Government released an economic statement entitled, *Victoria: Leading the Way* (VDPC, 2004). As a blueprint for future development of the Victorian economy, the economic statement included 19 new 'actions' aimed at:

- augmenting the competitiveness of the Victorian economy;
- stimulating private sector investment and increasing new job growth;
- boosting public sector investment in infrastructural projects to improve the transportation of goods to new and emerging markets;
- facilitating the growth of export-oriented businesses;
- reducing the extent of overbearing and costly government regulation (including tax relief for the business sector);
- maximising the sustainable returns from Victoria's natural resource assets.

There are undoubtedly a number of very good proposals embodied in this economic statement and we wholeheartedly support many of them. However, we believe that a number of proposed policy measures are primarily designed to boost Victoria's GSP. As we have seen in Chapter 4, Victoria's per capita GPI(3) failed to keep pace with the growth in its per capita GSP and, in some years, declined when per capita GSP increased. One of the main reasons behind this was the rapid rise in the social and environmental impacts of GSP growth — in particular, the increased cost of lost natural capital services.

Strangely, not one of the 19 actions outlined in the economic statement was devoted to the natural environment. While Action 19 refers to the 'sustainable' utilisation of Victoria's non-renewable coal reserves and the assessment of potential geosequestration sites for carbon dioxide emissions, there is no recognition of the fact that Victoria's economy — like all economies — is a subsystem of the natural environment and entirely dependent upon it for sustenance. Nor is there any reference to inequities in the current system and how they can be successfully ameliorated. We are therefore sceptical as to whether, in aggregate, the proposals put forward in the economic statement will: (a) increase Victoria's per capita GPI(3)[1], and (b) ensure that whatever level of welfare is generated by the Victorian economy will be ecologically sustainable in the long-run.

Many observers would argue that environmental policies belong in an environmental statement, not an economic statement. We, however, believe that the failure to link economic, social, and environmental policies is one of the main reasons behind the stifled rise in Victoria's GPI. Moreover, we are of the view that all benefits and costs are effectively 'economic' — no matter what their origin — and need to be taken on board when designing policies to increase Victoria's sustainable well-being.

6.2.1. Tax Cuts to Business

One of the policies put forward in *Victoria: Leading the Way* is the delivery of tax cuts to business (Action 13). While the promised tax relief will no doubt reduce the cost of operating a business in Victoria, we believe the tax system is an ideal mechanism to encourage and facilitate 'desirable' business .behaviour and penalise activities that inflict harm on both society and the natural environment. The economic statement of the Victorian Government goes only a very small way towards using the tax system in this manner.[2]

The reduction in payroll tax, for example, is a positive step to encourage greater employment of labour that, in turn, can reduce the damaging cost of unemployment and family breakdown. However, there is no indication that the Victorian Government plans to alter the mix of tax impositions to encourage value-adding in production and penalise resource depletion, resource waste, and pollution. Neither are there tax incentives and/or subsidies to promote research and development into 'green' technologies that, apart from reducing environmental costs, will unquestionably form the basis of tomorrow's growth industries.

6.2.2. Infrastructural Investment

Given the much lower welfare generated by publicly-provided service capital in 2003 compared to 1986, the Victorian Government's plan to increase its investment in infrastructural projects is a welcoming trend. Our concern is that much of this investment is narrowly aimed at extensively upgrading port facilities and redeveloping the Melbourne wholesale markets (Actions 1, 2, and 3). These large-scale investments will unquestionably be of great benefit to Victoria, however, we believe governments can play a key role in kick-starting the development of high-tech, value-adding, and resource-saving industries.

Very often, new industries suffer from a dearth of infrastructural support and the lack of economies of scale advantages commonly possessed by incumbent industries. These difficulties are further compounded by the lack of tax-based incentives already mentioned and the often undue tax advantages enjoyed by existing industry sectors. We believe that greater and better targeted infrastructural investment would assist in the emergence and development of tomorrow's key industries. This would enable Victoria to significantly raise its productivity, increase its efficiency of energy use, and elevate standards of production excellence to new heights.

It is interesting to note that a recent report by the *Melbourne 2030 Implementation Reference Group* has also raised concerns about the lack of appropriate infrastructural investment by the Victorian Government (DSE, 2004). However, the problem is not confined to Victoria. The Governor of the Reserve Bank of Australia has also highlighted an apparent lack of infrastructural investment throughout Australia that is likely to impact negatively on sustainable well-being for some time to come (Brown, 2005).

6.2.3. Opening Doors Export Plan

The *Opening Doors Export Plan* (Action 9) is designed to complement Federal Government export initiatives and to raise the profile of Victoria's strategic export capabilities (VDPC, 2004, p.18). Through this plan, the Victorian Government aims to ensure the state reaches a target of $30 billion worth of exports by 2010.

In view of the major impact of foreign debt on Victoria's per capita GPI(3), a dramatic rise in export income can potentially raise the welfare of the average Victorian. We say potentially because the recent growth in export income has been more than offset by higher import spending. We do not wish to downplay the significance of increased export revenue. Nevertheless, we believe that not enough policy emphasis is being placed on 'import-replacement'. An import-replacement policy is not, as some believe, 'anti-trade'. Nor does it require the imposition of tariffs and quotas to protect inefficient and under-performing industries.[3] What it does require, however, is a competitive industry base and the facilitation of high-tech, value-adding, and resource-saving industries. Indeed, value-added industries, by producing highly demanded high-priced goods, can increase export revenue as well as reduce import spending.

Of course, the balance of trade implications of an extra dollar of export revenue is no different to one less dollar of import spending. On the surface, at least, a successful import-replacement policy appears no more efficacious than a successful export-based policy. However, an overemphasis on export-oriented policies can result in the over-specialisation in the production of a limited range of goods. This can reduce a state's self-sufficiency and increase its exposure to volatile global market forces. Furthermore, over-specialisation can render a state more reliant on exports as a source of income that, in turn, renders it "less free not to trade". An import-replacement policy can do much to avoid this potential dilemma.

6.2.4. Exporting Education

As a way of boosting the income generated from the export of higher education services, the Victorian Government is committing $5.8 million during the 2005-2007 period to attract a larger number of overseas students to Victoria's higher education institutions (Action 10). With direct benefits worth an estimated $1.5 billion per annum to the Victorian economy, this policy is a clear reinforcement of Action 9 (VDPC, 2004, p. 19).

We are not so much concerned about the export of higher education services *per se*, but more so the possibility that competition for the higher education dollar could lower education standards. Victoria currently possesses three of Australia's top ten ranked universities of which the University of Melbourne is ranked number one (Williams and Van Dyke, 2004). Its regional universities are also ranked amongst the highest of their type in Australia.

We believe that Victoria's excellence in higher education is a major asset that generates enormous spillover benefits to the Victorian economy and Victorian society at large. We are convinced that it has contributed to Victoria's superior performance relative to the Rest-of-Australia. Unfortunately, unless minimum standards are established by legislative decree, competition need not always be standards-raising. It would be to the great detriment of Victoria if its higher education standards declined simply to secure a marginal increase in export revenue. As limited as its powers are in relation to higher education, the Victorian Government should do everything it can to protect its higher education institutions from the potential degenerative effects of standards-lowering competition.

6.2.5. Competition and Efficiency

On a number of occasions, we have referred to the need for Victoria to reduce the inefficiency of its resource use — in particular, the use of energy sources. Greater efficiency not only lowers production costs and increases competitiveness, it reduces the pressure of a per unit of economic activity on the natural environment, thereby reducing the environmental costs that are currently weighing down Victoria's per capita GPI(3).

Action 15 refers to the Victorian Government's creation of a Competition and Efficiency Commission (VDPC, 2004, p. 26). The main role of the Commission will be the examination, reduction, and streamlining of existing government regulation to reduce compliance costs and speed up the approval process for development projects in Victoria.

Understandably, there is little reference to competition policy — vital to ensure efficiency within the Australian economy as a whole — given that competition policy is a Federal Government responsibility carried out on its behalf by the Australian Consumer and Competition Commission (ACCC). It is, however, in the interests of the Victorian Government to apply pressure on the Federal Government should it appear to weaken its stance on competition matters, particular as they relate to corporate mergers and the misuse of market power by large corporations (sections 45-50 of the Trade Practices Act, 1974).

There are three crucial points we would like to make in relation to efficiency and regulatory reform that are pertinent to Victoria's sustainable well-being. First, efficiency is not just about lowering the cost of operating a business. It is also about ensuring the relative division of the incoming resource flow is allocated to where it will generate the highest welfare for Victorians. As such, there is no point in reducing regulation if it leads to a rise in unpriced spillover costs that the regulation itself is initially designed to minimise. Apart from equity considerations, the Victorian Government would, if it took this course of action, run the risk of imposing net costs on Victoria that would place downward pressure on Victoria's GPI (even though it might increase the state's GSP). Clearly, the Victorian Government needs to establish the best and most cost-effective means of regulation so it can reduce compliance costs yet also protect Victorians from the damaging side-effects of undesirable production activities — an obvious role for the new Competition and Efficiency Commission.

Second, if the Victorian Government is serious about efficiency, it needs to do more to internalise the unpriced externalities at the root of many social and environmental costs of economic activity. Again, this can be achieved by way of the tax system, licence fees, and tradeable depletion and emission permits. Subsidies can also be used to encourage and reward desirable business behaviour (i.e., business activities that generate positive spillover benefits). We believe that taxes and licence fees are an ideal way to initiate the cost internalisation process, while tradeable permits offer a better long-term solution. We shall have more to say on this soon.

Third, we are also concerned that the tax system encourages private sector investment into non-productive, 'rent-seeking' ventures. Economic rent in the pure sense refers to the income earned from asset possession that exceeds the initial opportunity cost of acquiring or creating an asset (i.e., the minimum amount that would need to be earned to induce the initial creation or supply of the asset) (Connolly and Munro, 1999). When someone is earning an economic rent, they receive an income far greater than the true value generated by the asset they possess. Thus, the income they receive does not reflect the genuine contribution they have made to the creation and maintenance of society's wealth.

We believe that the tax system in Australia has led to excessive rent-seeking in the form of real estate acquisition and property construction. This, in our view, is largely unproductive and partly to blame for the lack of investment in productive, resource-saving, and high-value adding ventures, including a lack of private investment in workforce training that now leaves Australia with a shortage of skilled workers despite at least 500,000 Australians continuing to remain unemployed. Our position on this appears to be supported by recent statements made by the Governor of the Reserve Bank of Australia (RBA, 2005).

Governments therefore need to alter the investment incentives and disincentives currently embodied in taxation legislation to reduce the extent of inefficient and inequitable rent-seeking behaviour. While many of the taxation modifications required to increase productive investment necessitates action from the Federal Government, the Victoria Government can also make a contribution in this area via changes in land and wealth taxes.

6.2.6. Industrial Relations Reform

Increasing productivity at the workplace level is vital if Victoria is to maintain competitiveness, improve the efficiency with which it uses its scarce natural resources (in particular, energy and water), and augment the production of high value-added goods. Through Action 17, the Victorian Government aims to increase workplace productivity by funding the development of model ways to promote greater workplace flexibility (VDPC, 2004, p. 28).

While the increase in workplace flexibility is an important ingredient in any attempt to boost workplace productivity, we believe that workplace flexibility cannot be truly and equitably achieved without a genuine move towards greater labour market flexibility. Current labour market inflexibility forces many people to work excessive hours at a time when some people are underemployed while others cannot find work at all (Tiffen and Gittins, 2004).

Although labour market rigidities have been reduced over the last decade, a number of observers believe that the rapid rise in casual employment is a measure of the inadequate nature of many industrial relations reforms (Cowling et al., 2003). Moreover, there have been instances where modifications to industrial relations systems have led to the erosion of workers' wages and conditions of employment. In addition, workers are often faced with the restrictive choice of either having to work more than their desired number of hours in a full-time occupation or a more appropriate number of hours in a casual job. Clearly, policy-makers need to install a form of labour market flexibility that protects workers' pay and conditions and increases their work-leisure-family options. Only then will a desirable balance between the needs of Victorian businesses and workers emerge that would simultaneously:

- raise business competitiveness and productivity;

- increase the potential for job-sharing and thus help lower unemployment;
- reduce the high current cost of underemployment caused by the growing casualisation of the workforce;
- lower the cost of family breakdown by providing employment security and flexibility.

As for promoting more productive workplaces, this depends largely on the levels of trust and commitment engendered at the enterprise level (Blandy and Brummitt, 1990). Both of these factors can be facilitated by the type of labour market flexibility just discussed as well as the establishment of well-defined internal career paths backed by a dual employer-employee commitment to on-going training and skills development.

Of course, when referring to industrial relations reforms, it should be acknowledged that the Victorian Government has limited legislative powers in this policy domain. It is often at the mercy of many Federal Government reforms that may or may not be beneficial to Victoria's sustainable well-being. The Victorian Government should therefore apply pressure to the Federal Government to instigate desirable industrial relations reforms and vent its concern should proposed Federal reforms not be in Victoria's best interests.

6.2.7. Energy Policy

The final initiative outlined in *Victoria: Leading the Way* relates to the Victorian Government's desire to maintain a low-cost and reliable energy supply in Victoria (Action 19). While there is mention of support for leading-edge research into sustainable energy alternatives, the funding commitment of the Victorian Government ($1.5 million per year) does not befit the urgency with which Victoria should be making the transition to renewable energy sources.

In addition, the support for carbon geosequestration demonstrates that Victoria's energy policy is decidedly supply-side-oriented. There is very little being offered to reduce the demand for energy by way of measures to facilitate the increase in energy efficiency. We also believe that an economic statement outlining the importance of food production (Action 12) ought to include policy initiatives to limit land degradation and the unsustainable and inefficient use of inland river water resources.

6.3. POLICY RECOMMENDATIONS

In this section, we will be outlining a number of specific policy initiatives to increase Victoria's sustainable well-being. Given the extent to which the environmental costs have played such a significant part in the stifled increase in Victoria's per capita GPI(3), we will focus a considerable amount of our attention on a policy approach commonly referred to as 'ecological tax reform'. We shall also have something to say about the need to encourage better rather than more production, as well as the cost of unemployment and how it can be remedied.

6.3.1. Ecological Tax Reform

In its generally accepted form, ecological tax reform involves the reduction of taxes on income, profits, and labour and the imposition of taxes on resource depletion and pollution (O'Riordan, 1997; Roodman, 1998; and Lawn, 2000b). Although we haven't explicitly used the term up until now, it is clear that we have already discussed numerous aspects relating to this particular policy initiative.

What is the benefit of ecological tax reform? First, the reduction in taxes on income and profits encourages value-adding in production that qualitatively improves the stock of human-made capital (i.e., producer goods and consumer goods). Second, the cutting of taxes on labour (e.g., payroll taxes) induces a subtle substitution towards the use of labour in production. This assists in reducing the cost of unemployment. Finally, the imposition of depletion and pollution taxes (i.e., throughput taxes) helps to increase the efficiency of resource use that, in turn, reduces the pressure of a per unit of economic activity on the natural environment.[4] Crafted in a responsible fashion, ecological tax reform can be a tax-neutral policy — that is, the aggregate tax burden on the private sector need not change. Indeed, the tax burden should ultimately decline for those engaged in welfare-increasing business ventures.

As pointed out in section 6.2.1, the Victorian Government is planning to reduce payroll taxes and is therefore making a useful contribution on the employment front. But it is failing in terms of throughput taxes. The Victorian Government could, as is sometimes the case, introduce licences whereby the fees charged to obtain a licence can serve as a tax to partly reflect the cost of depletion and pollution-related activities (e.g., water extraction, forestry, fishing, and pollution licences). However, this course of action is not as effective or as efficient as per unit taxes. It would, nonetheless, mark an improvement on current policy stances.[5]

Despite political concerns about any new form of tax, we believe depletion and pollution taxes could be introduced gradually by the Victorian Government to give businesses time to make suitable adjustments. This would prevent any immediate damage to the Victorian economy (note: not all businesses would be affected by these taxes). Subsidies could also be offered to firms in order to encourage them to engage in the research and development of green, resource-saving technologies. Subsidies or tax rebates could also be provided to encourage their eventual uptake. Having said this, the Federal Government is often better placed in this regard than state governments.

From a long-term perspective, we believe that ecological tax reform would be more successfully conducted through the introduction of tradeable depletion and pollution permits. We favour permit systems because, as much as throughput taxes facilitate the more efficient allocation of the incoming resource flow, they do not guarantee the ecological sustainability of economic activity.

Why is this so? Throughput taxes merely reduce the resource throughput (environmental impact) per unit of economic activity (Daly, 1996; Lawn, 2000b and 2004b). This may seem a cause for gratification until one considers the potential environmental impact if the percentage decline in resource throughput per unit of economic activity is exceeded by a larger percentage increase in all economic activities. The net effect is, of course, the diminution of natural capital which, if left unchecked, eventually results in a nation's or state's ecological footprint surpassing the biocapacity of its natural environment (i.e., ecological unsustainability). In order for the market alone to prevent this from occurring, resource prices — and this includes resource prices manipulated by the use of throughput taxes — must be capable of reflecting the *absolute scarcity* of all resources. Unfortunately, at best, resource prices can only reflect the *relative scarcity* of different resources types (i.e., how scarce one resource is relative to another). It is the ability to reflect the latter that allows manipulated resource prices to facilitate a more efficient allocation of the incoming resource flow. But it is the inherent failure to reflect the former that ensures manipulated resource prices cannot prevent the aggregate rate of resource throughput exceeding the maximum rate that can be sustainably supplied by the natural environment (Howarth and Norgaard, 1990; Norgaard, 1990; Bishop, 1993; Daly, 1996; Lawn, 2004b).

To ensure the rate of resource throughput does not deplete the stock of natural capital, it is necessary to impose quantitative restrictions on both the rate of resource use and the rate at which pollution is generated. This can be achieved by a system of tradeable depletion and pollution permits that, if properly designed, need not sacrifice the efficiency benefits of throughput taxes.

How would such a system work? Consider a system of tradeable water permits within the Murray-Darling Basin. A government authority (e.g., Victorian Department of Sustainability and Environment) would initially determine the maximum sustainable rate of water extraction from Victorian-located rivers.[6] It would then auction off a limited number of water extraction permits to the highest bidders. A permit would grant the possessor the right to extract a certain amount of water over a specified period — for example, ten megalitres of water a year. Consequently, someone wanting to extract 100 megalitres of water in a year would need to purchase ten permits.

The auctioning process would be undertaken each year to allow the government authority to vary the number permits in line with fluctuating water flows. This would mean that a permit would expire at the end of each year even if it was unused. Expired permits would not be redeemable. To maintain competitive markets, there would be a limit on the number of permits any single individual or firm could purchase. All permits could be resold to another individual or firm: (a) during the period prior to their expiration, and (b) so long as the buyer was not already in possession of the maximum number of permits.

To safeguard past investments in water-using activities, existing water users could be given first preference in the auctioning process for the first five years following the introduction of the permit system (i.e., by setting aside and auctioning off a certain number of the limited permits to current water users). This would give inefficient or marginal water users sufficient time to improve their performance or gradually exit the industry they currently operate in.

Three important objectives would be achieved with the introduction of such a scheme. First, by limiting the number of permits sold, the quantity of water extracted from Victorian-located rivers would be restricted to the levels required to maintain environmental flows in the Murray-Darling Basin. This would guarantee achievement of the sustainability objective.

Second, because it is necessary to buy a permit to extract water, a water user would be compelled to pay a premium for each megalitre of water used. The premium is equivalent to a throughput tax that would facilitate the efficient allocation of water among alternative product uses. That is, the premium would ensure that the annual quantity of extracted water is allocated to water-using activities generating the highest welfare benefits. Note, therefore, that there is no need for a government authority to calculate and impose a water tax — the tax rate is determined by the interaction of the demand and constrained supply forces in the water permit market.

Finally, the revenue raised by the sale of water permits could be redistributed to the poor and/or be used to compensate people affected by the undesirable actions of certain water users. This would enable the Victorian Government to bridge the gap between the rich and poor and thus achieve its equity goals.

The beauty of the tradeable permit system is that it could be applied to other renewable resource types (e.g., timber and fishery resources). It could also be tailored to meet the unique circumstances of a particular region. For example, a system of tradeable water permits in the Murray-Darling Basin would differ to a permit system in another river basin. Also, given that environmental conditions can vary significantly within a particular region, it is highly probable that multiple trading systems would be applied to specific environmental systems. Referring to the river basin context again, separate permit systems could be applied to the upper and lower reaches of a particular basin in recognition of their different water flows, ecosystem values, and soil and vegetation types.

Of course, it is unlikely that a tradeable permit system could be instituted overnight. Given the path-dependent nature of economic systems (David, 1985; Arthur, 1989; Dosi and Metcalfe, 1991), there is the possibility that the introduction of such a system could send undesirable shock-waves throughout the economy. For the following reasons, we believe that taxes and subsidies are the ideal way to introduce an ecological tax reform policy:

- Taxes and subsidies can be gradually imposed to prepare the economy and its participants for a different set of relative price signals;
- Taxes do not require a radical change in the way resource users purchase the resources they require (unlike a system of tradeable resource permits);
- Taxes can effect a gradual but not disruptive shift in the allocation of resources from dirty, low value-adding industries to clean, green, high value-adding industries.

Once taxes and subsidies have played their role in altering the allocation of resources, tradeable permit systems should then be introduced. Not unlike the throughput taxes imposed initially, permit systems can also be introduced in a gradual manner — that is, by sanctioning a rate of resource throughput equal to that in place at the time of the system's introduction and then reducing it over time to the desired rate (e.g., to one where the ecological footprint of a nation or state could be kept permanently within the biocapacity of its natural environment).[7] The possibility of having to reduce the rate of resource throughput may require governments to purchase some of the resource rights currently held by resource users.

Instituted in the manner described above, permit systems can overcome the high growth rate predilection that appears to be having a negative impact on sustainable well-being. Moreover, they are likely to play a key role in facilitating the transition from quantitative expansion (growth) to that of qualitative improvement (development).

6.3.2. Government Investment in Land and Soil Conservation

Agricultural land is not directly harvested but exploited for its propagating properties. Thus, unlike a flow of timber that is sustained by ensuring the harvest rate from a forest/plantation does not exceed its capacity to regenerate, the sustainable use of agricultural land cannot be achieved via controls on the incoming resource flow into the economy. Short of having to directly regulate all agricultural activities, we believe the sustainable use of agricultural land can best be achieved by encouraging farmers to adopt sustainable land use practices. This is best facilitated by a policy mix that: (a) places the practical responsibility of land management on the land owner, and (b) places the financial responsibility of sustainable land use practices largely on the government. Having the financial responsibility rest predominantly with the government is entirely legitimate given that the condition of 'sustainability' is essentially a *public good* and therefore requires government intervention to be achieved.

The first major component of a sustainable land use policy is the use of subsidies and substantial tax rebates to assist farmers to adopt sustainable land use practices. The second policy component is the levying of penalties on farmers who fail to fulfil their stewardship responsibility. The extent of the penalty would depend on the degree of land degradation and would be paid through the tax system not unlike university students pay their tuition fees through the Higher Education Contribution Scheme (HECS).

How would the penalty be assessed? Taking into account prevailing environmental conditions that can impact on the condition of agricultural land at a particular point in time (e.g., drought), representatives of the Victorian Department of Primary Industries would conduct random inspections of farms to assess their overall condition. Should it be clear that a farmer's land exists in a sustainably productive state, they would not incur a penalty. However, worst-case offenders would incur both the highest penalty and a 'yellow card'. Three yellow cards would equate to a 'red card' and compulsory acquisition of the farm. The farmer would receive the market value of the property less any outstanding penalties and would be barred from engaging in agricultural activities for a specified period (not unlike professionals and tradespeople can be barred for engaging in negligent or sub-standard practices).

Of course, acquiring properties is not a trivially inexpensive exercise. We believe the Natural Heritage Trust that came into existence following the part sale of Telstra is an ideal source of funds to acquire the properties of negligent farmers.[8] Although the Natural Heritage Trust fund is a Commonwealth asset, we believe some of it should be allocated to the states to help reduce land degradation in the manner just described. It should also be noted that acquired properties would be resold to anyone willing to use the land for agricultural or any other productive purpose. Thus, a state government is unlikely to be in the possession of a significant amount of confiscated land at any one time.

It is often shown that the dire economic circumstances of a farmer is the main factor contributing to the use of unsustainable land practices — i.e., farmers, in their efforts to remain financially viable, invariably over-extend the productive capacity of their land. We are well aware of this but do not believe the penalty system would compound such a problem. However, to further assist farmers in this matter, we believe the Natural Heritage Trust should also be used to enable struggling farmers to exit the agricultural industry and either:

(a) resettle and gain employment elsewhere, or (b) obtain qualifications in a new field where employment can be found locally. Where a marginal farming region is most at risk, we believe the Natural Heritage Trust can be used to invest in a community level project to establish a replacement industry.

Importantly, a similar approach could also be applied in the case of the forestry, mining, and irrigation industries. While many would query the possible high cost of this restructuring process, we are confident that it would amount to much less than the eventual social and environmental cost of failing to adopt a proactive stance. Indeed, we believe that the failure of governments to be proactive on this front has played a significant role in weighing done the GPI of both Victoria and the remainder of Australia.

6.3.3. Preservation of Remnant Vegetation and Critical Ecosystems

To maintain the level of biodiversity that is needed to sustain the natural environment's life-support services, critical ecosystems require preservation and, in some instances, rehabilitation. Ideally, somewhere in the vicinity of twenty percent of a nation's or state's land area should be preserved as habitat for wildlife conservation (Wilson, 1992).[9] Nevertheless, more land should be preserved as native vegetation refuges and as vegetation corridors to connect critical ecosystems.

It was explained in Chapter 3 that native vegetation plays a critical role in the maintenance of soil productivity and important ecosystems. As such, future land clearance should be kept to a minimum, if not be entirely prohibited. Strict controls over native vegetation clearance have already been introduced in some states in Australia, however, in our view, something like the Native Vegetation Clearance Act of South Australia (1990) needs widespread introduction. The Native Vegetation Clearance Act has resulted in the complete cessation of wholesale land clearance in South Australia. Under this Act, farmers require permission to clear native vegetation — which is often denied — however, unsuccessful applicants are provided with the funds required to fence off native vegetation and manage it effectively.

Having said this, legislation of this type requires strengthening in the form of adequate land owner compensation for the potential loss of agricultural production. Compensation is also necessary to meet equity considerations. We believe the Natural Heritage Trust fund could also be used to finance land clearance control policies. Again, some of the Trust fund should be allocated to the states to help minimise the unacceptable rate of land clearance.

6.3.4. The Treatment of Non-renewable Resource Profits

In sub-section 3.4.14, we pointed out that the cost of non-renewable resource depletion is best determined by calculating the proportion of depletion profits that need to be set aside to establish a suitable replacement asset. The method we have used to calculate this cost is a variation on El Serafy's 'user cost' approach (Lawn, 1998).

El Serafy's (1989) method attempts to overcome the current error of treating the entire proceeds from non-renewable resource depletion as income. This error arises because a proper measure of income must take into account the need to keep the stock of income-generating capital intact (Hicks, 1946).

Since, by definition, non-renewable resource use involves the diminution of the stock of income-generating natural capital, at least some of the proceeds from non-renewable resource depletion must be set aside to establish a suitable replacement asset. The implications of this, according to El Serafy, are that any estimation of sustainable income requires a non-renewable resource earmarked for depletion to be converted into a perpetual income stream. This requires a finite series of earnings from the sale of the resource to be converted to an infinite series of true income such that the capitalised values of the two series are equal (El Serafy, 1989).

To do this, an income and capital component of the finite series of earnings must be identified. If correctly estimated, the income component constitutes an amount that can be consumed without any fear of undermining the capacity to sustain the same level of consumption over time. The capital component, on the other hand, is an amount that needs to be set aside each year to ensure a perpetual income stream of constant value, both during the life of the resource as well as following its exhaustion. It is this capital component that constitutes the true 'user cost' of resource depletion. To identify the income and capital components, El Serafy has suggested the use of the following equation:

$$X / R = 1 - \frac{1}{(1+r)^{n+1}} \tag{6.1}$$

where:

- X = true income (resource rent)
- R = total net receipts (gross receipts less extraction costs)
- r = discount rate
- n = number of periods over which the resource is to be liquidated
- $R - X$ = user cost or the amount of total net receipts that must be set aside to establish a replacement asset to ensure a perpetual income stream.

The two key parameters in the determination of the income and capital components are the number of periods over which the resource is to be liquidated and the chosen discount rate. The greater are the values of these two parameters, the more substantial is the income component and the smaller is the amount that needs to be set aside each period to ensure a perpetual income stream.

The number of periods over which the resource is to be liquidated is relatively easy to estimate and, in the majority of cases, depends on the size of a non-renewable resource deposit as well as expected future resource prices. The major difficulty lies in determining the most appropriate discount rate. According to El Serafy, the chosen discount rate should reflect prudent behaviour on the part of the resource liquidator.

It is at this point where our user cost approach differs to that of El Serafy. El Serafy is of the view that the replacement asset can be of any particular form, whether it be a human-made asset, a natural capital asset, or even a financial asset (El Serafy, 1996). Since this view assumes the substitutability of human-made for natural capital, El Serafy's method of measuring Hicksian income is one of the weak sustainability kind. Our position is that human-made and natural capital are complements and, as such, the only true measure of Hicksian income is one of the strong sustainability kind (see sub-section 7.1.4 for more on the difference between weak and strong sustainability). Since the strong sustainability approach requires both natural and human-made capital to be kept intact, a non-renewable resource must be replaced by a suitable *renewable* resource substitute.

What does this mean in terms of the user cost formula? Not a great deal except in relation to the choice of discount rate. A weak sustainability advocate would probably suggest a discount rate equal to the real interest rate earned on alternative assets, whether it be human-made capital or a financial asset, since the real interest rate reflects the likely real returns on the re-investment.

Our view is that the chosen discount rate should be equivalent to the real interest rate on the cultivated renewable resource. This happens to be its natural regenerative rate (Lawn, 1998). Thus, in order to put the strong sustainability approach into practice, the discount rate used in the user cost formula must be replaced with the regenerative rate of the proposed renewable resource substitute.

We believe that our variation of the El Serafy Rule can be made operational by compelling resource liquidators to establish a 'capital replacement' account in the same way business managers are required to establish a superannuation fund for employees. This could be done through changes in accounting legislation. Ideally, the legislative changes would include a strict schedule of discount rates and average mine lives to apply when calculating the set-aside component for each non-renewable resource type. The capital replacement accounts would be held by government-approved resource management companies whose task it would be to establish renewable replacement assets on behalf of the non-renewable resource liquidators.

6.3.5. Government Investment in Service Capital

We indicated in sub-section 6.2.2 that the Victorian Government's plan to increase its commitment to infrastructural investment (Actions 1, 2, and 3) will be of considerable benefit to Victorians. However, we also mentioned that more needs to be achieved through well-targeted infrastructural investment to kick-start the development of high-tech, value-adding, and resource-saving industries. We will not, therefore, repeat ourselves. But we would like to again stress that production excellence is vital if Victoria is to improve its stock of human-made capital that, in turn, would generate higher profits for businesses and higher real wages for workers.

Not only can better rather than more production increase the export of high-valued products and assist in reducing the burgeoning import bill, it can help reduce the cost of unemployment by allowing workers to work fewer hours without having to forego consumption-related benefits (e.g., through job-sharing). Of course, this depends very much on the genuine flexibility of labour markets, as previously discussed. It also relies very heavily on Victoria's commitment to excellence in education where it already has a decisive advantage over the remainder of Australia.[10]

One final point. The Victorian Government can play a significant role in the establishment and development of high-tech, resource-saving industries by taking a greater lead in the procurement of products containing recycled materials, and of plant, machinery, and equipment powered by renewable energy sources. The construction of low energy-using public buildings would also benefit significantly. Green procurement policies help to develop ready markets for low environmental impact goods that allow emerging green industries to rapidly attain the critical mass and economies of scale required to compete against traditional industries.

It is true that a green procurement policy can increase the direct costs of government spending, however, it is likely to improve the government budget position in the long-run. For example, a strict green procurement policy, by helping to reduce the negative spillover effects of economic activity, can lower the cost of public sector operations (e.g., by lowering government defensive and rehabilitative expenditures). Moreover, should it lead to increased profits and higher real wages of workers, it can help generate higher tax revenues. Overall, there is no reason why a green procurement policy should lead to a deterioration of the government budget position.

6.3.6. A Commitment to Full Employment

This last policy recommendation is very much dependent on the policy stance of the Federal Government. It might also be regarded by some readers as the most radical of the policies we are proposing. This aside, we believe that central governments should restore full employment as the centrepiece of macroeconomic policy. By full employment, we mean a situation where enough hours of work can be generated to match the work preferences of the labour force (Mitchell and Mosler, 2001).

In terms of this definition, full employment is obtained when the level of aggregate demand within the macroeconomy is sufficient to bring about a level of national income consistent with what is needed to eliminate all but frictional unemployment.[11] Clearly, structural unemployment will exist if 'employed' people are working fewer hours than the amount desired at going real wage rates. Thus, full employment is not achieved if members of the labour force are underemployed.

There are three main reasons why we believe that full employment should again be the focus of macroeconomic policy:

1. Unemployment, underemployment, and labour underutilisation impose significant welfare costs on society (Mitchell et al., 2003);[12]
2. Persistent unemployment reflects a failure on the part of governments to meet their equity obligations (Sen, 1997);
3. Unemployment is a severe example of inefficient resource use and, as such, every efficiency-concerned government should be disturbed by the enormous waste that it represents.

At present, the preferred macroeconomic policy stance in most developed countries is based on the supposed need to 'fight inflation first'. It is a policy stance that is predicated on two widely held beliefs. The first is the existence of an unemployment rate at which inflation remains steady — the so-called non-accelerating inflation rate of unemployment (NAIRU). Should the unemployment rate fall below the NAIRU, it is argued that growing labour market pressure results in non-productivity-based wage rises. This, in turn, leads to an accelerating rate of inflation. Should the unemployment rate rise above the NAIRU, the opposite occurs (Norris, 1989).

Second, the NAIRU is premised on the view that macroeconomic performance depends on the extent to which a government is able to control the rate of price inflation. Should a government increase aggregate demand to reduce or eliminate unemployment, inflationary pressure builds up within the economy as the unemployment falls below the NAIRU and leads, ultimately, to an unemployment rate higher than the rate that existed prior to the demand stimulus.

There is no doubt that an indiscriminate fiscal or monetary expansion by a central government can lead to an inflationary episode that must eventually be addressed by a deflationary and, indeed, unemployment-increasing response (Cowling et al., 2003). There is, therefore, considerable truth in the importance of controlling inflation and the need to wisely undertake expansionary fiscal and/or monetary policies.[13] However, some observers question whether the possibility and not the high probability of hyper-inflation occurring demands a macroeconomic obsession with inflation control (e.g., Blinder, 1987; Modigliani, 2000).

The unfortunate feature of a NAIRU or 'inflation first' policy is obvious — its success relies on the existence of an unemployed pool of labour. NAIRU advocates respond by arguing that productivity increases, supply-side initiatives, and the lowering of inflationary expectations can reduce the NAIRU over time and attenuate the number of disadvantaged citizens. While the evidence indicates a lowering of the NAIRU in Australia over the past decade, the NAIRU approach has been unsuccessful in bringing about full employment. Moreover, it is unlikely to do so unless full employment becomes an explicit macroeconomic policy objective. The NAIRU approach simply does not generate the level of aggregate demand needed to eliminate all but frictional unemployment.

We will not go into explicit and lengthy details, but we are convinced by the arguments put forward by the Centre of Full Employment and Equity (University of Newcastle) and the Centre for Full Employment and Price Stability (University of Missouri-Kansas City) that:

- full employment can only be achieved if a central government is willing to make up the necessary short-fall in aggregate expenditure;
- central government budget deficits need not be inflationary nor interest rate-increasing;
- government expenditure does not necessarily crowd out private sector activity.

Since an indiscriminate fiscal expansion by a central government can be undesirable, the Centre of Full Employment and Equity has proposed the idea of a Job Guarantee. The Job Guarantee is a demand-side policy whereby the government acts as a buffer stock employer to continuously absorb unemployed labour displaced by the private sector (Mitchell and Watts, 1997). In other words, any person unable to secure employment in the private sector (or, indeed, conventional public sector) automatically receives a job under the Job Guarantee scheme. All Job Guarantee employees are paid a minimum award wage to ensure they live decently. Importantly, the minimum wage establishes a wage floor for the entire economy.[14] Spending by the government on the Job Guarantee increases (decreases) as jobs are lost (gained) in the private sector. In doing so, the Job Guarantee achieves 'loose' full employment.

From a Victorian Government perspective, a full employment objective is out of its reach in the sense that it is not in a position equivalent to the Federal Government to offset any shortfall in aggregate expenditure within the economy. Having said this, the Centre of Full Employment and Equity has recently put forward a Community Development Job Guarantee proposal that, despite requiring Federal Government assistance, can be introduced at the localised level to deal more effectively with youth unemployment and long-term unemployment (i.e., those most at risk from the vagaries of fluctuating labour market conditions) (Mitchell et al., 2003). We strongly recommend this report to Victorian policy-makers and believe they should exert pressure on the Federal Government to provide the funding necessary to put the Community Development Job Guarantee proposal into operation where it is most required in the state of Victoria.

There is one other benefit of the Job Guarantee worthy of mention. As an employer-of-last-resort scheme, the Job Guarantee enables people to maintain the human capital skills they would otherwise lose during an extended period of unemployment. Moreover, the scheme can also be used to impart new skills and retrain Job Guarantee employees. Both the maintenance of previously acquired skills and the acquisition of new skills can help alleviate skill shortages that often emerge when unemployment rates are low — or, in the case of the Job Guarantee scheme, when the number of Job Guarantee employees is small. This, in turn, can minimise the potential mismatch between labour supply and demand that is currently leading to a paucity of proficient workers in some Australian industries.

NOTES

[1]   Or, for that matter, prevent the GPI from eventually falling.

[2]   It must be said that state governments are constrained in using taxes to alter the mix of desirable/undesirable activities to increase the GPI.

[3]   Of course, both tariffs and import quotas are beyond the jurisdictional powers of the Victorian Government.

[4]   Depletion and pollution taxes are often referred to as 'throughput' taxes because depletion concerns the 'input' of resources and pollution concerns the 'output' of wastes. Throughput is a term commonly used to describe the combined effect of resource inputs/waste outputs.

[5]   The preferred method of dealing with environmental misdemeanours continues to be the use of depletion and pollution standards. Evidence suggests that the setting of environmental standards is an inefficient way of dealing with environmental externalities (Pearce and Turner, 1990).

[6]   Given the complexity of water issues relating to the Murray-Darling Basin, the extraction rate determined by the Victorian Department of Sustainability and Environment would presumably be made in consultation with the Murray-Darling Basin Commission, the Federal Government, and the Queensland, New South Wales, and South Australian governments. Consultation would be needed to ensure sustainability was determined from an overall 'basin' perspective, not just the Victorian perspective.

[7]   The desired rate is likely to be less than the maximum sustainable rate. This is because the maximum rate is too difficult to calculate with precision. In addition, ecosystems are subject to novel and unforseen changes that are often triggered off by operating consistently at their sustainable limits.

[8] In saying this, we are not necessarily advocating the sale of public assets to finance environmental initiatives. We believe governments should finance the protection of the natural environment in the same way they finance general policy matters.

[9] Indeed, Wilson believes it should be more in the region of 50%.

[10] Once more, this is very much a function of the Federal Government's policy on Australia's higher education. The Victorian Government can, however, play its role in terms of primary and secondary school education, as well as tertiary and further education outside the university system (e.g., TAFE colleges).

[11] Frictional unemployment is the unemployment arising from individuals making the transition from one job to another and quitting jobs to seek a job more in keeping with their preferences (Dornbusch and Fischer, 1990).

[12] In our calculation of the cost of unemployment (broadly defined), we ignored the cost in terms of lost output because it is reflected in the GPI by a lower than potential consumption level. Hence, the full cost of unemployment is much larger than that revealed in Chapter 4.

[13] NAIRU proponents go much further and argue that expansionary fiscal and monetary policies are almost always undesirable and should be avoided.

[14] One of the other benefits of a Job Guarantee scheme is that allows a government to indirectly implement a progressive industrial relations policy. For example, a government could introduce post-industrial workplace practices (i.e., greater participatory democracy through the devolution of power in the workplace) that would give people the choice between a potentially demeaning but higher-paid job in the private sector or a self-actualising but lower-paid Job Guarantee job. In the same way the Job Guarantee wage acts as a disincentive for the private sector to pay very low wages, so the Job Guarantee scheme can act as a disincentive for the private sector to generate demeaning jobs and/or introduce draconian workplace practices.

Chapter 7

THE WEAKNESSES OF THE GPI

7.1. SHORTCOMINGS OF THE GPI AND HOW THEY CAN BE OVERCOME[1]

Our assessment of the performance of the Victorian economy has relied exclusively on the results of our GPI study. Naturally, the credibility of our assessment depends on how accurately the GPI reflects the sustainable well-being of Victorians. As it is, there are many critics who claim the GPI is riddled with too many flaws to possess any policy-guiding value.

Although considerable time was spent substantiating the application of the GPI in Chapters 2 and 3, we believe it is now necessary to discuss some of its weaknesses. In the process of doing this, we will reply to some of the criticisms levelled at the GPI. While there is little doubt that the GPI is a less-than-perfect indicator of sustainable well-being, we aim to show that: (a) some of the criticisms directed towards the GPI are unjustified, and (b) via the establishment of a more informative indicator framework, better data sources, and improved valuation methods, the few existing weaknesses of the GPI can be overcome. This, in turn, would greatly improve the reliability of future GPI studies.

7.1.1. Lack of an Exhaustive List of Items

The first and most obvious weakness of the GPI stems from the fact that the list of benefit and cost items used in its calculation is not at all exhaustive. Examples of absent welfare-related factors in our GPI study include the imputed value of leisure time, the cost of noise pollution and increasing urbanisation, the irksome nature of certain forms of employment, and the environmental costs of solid-waste pollution, coral reef destruction, and dwindling fish stocks. It is true that many of these items have been incorporated into previous GPI studies (e.g., Daly and Cobb, 1989; Lawn and Sanders, 1999; Hamilton, 1999; Clarke and Islam, 2004). Nevertheless, the very extensive range of benefit and cost items used in some GPI studies does not seem to have prevented at least one major welfare-related factor from being overlooked or omitted.

In defence of the GPI, the omission of crucial benefit and cost items is often attributable to the lack of available data sources required to make reliable monetary estimates of certain items. Thus, this first weakness of the GPI could be partially overcome if an indicator framework was specifically established to procure the necessary data to make GPI calculations. This issue is taken up again in section 7.2.

7.1.2. The Overwhelming Effect of Dominant items

The second major weakness of the GPI is that small variations in a dominant item (e.g., consumption-related welfare) can overwhelm large variations in a lesser item (e.g., cost of urban waste-water pollution) (Neumayer, 1999). Whether this is a problem at all is debatable. We believe that the domination of one item over another simply indicates that it has greater welfare significance. In addition, a dominant item invariably constitutes the aggregation of smaller related items. For example, consumption-related welfare involves a wide variety of goods and services that serve different welfare-related functions. Thus, it might be useful to disclose each consumption category as a separate item. Even so, disaggregation of a dominant item would not alter the final GPI value.

As it is, we have disaggregated consumption expenditure into the various national accounting categories (e.g., food; cigarettes and tobacco; transport services; and hotels, cafes, and restaurants; etc.) to conduct the welfare-related adjustments described in Table 3.2 (see also Tables 9.2, 9.3, and 9.4 in Chapter 9). We could have maintained each category as an individual item but chose, instead, to re-aggregate them. A similar exercise could also have be undertaken in relation to non-paid household and volunteer labour since both items involve work that provides a vast array of different services. In all, the domination of certain items is more of a presentation issue and does not undermine the GPI.[2]

7.1.3. Inadequate Valuation Methods

The validity of the criticisms levelled at the GPI is greatest in relation to its third major weakness — namely, the valuation methods used in its calculation (see Maler, 1991; Atkinson, 1995; Hamilton, 1994 and 1996; and Neumayer, 1999 and 2000). The majority of the criticism has been directed at the valuation of the following GPI items: consumption-related welfare; the Distribution Index (DI); defensive and rehabilitative expenditures; the cost of non-renewable resource depletion; and, finally, the tendency to deduct the 'cumulative' cost of various environmental damages (e.g., lost agricultural land and excessive irrigation water use). To respond to these criticisms, we will now deal with each item individually, starting with consumption-related welfare.

Consumption-related Welfare

There are two aspects to consumption-related welfare that have attracted criticism. The first relates to the qualitative dimension of consumption; the second relates to the use of *real* values or constant prices in the valuation of consumption-related welfare. As to the first aspect, it is argued that a consumption-based item cannot capture the qualitative features of the various goods and services consumed. We have already alluded to this problem in Chapters 2 and 3 and, to some extent, have overcome it by treating all expenditure on cigarettes and tobacco, and half of all expenditure on alcoholic beverages as non-welfare-enhancing (see Table 3.2). But, certainly, more needs to be done to deal with this issue adequately.

In relation to the second aspect, consumption expenditure is measured in real rather than nominal money values in order to reflect the change in the physical quantity of goods consumed over time (see the explanation on the efficacy of using real monetary values in section 2.1). However, for two good reasons, an increase in real consumption expenditure cannot be directly equated with a proportionate increase in well-being. The first is due to the principle of 'diminishing marginal utility' which suggests that as one augments their consumption of physical goods, the benefits they enjoy increases at a diminishing rate. The second is due to the fact that an increase in the rate at which certain goods are consumed may not increase the benefits they yield. Consider, for example, the lighting of a room by a light bulb. Is more welfare experienced if three light bulbs are worn out or 'consumed' over one year compared to just one light bulb that lasts the full year? No, the total welfare in both cases is the same yet, in the former instance, more goods have been consumed.

Despite these potential accounting flaws, real consumption expenditure may still prove to be a worthy reference point in the estimation of consumption-related welfare. Why? It is generally recognised that people will pay a higher price for a good embodying superior welfare-yielding qualities. Consequently, a measure of consumption-related welfare ought to be computable through the use of market prices. For instance, the rental value of a car, a house, a TV, or a refrigerator — i.e., the amount paid to rent durable goods for a one year period — is widely considered a proxy measure of the annual services they yield. On this basis, the full market price of a non-durable good should approximate the service it yields during the accounting period in which it was initially purchased and ultimately consumed (Daly, 1991).

Unfortunately, the market prices and rental values of goods vary for reasons other than the change in their welfare-yielding qualities. The price of a good is also affected by: (a) the relative prices of the different forms of resources used in its production; (b) the actual quantity or supply of the good itself; and (c) changes in taxes, the nominal money supply, and the opportunity cost of holding money. Clearly, for market prices to remain a proxy indicator of well-being, it is necessary to eliminate all price-influencing factors other than those related to a good's welfare-yielding qualities. Given that this is a near impossible task, there are two choices available. The first option is to leave prices as they are — that is, to rely on current or nominal prices. The second option is to deflate the nominal annual value of consumption expenditure by an aggregate price index. If the former option is chosen, the nominal value of all consumption expenditure will embody unwanted price influences over and above any welfare-related influences. If the latter option is chosen, one obtains the real value of all consumption expenditure. But, in so doing, one also eliminates the price-influencing effect of a variation in the welfare-yielding qualities of all goods — the very influence that one wants to maintain in order for prices to constitute an approximate measure of well-being.

We believe that the latter option — the one we adopted for our study — is desirable for the following reason. While the principle of diminishing marginal utility suggests that an increase in well-being will be proportionately less than the increase in the quantity of physical goods consumed, the principle is based on the assumption that there is no change in their welfare-yielding qualities. It is reasonable to assume that, through technological progress, the welfare-yielding qualities of most goods will continue to increase for some time to come. If so, this will largely offset the effect of the principle of diminishing marginal utility. To what extent it does so, one cannot ascertain, however, it should be sufficient to ensure that any positive impact that consumption-related welfare has on the GPI is well reflected by an increase in real rather than nominal consumption expenditure.[3]

The Distribution Index (DI)

The criticism directed towards the next particular item — the Distribution Index (DI) — was outlined in sub-section 3.4.5. While we have followed one of the valuation methods denounced in some quarters, we believe the criticism is invalid. We have explained why in sub-section 3.4.5 and invite all non-recollecting readers to revisit it.

Defensive and Rehabilitative Expenditures

The policy of subtracting defensive and rehabilitative expenditures in the calculation of the GPI has been widely questioned (Maler, 1991; Lebergott, 1993; United Nations 1993; Hamilton, 1994 and 1996; and Neumayer, 1999). It has been suggested that the concept of defensive expenditure is very dubious because it is impossible to draw the line between what does and does not constitute a defensive form of expenditure. For example, as Neumayer (1999, p. 83) argues: "If health expenditures are defensive expenditures against illness, why should food and drinking expenditures not count as defensive expenditures against hunger and thirst? Are holiday and entertainment expenditures defensive expenditures against boredom? Should they all be subtracted from personal consumption expenditures?" Furthermore, a United Nations review of national accounting has argued that when the concept of defensive expenditures is pushed to its logical conclusion, scarcely any consumption expenditure contributes to an improvement in human welfare.

There is some degree of truth in the above criticism. However, there is a fundamental difference between expenditures over and above the amount deemed necessary to satisfy base-level needs and expenditures people feel increasingly required to make to protect themselves against the unwanted side effects of economic activity. It is safe to say that the latter are defensive in character and the majority of the former are not. In addition, if all consumption expenditure was purely defensive, a lot less spending would take place since, for example, expenditure on gourmet food at a restaurant would be pointless. Why pay a large sum for high quality food and waiting service if one can pay a much smaller sum to meet their defensive consumption needs?

There is no doubt that the assumptions we have made regarding defensive and/or rehabilitative forms of expenditure are purely arbitrary. What's more, they also result in a significant adjustment to consumption expenditure — particularly in the case of CON(3). However, we believe the assumptions are reasonable for the simple reason that, as Neumayer himself suggests, a great deal of consumption expenditure *is* defensive and/or rehabilitative in nature.

The Cost of Non-renewable Resource Depletion

The criticism directed at the valuation methods used in calculating the cost of non-renewable resource depletion is twofold. In the first instance, it is argued that the wide variety of techniques used reflects a general lack of methodological consistency on the part of GPI advocates. We, to a considerable extent, agree. Indeed, we believe there is a genuine need to establish a standardised set of items and valuation techniques. Not only would this strengthen the case for the GPI, it would also allow for more meaningful welfare comparisons across different nations, states, and provinces.

In the second instance, Neumayer (2000) has been particularly critical of the widespread use of the replacement cost approach. Neumayer believes a resource rent approach should be used. Although the resource rent method has been employed in a number of GPI studies, it typically involves a deduction of the *total* cost of non-renewable resource depletion. In many instances, it also involves the assumption of escalating non-renewable resource prices (e.g., Daly and Cobb, 1989). Neumayer argues against the deduction of the total cost of non-renewable resource depletion by claiming that El Serafy's (1989) 'user cost' formula is the correct means of calculating resource rents (see equation 6.1). The significance of El Serafy's user cost formula is that only a portion of the total cost of resource depletion is deducted — not the total cost as is widely practiced.

We agree entirely with Neumayer regarding the El Serafy user cost formula. As mentioned in Chapters 3 and 6, it is the method we have used to calculate the cost of non-renewable resource depletion. Where we depart from Neumayer's argument is his objection to using a replacement cost approach. Neumayer dislikes the replacement cost approach because he believes there is no reason why non-renewable resources need to be fully replaced in the present when there are reserves available for many years to come. If there is no current requirement to fully replace non-renewable resources then, according to Neumayer, it is wrong to use a replacement cost approach to calculate the cost of depletion.

We disagree with Neumayer because, in our view, the GPI seeks to incorporate a Hicksian sustainability element. As such, the GPI is designed to capture the sustainable nature of economic activity as well as the economic welfare it generates. While the present quantity of resources being extracted from non-renewable resource stocks can be sustained for some time without having to find or establish a renewable resource replacement, this doesn't mean that it can be sustained indefinitely. And while it may not be necessary to think about a replacement resource for some time, for proper accounting purposes, the actual cost of establishing a renewable resource substitute must be attributed to the point in time when the depletion took place. Indeed, this is the basis behind the El Serafy user cost method.

It might be argued that we are being inconsistent here — after all, we are arguing in favour of the replacement cost approach while also promoting the use of El Serafy's user cost formula. The El Serafy user cost formula is regarded as just one of many ways to execute the resource rent approach.

However, the beauty of the El Serafy user cost formula is that it can be used to calculate resource rents and replacement costs. It is a resource rent method in that the portion of the proceeds from resource extraction that does not constitute a user cost is a genuine resource rent (X). It is also a replacement cost method in that the portion of the proceeds from resource extraction that constitutes a user cost is, in fact, the genuine cost of resource asset replacement ($R - X$). Since it is the user cost that ought to be deducted when calculating the GPI, the El Serafy formula serves its purpose as a replacement cost means of estimating the cost of resource depletion. Therefore, it is not correct to say that the user cost approach is exclusively a resource rent method.

Assuming the Escalation of Resource Prices over Time

It was pointed out above that the cost of non-renewable resource depletion is often calculated on the assumption of escalating resource prices over the study period. This, too, has been criticised given that most commodity prices have historically fallen in real terms (Neumayer, 2000).

Neumayer's observation that most commodity prices have not increased in real terms is entirely correct. So why have we made a conflicting assumption? In view of the expected life of many non-renewable resources and the projected rates of depletion, the price of non-renewable resources should have already begun to rise to reflect their impending absolute scarcity. That they have not simply demonstrates that markets, while very good at signalling relative scarcities (e.g., the scarcity of oil relative to coal), are woefully inadequate at signalling the absolute scarcity of the total quantity of all resources available for current and future production (Howarth and Norgaard, 1990; Norgaard, 1990; Bishop, 1993; Daly, 1996; and Lawn, 2004b).

Should one use the actual market prices of non-renewable resources to assist in the calculation of the GPI if they fail to reflect their increasing absolute scarcity? We think not. To get an accurate picture of sustainable well-being, one should use the best estimate of rising non-renewable resource prices. Many studies have used a 3% escalation factor. In our calculation of the GPI for Victoria, Australia, and the Rest-of-Australia, a 2% escalation factor was assumed. In all, an assumed escalation of non-renewable resource prices seems in our mind justified.

Cumulative Environmental Costs

The final contentious valuation issue relates to whether the deduction term for the cost of lost agricultural land, excessive irrigation water use, and long-term environmental damage should, in each case, be a cumulative total. By cumulative we mean that the amount deducted for each year is equal to the annual cost plus the accumulated cost from previous years. Neumayer (2000) believes this practice is flawed since it involves double counting. He believes that only the present cost should be deducted.

Neumayer has a very good point here and unless accumulation of the cost can be adequately justified, it should be abandoned. However, we believe accumulation can be justified because the GPI attempts to measure the sustainable well-being of a nation or state at the time it is being experienced. In the case of lost agricultural land, excessive irrigation water use, and long-term environmental damage, the impact on the sustainable well-being in a given year depends very much on actions taken in the past. Hence, the total cost in any given year must reflect the amount required to compensate a nation's or state's citizens in that year for the cumulative impact of past as well as present economic activities.

7.1.4. The GPI is not a True Measure of 'Sustainable' Well-being

Although the fundamental aim of the GPI is to measure the sustainable well-being of a nation or state, it has been suggested that the GPI fails in terms of the 'sustainability' side of the coin. To understand why, we need to reconsider the Hicksian concept of sustainability outlined in Chapters 2 and 3.

In the specific case of sustainable well-being, the key aspect of Hicks' concept is the need to keep welfare-generating capital intact. As mentioned a number of times during this report, capital comes in essentially two forms: (a) human-made capital, such as producer goods (plant, machinery, and equipment) and durable consumer goods; and (b) natural capital, such as forests, sub-soil assets, fisheries, water resources, and critical ecosystems.

There are, however, two schools of thought as to what form of capital must be kept intact to 'sustain' the well-being of a nation's or state's citizens. The first is commonly referred to as the 'weak' sustainability school. To achieve weak sustainability, it is only deemed necessary to maintain a combined stock of human-made and natural capital. It matters not whether one of the two forms of capital is in decline since it assumed that both forms of capital are adequate substitutes for each other (Pearce and Turner, 1990; Daly, 1996).

The second school of thought is the 'strong' sustainability school. Advocates of strong sustainability believe that natural capital provides a range of critical sustainability services that human-made capital is unable to fully replicate. They therefore believe that human-made and natural capital are complements not substitutes and, in order to achieve sustainability, the two forms of capital must be individually kept intact — especially natural capital.

We belong to the strong sustainability school for the simple reason that we believe human-made and natural capital are complementary forms of capital. It is undeniably true that advances in the technology embodied in human-made capital can, for some time at least, reduce the resource flow required from natural capital to produce a given physical quantity of physical goods. However, for three related reasons, this does not amount to substitution (Lawn, 1999). First, technological progress only reduces the high entropy waste generated in the transformation of natural capital to human-made capital.[4] It does not allow human-made capital to "take the place of" natural capital.

Second, because of the first and second laws of thermodynamics, there is a limit to how much production waste can be reduced by technological progress. This is because 100% production efficiency is physically impossible; there can never be 100% recycling of matter; and there is no way to recycle energy at all.

Third, a value of one or more for the elasticity of substitution between human-made and natural capital is necessary to demonstrate the adequate long-run substitutability of the former for the latter. It has recently been shown that the value of the elasticity of substitution derived from a production function obeying the first and second laws of thermodynamics is always less one (Lawn, 2004c). Thus, the production of a given quantity of human-made capital requires a minimum resource flow and, therefore, a minimum amount of resource-providing natural capital (Meadows et al., 1972; Pearce et al., 1989; Costanza et al., 1991; Folke et al., 1994; Daly, 1996). It is for these reasons that we believe that natural capital maintenance is required to ensure the ecological sustainability of economic activity.

The problem with the GPI is that it merely counts the cost of the various natural capital services lost in the provision of welfare-yielding goods. While it is vital to obtain a better measure of well-being by subtracting the cost of environmental damage, it is equally important to know when a nation's or state's stock of natural capital has declined to such an extent as to render the welfare it enjoys ecologically unsustainable. The GPI does not provide this information. As such, the GPI requires supplementation to accurately reveal the 'sustainable' well-being of a nation or state.

Given the need to keep natural capital intact, we believe it is advisable to undertake biophysical assessments of resource stocks and critical ecosystems and present the information in something akin to a natural capital account. Diminution of natural capital over time would indicate that a nation's or state's well-being — whether rising or falling — is becoming increasingly unsustainable.

As a back-up to the natural capital account, a comparison between a nation's or state's ever-changing ecological footprint and biocapacity could also be provided (see Wackernagel et al., 1999). In this particular instance, the surpassing of the latter by the former would also indicate the unsustainable nature of economic activity.

7.1.5. The GPI Fails to Reflect the Potential Future Impact of Present Actions

The final weakness of the GPI relates to its failure to reflect the potential impact of present actions and policies. For example, while the GPI conveys useful information about the current manifestations and immediate effects of past and present activities, it reveals little if anything about the potential impact of current activities. This weakens the policy-guiding value of the GPI.

It might, therefore, be expedient to calculate a second GPI value that incorporates the probable future benefits and costs of current actions (i.e., attributes future benefits and costs to the present calculation of the GPI.). This could be achieved by employing forecasting techniques put forward by Asheim (1994 and 1996), Pezzey (1993), and Pezzey and Wiltage (1998). Ideally, if a nation or state introduced policies to move the economy towards a more sustainable, just, and efficient mode of operation, the value of the second GPI value would be higher than the standard GPI to reflect the forecasted net benefits. A lower accompanying measure of economic welfare would reflect the failure of present policies. Indeed, if our evidence is valid concerning the potential harm of high rates of economic growth to sustainable well-being, the implementation of growth-based policies should result in a lower rather than higher supplementary GPI value. In addition, the failure to introduce qualitative improvement initiatives ought to be reflected by a gradual widening of the gap between the supplementary GPI and the standard GPI.

7.2. THE NEED FOR A MORE INFORMATIVE INDICATOR AND DATA-COLLECTING FRAMEWORK

Our assessment of the performance of the Victorian economy *vis-a-vis* the Rest-of-Australia was made inordinately difficult by the lack of appropriate data sources. It not only forced us to confine our study to the period from 1986 to 2003 (we would have preferred to have gone back to the 1960s) it meant that certain items could not be calculated using our preferred valuation method. For example, it was necessary to obtain and use data for both Australia and Victoria that clearly involved a consistent data gathering process. While we were able to locate data that met this requirement, the data was not always as comprehensive as we would have liked. Often the more suitable and valuation-friendly data existed in an inconsistent form or at the national level only.

The impact of data limitations on our study was obvious — we were often forced to make heroic valuation assumptions that meant some items were destined to be, at best, distant approximations of their correct value. Having said this, we applied each valuation method consistently over the study period and were at pains to ensure our estimations of the social and environmental costs erred on the conservative side. Hence, while the total GPI values may not be entirely accurate, we are relatively confident that the trend movement in per capita GPI(3) for both Victoria and the Rest-of-Australia are reliable indications of the changing well-being of Victorian and remaining Australian citizens over the study period. Since we have not provided ecological footprint estimates or a natural capital account for both Victoria and the Rest-of-Australia, we are far less confident that the respective GPIs reflect a level of well-being that can be 'ecologically sustained' into the distant future. However, we are adamant that per capita GPI(3) is a better indicator of sustainable well-being than per capita GSP (Victoria) and per capita GDP (Australia and Rest-of-Australia).

To improve the reliability of future GPI estimates, we believe it would be efficacious to establish an indicator framework that is specifically designed to accurately measure the values of each component item. An indicator framework of this nature would be doubly valuable because it would: (a) provide researchers and policy-makers with detailed statistical information concerning each item, and (b) advance their capacity to address concerning issues through the formulation of appropriate remedial measures.[5]

On the whole, economic data already exists in quite detailed form at both the national and state levels in Australia. It must be said, however, that the value of the stock of consumer durables is not available at the state level. To maintain consistency, we were forced to abandon the Australia-wide data and employ our own valuation approach to both Victoria and Australia.

Social and environmental data, particularly the latter, exists in an inconsistent and incongruous form that would appear to reflect the often piecemeal approach to policy-making in these two areas. State-based data is particularly difficult to access. To the credit of the Australian Bureau of Statistics, significant improvements have been made in the collection of social and environmental data. However, its compilation is often the product of irregular studies whereby the data gathering process and the valuation methods employed differ over time. This renders the use of data across time ineffectual. It is also why, in our study, we often had to select a point value estimate of a benefit or cost item and establish an index to weight the value over the study period.

From the point of view of environmental data, there is an urgent need to establish stock and flow accounts of the various resource types and other natural capital assets at both the national and state levels. Regular ecosystem monitoring and annual updates of ecosystem health are also crucial. We find at extraordinary that data of this type does not exist in a comprehensive and user-friendly form.

Also desperately required are regular valuation studies to estimate the different social and environmental benefits and costs of economic growth. Of course, to be of value, these studies would ideally make use of annually updated data so as to ensure the consistency of valuations across time. We also think it is bewildering that the cost of such things as native vegetation clearance, loss of old growth forests, and dryland salinity is not regularly and scrupulously estimated by relevant government departments. In all, much could and should be done to facilitate more accurate estimates of the GPI and other alternative indicators of sustainability and human well-being.

NOTES

[1]   Much of what is discussed in section 7.1 is drawn from Lawn (2005).
[2]   If it has one negative aspect, it is the fact that it may render causality between the GPI and its component items more difficult to establish.
[3]   There are attempts being made to capture the qualitative dimension of goods, in particular, producer goods, through the use of hedonic pricing techniques (Moulton, 2001). We are currently engaged in experimental work to adjust the prices of certain types of goods (e.g., computers and telecommunication goods) to reflect their rapid qualitative improvement in recent years.
[4]   To understand what is meant by low and high entropy matter-energy, the importance of the first and second laws of thermodynamics must be revealed. The first law of thermodynamics is the *law of conservation of energy and matter*. It declares that energy and matter can never be created or destroyed. The second law is the *Entropy Law*. It declares that whenever energy is used in physical transformation processes, the amount of usable or 'available' energy always declines. While the first law ensures the maintenance of a given quantity of energy and matter, the Entropy Law determines that which is usable. This is critical since, from a physical viewpoint, it is not the total quantity of matter-energy that is of primary concern, but the amount that exists in a readily available form.

The best way to illustrate the relevance of these two laws is to provide a simple example. Consider a piece of coal. When it is burned, the matter-energy embodied within the coal is transformed into heat and ash. While the first law ensures the total amount of matter-energy in the heat and ashes equals that previously embodied in the piece of coal, the second law ensures the usable quantity of matter-energy does not. In other words, the dispersed heat and ashes can no longer be used in a way similar to the original piece of coal. To make matters worse, any attempt to reconcentrate the dispersed matter-energy, which requires the input of additional energy, results in more usable energy being expended than that reconcentrated. Hence, all physical transformation processes involve an irrevocable loss of available energy or what is sometimes referred to as a 'net entropy deficit'. This enables one to understand the use of the term *low entropy* and to distinguish it from *high entropy*. Low entropy refers to a highly ordered physical structure embodying energy and matter in a readily available form, such as a piece of coal. Conversely, high entropy refers to a highly disordered and degraded physical structure embodying energy and matter that is, by itself, in an unusable or unavailable from, such as heat and ash. By definition, the matter-energy used in economic processes can be considered low entropy resources whereas unusable by-products can be considered high entropy wastes.
[5]   Having said this, many of the items are interrelated and thus, from a policy perspective, cannot be dealt with in isolation. Given that a high rate of economic growth appears to be a major underlying cause of escalating environmental costs, policies to reduce environmental damage will need to focus on 'scale-related' issues and not so much on improved environmental management.

Chapter 8

SUMMARY AND CONCLUSIONS

Measuring genuine progress is vital if we wish to be better informed of the impact that our policy-makers are having on our sustainable well-being. Improved indicators of genuine progress also enable policy-makers to properly assess the worthiness of past policies and the reasons underlying their failure or success.

Unfortunately, policy-makers continue to steer national and state economies using Gross Domestic Product (GDP) and Gross State Product (GSP) as their genuine progress compasses. GDP and GSP fail to encapsulate the full impact of a growing national or state economy on sustainable well-being. GDP and GSP not only ignore non-market production, they overlook many social costs and make no allowance for the impact that a change in the distribution of income can have on aggregate welfare.

GDP and GSP are also deficient in that their calculation assumes that all current consumption expenditure is welfare-enhancing in the present when, in fact, current expenditure on consumer durables generates welfare benefits in future years. The same also applies to the treatment of publicly-provided service capital and net capital investment.

We think it is high time that policy-makers utilise a more appropriate compass when designing welfare-enhancing policies and believe the Genuine Progress Indicator (GPI) is a useful starting point. Comprised of economic, social, and environmental benefit and cost items, the GPI integrates the wide-ranging impacts of economic growth into a single monetary-based index. Whilst the GPI includes some of the national accounting values used in the computation of GDP and GSP, its calculation accounts for a number of benefits and costs that invariably escape market valuation.

We do not deny that the GPI has some deficiencies. However, we believe the GPI has a sound theoretical foundation and is the best indicator of sustainable well-being so far devised. Should a more informative indicator framework, better data sources, and improved valuation methods be established, we are convinced that the existing weaknesses of the GPI can be eliminated.

Our GPI study reveals that Victoria's per capita GPI(3) fluctuated over the study period (1986-2003) but, overall, rose from a value of $18,839 per Victorian in 1986 to $22,951 per Victorian by 2003. This constituted a 21.8% rise in sustainable well-being over the study period or an average rate of increase of 1.46% per annum.

It is also clear to us that Victoria's per capita GSP greatly overstated the sustainable well-being of the average Victorian. For instance, our study shows that the difference between

Victoria's per capita GSP and per capita GPI(3) averaged around $9,500 per Victorian over the study period. Beginning with a disparity of $7,905 per Victorian in 1986, the difference between per capita GSP and per capita GPI(3) increased to $11,136 per Victorian by 2003.

Interestingly, despite a dramatic decline in the growth rate of the Victorian economy between 1989 and 1992, Victoria's per capita GPI(3) did not decline over this period ($19,957 per Victorian in 1989 and $20,535 per Victorian in 1992). Moreover, one of the largest increases in Victoria's per capita GPI(3) occurred in 1994 — a low-growth year that followed three previous years of low growth. Conversely, the high rate of growth of the Victorian economy between 1995 and 2000 did not significantly increase Victoria's per capita GPI(3) ($25,335 per Victorian in 1995 and $26,499 per Victorian in 2000). Indeed, Victoria's per capita GPI(3) fell in 2000 — a high-growth year.

It would appear to us that the high growth rates of the Victorian economy over the past decade have failed to translate effectively into the sustainable well-being of the average Victorian. This suggests that the extra benefits generated by high rates of growth were largely offset by the ever-increasing rise in social and environmental costs. We therefore believe that Victoria's per capita GPI(3) would have been higher in 2003 if the Victorian economy had been physically smaller but qualitatively better (i.e., if better goods were produced rather than a lot more goods).

A number of factors impacted on Victoria's per capita GPI(3) over the study period. The minor influences were:

- the rise in the service from consumer durables (SCD) after 1996;
- the decrease in the welfare from publicly-provided service capital (WPPSC) between 1992 and 1997;
- the increase in the combined cost of crime and family breakdown after 1996.

The major influences on Victoria's per capita GPI(3) included:

- the sheer magnitude of weighted CON(3) and its sharp increase after 1997;
- the steep rise in the Distribution Index (DI) between 1992 and 1997;
- the value of unpaid work (non-paid household work plus volunteer work);
- the rapid increase in the cost of unemployment (broadly defined) between 1990 and 1994 and the continuing relative high cost of unemployment between 1996 and 2003 despite the significant fall in the official unemployment rate;
- the wild fluctuations throughout the study period of Victoria's share of the change in Australia's foreign debt;
- the increasing cost of environmental damage (lost natural capital services) — in particular, the rising cost of long-term environmental damage caused by Victoria's excessive rate of energy consumption.

As for the performance of Victoria compared to the Rest-of-Australia (Australia minus Victoria), our study shows that the sustainable well-being of the average Victorian was consistently higher than that of the average person living elsewhere in Australia. Beginning with a difference in per capita GPI(3) of $2,105 per person in 1986, the disparity between Victoria and the Rest-of-Australia increased to $4,331 per person by 2003. In percentage terms, the per capita GPI(3) of the Rest-of-Australia increased by 11.3% compared to the 21.8% rise in Victoria's per capita GPI(3). Crucially, the difference between the per capita GPI(3) of Victoria and the Rest-of-Australia grew most intensely between 2000 and 2003.

Not unlike the circumstances existing in Victoria, we found that the continuing high growth rates of the Rest-of-Australian economy had a detrimental impact on sustainable well-being. Indeed, the similar relationship between per capita GPI(3) and the prevailing growth rates of the Victorian and Rest-of-Australian economies reaffirms out belief that the average Australian would have been better off had the policy emphasis throughout Australia been directed towards distributional equity, resource use efficiency, and natural capital maintenance.

Minor factors underlying the difference between the per capita GPI(3) of Victoria and the Rest-of-Australia were:

- Victoria's lower per capita cost of unemployment (broadly defined) in the latter years of the study period resulting from Victoria's capacity to create a larger number of full-time jobs;
- Victoria's higher Ecosystem Health Index (EHI) arising from its much smaller rate of native vegetation clearance over the study period.

Major reasons for Victoria's superior per capita GPI(3) include:

- Victoria's lower per capita cost of non-renewable resource depletion, particularly after 1993;
- Victoria's significantly lower per capita cost of lost agricultural land;
- overall, and given the similar per capita consumption-related welfare of Victoria and the Rest-of-Australia throughout the study period, Victoria's much lower social and environmental costs. Victoria's environmental performance was vastly superior as reflected by its considerably lower per capita cost of lost natural capital services.

Having said this, Victoria was outperformed by the Rest-of-Australia in terms of:

- excessive rates of irrigation water use;
- per capita energy consumption;
- and, to a lesser extent, air pollution.

From a policy viewpoint, we admit that the Victorian Government is limited in its capacity to increase Victoria's GPI because a great deal of what impacts on the Victorian economy remains the exclusive policy domain of the Federal Government. This aside, we believe that the Victorian Government can play a significant role in boosting the sustainable well-being of the average Victorian as well as maintain if not accentuate the superior relative performance of Victoria.

On examination of the Victorian Government's recent economic statement *Victoria: Leading the Way*, we feel it is primarily designed to boost the state's GSP. Given our reservations regarding the relationship between GSP growth and sustainable well-being, we believe the Victorian Government should be doing more to integrate economic, social, and environmental policies rather than treating each policy domain separately. More should also be done to treat all benefits and costs alike since, regardless of their origin, they impact equally on Victoria's sustainable well-being even if they are not reflected in Victoria's GSP.

Some of the policies we believe would increase Victoria's GPI include:

- the introduction of tax incentives and/or subsidies to promote research and development into 'green' technologies;
- better targeted infrastructural investment to assist in the emergence and development of tomorrow's key industries — i.e., industries that will significantly raise productivity, increase Victoria's rate of energy efficiency, and elevate standards of production excellence to new heights;
- an import-replacement policy centred around a competitive industry base and the facilitation of high-tech, value-adding, and resource-saving industries;
- the maintenance of world-class universities, including protection from the potential degenerative effects of standards-lowering competition;
- a regulatory reform process that reduces compliance costs for Victorian businesses without forgoing the welfare benefits that regulations are designed to protect;
- industrial relations reform involving the establishment of genuinely flexible labour markets that provides workers with greater work-leisure-family options while simultaneously protecting full-time work entitlements. Industrial relations reform must also engender greater workplace trust and the establishment of well-defined internal career paths supported by a dual employer-employee commitment to on-going training;
- ecological tax reform that would initially involve the manipulation of the tax system to: (a) reward 'welfare-increasing' business behaviour (e.g., activities that add greater value in production); (b) encourage the development and uptake of resource-saving technologies; (c) reduce the proportion of private sector investment being directed into non-productive, 'rent-seeking' ventures; and (d) penalise environmentally-destructive behaviour (e.g., high energy-intensive and polluting activities). To ensure Victoria's ecological footprint is commensurate with the biocapacity of its natural environment, an ecological tax reform package must eventually be remodelled to include tradeable permit systems;
- finally, a Job Guarantee program based on a revitalised full employment commitment that would not only reduce inequities in the system, but would eliminate the destructive social cost of unemployment, underemployment, and labour underutilisation.

GPI CALCULATIONS AND DATA SOURCES

9.1. INTRODUCTION

This chapter is provided to transparently reveal the valuation methods and data sources used in the derivation of the items that make up the GPI. At the end of the chapter, tables are supplied to show exactly how the final value of each item was calculated. The items discussed correspond to those appearing in Tables 4.1 (Victoria), 5.1 (Rest-of-Australia), and 9.1 (Australia). It should be noted that the final values of each item shown in Tables 4.1, 5.1, and 9.1 appear in 'bold' in the tables provided at the rear of this chapter.

9.2. THE CALCULATION OF THE GPI ITEMS

In the case of some items, derivation of the annual values was not required — the values could simply be drawn from national and state accounting sources produced by the Australian Bureau of Statistics (ABS). This applied to most of the economic items. Conversely, the social and environmental benefit and cost items were generally calculated by assigning a monetary estimate to the social or physical environmental data relating to the particular item in question. In a number of instances, we relied upon a previous point estimate of a social or environmental cost and established an index to estimate the changing cost over the study period. This is not the ideal method of calculation. However, because of data limitations previously discussed in Chapter 7, this was often the only method available to us.

9.2.1. Items a, b, c: Consumption Expenditure (Private and Public) - CON(1), CON(2), and CON(3)

The values pertaining to consumption expenditure were sourced directly from published ABS national and state accounts. The values of CON(1), CON(2), and CON(3) were obtained by adjusting consumption expenditure as per Table 3.2. The values are revealed, in full, along with the adjustments to each consumption category in Tables 9.2 (Australia), 9.3 (Victoria), and 9.4 (Rest-of-Australia). The values for the Rest-of-Australia were determined by subtracting Victoria's consumption expenditure from that of Australia.

Data sources:

ABS, Catalogue No. 5204.0.
ABS, Catalogue No. 5220.0.
Foster, R. (1996), *Australian Economic Statistics: 1949-50 to 1994-95*, Reserve Bank of Australia Occasional Paper No. 8.

9.2.2. Item d: Expenditure on Consumer Durables (ECD)

Like the previous items, the expenditure on consumer durables (ECD) was sourced from ABS national and state accounts. The values for the expenditure on the different categories of consumer durables (e.g., clothing and footwear; furnishings and household equipment; and purchases of vehicles) are shown in italics in Tables 9.2 (Australia), 9.3 (Victoria), and 9.4 (Rest-of-Australia). The final ECD values for each year are the sum of the italicised values. They are also revealed in Table 9.5. Once again, the values for the Rest-of-Australia were determined by subtracting the Victorian values from that of Australia.

Data source: As per items *a*, *b*, and *c*.

9.2.3. Item e: Stock of Consumer Durables

To determine the annual service provided by consumer durables, it was first necessary to estimate the value of the existing stock. We assumed that the stock of consumer durables would, on average, endure for ten years. Thus, in order to calculate the value of the existing stock, we assumed that its value was the sum of the previous ten years' expenditure on consumer durables (i.e., consumer durables purchased eleven or more years ago were assumed to be fully 'consumed'). The annual values of the stock of consumer durables are revealed in Table 9.5.

Data source: As per item *d*.

9.2.4. Item f: Service from Consumer Durables (SCD)

The annual service from consumer durables (SCD) was calculated by multiplying the start-of-year stock value by 0.1 (10%). The annual service from consumer durables is revealed in Table 9.5.

Data source: As per item *d*.

Table 9.1: Genuine Progress Indicator (GPI) and real GDP for Australia, 1986-2003

Year	CON(1) ($)	CON(2) ($)	CON(3) ($)	ECD ($)	Consumer durables ($)	SCD ($)	Adjusted CON(1) ($)	Adjusted CON(2) ($)	Adjusted CON(3) ($)	Distribution index	Weighted CON(1) ($)	Weighted CON(2) ($)	Weighted CON(3) ($)
	a	b	c	d	e	f (e x 0.1)	g (a - d + f)	h (b - d + f)	i (c - d + f)	j (1986 = 100.0)	k (g/j) x 100	l (h/j) x 100	m (i/j) x 100
1985					321,874.8								
1986	347,090.0	284,441.8	216,911.5	-37,124.0	328,677.5	32,187.5	342,153.5	279,505.2	211,975.0	100.0	342,153.5	279,505.2	211,975.0
1987	352,549.0	288,815.3	219,224.5	-34,753.0	333,147.8	32,867.7	350,663.7	286,930.0	217,339.2	98.9	354,567.1	290,123.9	219,758.5
1988	364,010.0	298,176.3	226,434.5	-35,493.0	339,078.4	33,314.8	361,831.8	295,998.0	224,256.3	102.3	353,657.1	289,310.7	219,189.8
1989	378,490.0	310,179.0	236,498.3	-37,570.0	346,213.3	33,907.8	374,827.8	306,516.8	232,836.1	105.9	354,052.7	289,527.9	219,931.0
1990	395,052.0	323,966.0	247,125.0	-39,244.0	354,631.5	34,621.3	390,429.3	319,343.3	242,502.3	106.5	366,693.5	299,929.1	227,759.6
1991	400,592.0	327,902.3	249,570.3	-37,708.0	359,489.5	35,463.2	398,347.2	325,657.4	247,325.4	101.8	391,338.3	319,927.5	242,973.7
1992	408,219.0	334,322.3	254,829.3	-38,094.0	363,647.3	35,949.0	406,074.0	332,177.2	252,684.2	101.0	402,076.8	328,907.5	250,197.0
1993	415,385.0	340,306.8	259,893.8	-38,920.0	369,180.6	36,364.7	412,829.7	337,751.5	257,338.5	103.0	400,903.6	327,994.3	249,904.3
1994	424,401.0	348,206.0	266,899.5	-39,713.0	374,777.0	36,918.1	421,606.1	345,411.1	264,104.6	105.0	401,364.2	328,827.4	251,424.6
1995	442,345.0	363,922.5	279,371.0	-41,784.0	380,403.0	37,477.7	438,038.7	359,616.2	275,064.7	107.6	407,057.5	334,181.6	255,610.2
1996	460,225.0	379,175.3	291,306.0	-42,890.0	386,169.0	38,040.3	455,375.3	374,325.6	286,456.3	111.6	408,220.1	335,563.2	256,793.0
1997	472,111.0	389,060.3	299,263.8	-44,120.0	395,536.0	38,616.9	466,607.9	383,557.2	293,760.7	109.9	424,656.2	349,072.4	267,349.3
1998	493,282.0	407,433.8	313,995.8	-47,399.0	407,442.0	39,553.6	485,436.6	399,588.4	306,150.4	109.4	443,908.8	365,404.6	279,960.0
1999	515,843.0	426,712.5	328,804.0	-49,846.0	419,718.0	40,744.2	506,741.2	417,610.7	319,702.2	108.4	467,282.5	385,092.3	294,807.7
2000	535,894.0	443,963.3	341,834.8	-51,816.0	432,290.0	41,971.8	526,049.8	434,119.1	331,990.6	108.1	486,516.3	401,494.3	307,040.9
2001	549,805.0	454,876.5	350,098.5	-52,345.0	446,927.0	43,229.0	540,689.0	445,760.5	340,982.5	109.3	494,665.9	407,817.7	311,958.3
2002	566,553.0	468,399.8	361,073.5	-54,543.0	463,376.0	44,692.7	556,702.7	458,549.5	351,223.0	110.1	505,594.8	416,452.5	318,979.0
2003	589,067.0	486,963.8	376,237.3	-58,483.0	482,939.0	46,337.6	576,921.6	474,818.4	364,091.9	110.1	524,052.9	431,306.3	330,726.7

Note: All values are in millions of 2002-2003 dollars except where indicated

Table 9.1 (Continued): Genuine Progress Indicator (GPI) and real GDP for Australia, 1986-2003

Year	WPPSC ($) n	H/hold labour ($) o	Volunteer labour ($) p	Cost of u/e ($) q	Cost of crime ($) r	Cost of family b/d s	Foreign debt ($) t	Non-ren. res. dep. ($) u	Lost agric. land ($) v	Irrig. water use ($) w	Timber dep. ($) x	Air polln. ($) y	Urban w/w polln. ($) z
1985													
1986	15,697.4	225,124.2	16,950.7	-20,263.1	-10,782.7	-3,226.7	-43,623.9	-15,339.4	-34,622.1	-13,702.3	141.6	-5,941.9	-4,186.5
1987	16,460.9	228,378.9	17,905.4	-21,685.3	-11,904.7	-3,312.9	-15,398.0	-14,486.6	-34,935.5	-14,004.2	139.3	-6,022.5	-4,186.2
1988	13,497.5	231,547.0	18,860.0	-19,828.5	-11,788.6	-3,399.0	-12,685.2	-17,029.5	-35,254.6	-14,507.4	139.3	-6,282.8	-4,217.4
1989	12,642.3	234,630.1	19,814.6	-16,786.6	-11,978.6	-3,485.1	-23,858.6	-17,882.3	-35,579.4	-14,787.0	143.9	-6,470.8	-4,248.8
1990	15,543.7	237,629.4	20,769.2	-18,365.2	-12,593.2	-3,571.2	-21,762.1	-19,808.4	-35,910.0	-15,156.0	237.5	-6,645.8	-4,268.3
1991	17,311.8	240,546.3	21,723.8	-28,249.5	-13,103.8	-3,657.3	-15,445.1	-21,066.7	-36,246.3	-15,659.2	15.7	-6,573.6	-4,286.1
1992	18,942.2	246,934.1	22,678.4	-33,733.5	-13,510.2	-3,743.5	-23,702.3	-22,097.1	-36,588.3	-16,184.7	123.4	-6,526.0	-4,298.0
1993	17,392.9	253,171.8	23,561.5	-33,852.5	-13,812.6	-3,959.1	-18,197.2	-22,229.2	-36,934.9	-16,374.8	128.0	-6,698.0	-4,300.8
1994	16,005.8	259,261.8	24,479.0	-31,823.9	-13,653.3	-3,954.9	7,385.3	-22,622.8	-37,283.7	-16,710.3	-64.7	-6,889.7	-4,306.1
1995	16,874.2	265,206.4	25,432.3	-28,242.9	-13,803.0	-4,069.5	-23,155.7	-24,179.9	-37,637.2	-17,228.1	-65.1	-7,110.1	-4,322.9
1996	16,178.0	271,007.8	26,422.6	-28,630.2	-14,165.4	-4,295.0	-3,577.1	-26,041.3	-37,996.3	-17,707.3	-28.0	-7,338.9	-4,342.2
1997	14,925.6	272,227.4	27,451.5	-30,131.1	-15,321.0	-4,198.5	-16,878.1	-26,468.6	-38,361.2	-18,243.8	-28.0	-7,538.8	-4,348.7
1998	12,718.4	273,396.3	28,406.1	-29,515.8	-16,236.4	-4,205.2	-21,595.6	-27,342.4	-38,729.5	-18,738.4	463.8	-7,797.0	-4,353.4
1999	15,401.1	274,515.4	29,360.7	-27,692.7	-16,829.5	-4,303.1	-3,274.0	-27,227.6	-39,096.7	-19,172.4	463.8	-8,129.7	-4,363.5
2000	14,671.3	275,585.5	30,315.4	-26,308.4	-18,034.5	-4,085.4	-46,330.1	-28,765.5	-39,469.5	-19,400.8	463.8	-8,351.5	-4,376.3
2001	16,602.9	276,607.5	31,270.0	-27,891.7	-18,741.9	-4,529.4	-31,467.5	-30,907.5	-39,857.3	-19,906.5	463.8	-8,437.8	-4,366.0
2002	17,275.3	277,582.2	32,224.6	-27,289.3	-17,687.4	-4,420.9	-21,162.3	-30,815.5	-40,259.9	-20,361.3	161.9	-8,678.0	-4,408.1
2003	16,080.1	278,510.5	33,179.2	-27,923.9	-18,717.8	-4,506.1	-33,991.0	-30,926.7	-40,677.4	-20,782.4	463.8	-8,830.7	-4,421.6

Note: All values are in millions of 2002-2003 dollars except where indicated

Table 9.1 (Continued): Genuine Progress Indicator (GPI) and real GDP for Australia, 1986-2003

Year	L-T env damage ($)	LNCS ($)	EHI	Weighted LNCS ($)	GPI (1) ($)	GPI (2) ($)	GPI (3) ($)	Real GDP ($)	Aus. Pop. (thousands)	Per capita GPI (1) ($)	Per capita GPI (2) ($)	Per capita GPI (3) ($)	Per capita real GDP ($)
	aa	bb	cc	dd	ee	ff	gg	hh	ii	jj	kk	ll	mm
	u to aa		1986 = 100.0	(bb/cc) x 100						(ee/ii)	(ff/ii)	(gg/ii)	(hh/ii)
1985													
1986	-41,390.1	-115,040.8	100.0	-115,040.8	406,988.6	344,340.3	276,810.1	427,989.7	16,018.4	25,407.6	21,496.6	17,280.8	26,718.7
1987	-42,825.6	-116,321.3	99.8	-116,554.9	448,456.3	384,013.2	313,647.8	438,130.5	16,263.9	27,573.8	23,611.4	19,284.9	26,938.9
1988	-44,305.1	-121,457.7	99.5	-122,044.7	447,815.5	383,469.1	313,348.2	461,644.7	16,532.2	27,087.5	23,195.3	18,953.9	27,924.0
1989	-45,870.5	-124,694.9	99.3	-125,550.4	439,480.4	374,955.6	305,358.7	480,208.1	16,814.4	26,137.1	22,299.7	18,160.5	28,559.3
1990	-47,482.0	-129,033.0	99.1	-130,259.9	454,084.2	387,319.8	315,150.3	498,126.1	17,065.1	26,608.9	22,696.6	18,467.5	29,189.7
1991	-49,094.0	-132,910.1	98.9	-134,357.2	476,107.4	404,696.6	327,742.8	497,644.9	17,284.0	27,546.1	23,414.5	18,962.2	28,792.2
1992	-50,729.2	-136,300.0	98.8	-137,972.6	477,969.5	404,800.1	326,089.6	498,980.7	17,494.7	27,320.9	23,138.5	18,639.4	28,521.9
1993	-52,396.7	-138,806.3	98.7	-140,702.3	484,506.1	411,596.8	333,506.8	517,252.8	17,667.1	27,424.2	23,297.4	18,877.3	29,277.8
1994	-54,105.0	-141,982.3	98.5	-144,119.2	514,944.8	442,408.1	365,005.2	537,379.8	17,854.7	28,840.8	24,778.2	20,443.0	30,097.3
1995	-55,888.5	-146,431.7	98.4	-148,839.9	496,459.3	423,583.4	345,012.0	560,111.9	18,071.8	27,471.6	23,439.0	19,091.2	30,993.8
1996	-57,729.2	-151,183.2	98.2	-153,935.7	517,225.2	444,568.3	365,798.1	583,922.3	18,310.7	28,247.1	24,279.1	19,977.3	31,889.6
1997	-59,612.7	-154,601.8	98.0	-157,689.7	515,042.4	439,458.5	357,735.4	605,823.2	18,517.6	27,813.7	23,732.0	19,318.7	32,716.1
1998	-61,564.5	-158,061.4	97.9	-161,498.6	525,377.9	446,873.8	361,429.2	632,841.9	18,711.3	28,078.2	23,882.6	19,316.1	33,821.4
1999	-63,594.9	-161,121.0	97.7	-164,911.3	569,549.0	487,358.9	397,074.3	666,438.3	18,925.9	30,093.7	25,751.0	20,980.5	35,213.1
2000	-65,677.9	-165,577.6	97.5	-169,751.3	542,578.7	457,556.7	363,103.3	691,466.5	19,153.4	28,328.1	23,889.1	18,957.7	36,101.5
2001	-67,779.2	-170,790.5	97.4	-175,383.9	561,131.8	474,283.5	378,424.2	705,600.7	19,413.2	28,904.6	24,430.9	19,493.1	36,346.4
2002	-69,936.7	-174,297.7	97.2	-179,280.5	582,836.5	493,694.2	396,220.7	732,943.6	19,641.0	29,674.5	25,135.9	20,173.2	37,317.1
2003	-72,128.4	-177,303.4	97.1	-182,673.4	584,010.5	491,263.9	390,684.4	753,298.4	19,872.6	29,387.7	24,720.6	19,659.4	37,906.3

Note: All values are in millions of 2002-2003 dollars except where indicated

Table 9.1 (Continued): Genuine Progress Indicator (GPI) and real GDP for Australia, 1986–2003

Year	Per capita GPI (1) ($)	Per capita GPI (2) ($)	Per capita GPI (3) ($)	Per capita real GDP	INV ($)	INV* ($)	DEP ($)	DEP* ($)	NCI ($)	NCI/DEP* ($)	Growth strategy
	m	oo	pp	qq	rr	ss	tt	uu	vv	ww	xx
	1986 = 100.0	1986 = 100.0	1986 = 100.0	1986 = 100.0		$(rr + d)$		$(tt + n)$	$(ss - uu)$	(vv/uu)	
1985											
1986	100.0	100.0	100.0	100.0	88,436.0	125,560.0	57,464.0	89,651.5	35,908.5	0.40	high
1987	108.5	109.8	111.6	100.8	88,148.0	122,901.0	59,953.0	92,820.7	30,080.3	0.32	high
1988	106.6	107.9	109.7	104.5	95,257.0	130,750.0	63,633.0	96,947.8	33,802.2	0.35	high
1989	102.9	103.7	105.1	106.9	105,278.0	142,848.0	67,412.0	101,319.8	41,528.2	0.41	high
1990	104.7	105.6	106.9	109.2	106,005.0	145,249.0	68,444.0	103,065.3	42,183.7	0.41	high
1991	108.4	108.9	109.7	107.8	95,477.0	133,185.0	71,678.0	107,141.2	26,043.8	0.24	low/high
1992	107.5	107.6	107.9	106.7	90,690.0	128,784.0	74,530.0	110,479.0	18,305.0	0.17	low
1993	107.9	108.4	109.2	109.6	96,679.0	135,599.0	76,811.0	113,175.7	22,423.3	0.20	low
1994	113.5	115.3	118.3	112.6	103,042.0	142,755.0	79,880.0	116,798.1	25,956.9	0.22	low
1995	108.1	109.0	110.5	116.0	114,406.0	156,190.0	82,520.0	119,997.7	36,192.3	0.30	high
1996	111.2	112.9	115.6	119.4	116,673.0	159,563.0	85,124.0	123,164.3	36,398.7	0.30	high
1997	109.5	110.4	111.8	122.4	125,824.0	169,944.0	88,950.0	127,566.9	42,377.1	0.33	high
1998	110.5	111.1	111.8	126.6	137,876.0	185,275.0	93,773.0	133,326.6	51,948.4	0.39	high
1999	118.4	119.8	121.4	131.8	146,202.0	196,048.0	97,990.0	138,734.2	57,313.8	0.41	high
2000	111.5	111.1	109.7	135.1	158,349.0	210,165.0	103,794.0	145,765.8	64,399.2	0.44	high
2001	113.8	113.7	112.8	136.0	147,247.0	199,592.0	107,713.0	150,942.0	48,650.0	0.32	high
2002	116.8	116.9	116.7	139.7	162,553.0	217,096.0	114,217.0	158,909.7	58,186.3	0.37	high
2003	115.7	115.0	113.8	141.9	184,802.0	243,285.0	119,407.0	165,744.6	77,540.4	0.47	high

Note: All values are in millions of 2002–2003 dollars except where indicated

Table 9.2: Items *a, b, c, d, rr,* and *tt*: Consumption expenditure, expenditure on consumer durables (ECD), investment in producer goods (INV) and depreciation of producer goods (DEP) – Australia, 1986–2003

AUSTRALIA

Year		1986(1)	1986(2)	1986(3)	1987(1)	1987(2)	1987(3)
Components of consumption expenditure (CON)							
Food	(half is defensive in case (3))	36,134	36,134	18,067	36,194	36,194	18,097
Cigarettes and tobacco	(none adds to welfare in cases (2) and (3))	13,479	0	0	13,463	0	0
Alcoholic beverages	(half adds to welfare in cases (2) and (3))	7,077	3,539	3,539	6,867	3,434	3,434
Clothing and footwear	(consumer durables)	12,805	12,805	12,805	12,693	12,693	12,693
Rent and other dwelling services	(half is defensive in cases (2) and (3))	46,957	23,479	23,479	48,541	24,271	24,271
Electricity, gas and other fuel	(half is defensive in case (3))	5,709	5,709	2,855	5,967	5,967	2,984
Furnishings and household equipment	(consumer durables)	15,424	15,424	15,424	15,196	15,196	15,196
Health	(half is def. or rehab. in cases (2) and (3))	12,947	6,474	6,474	13,675	6,838	6,838
Purchase of vehicles	(consumer durables)	8,895	8,895	8,895	6,864	6,864	6,864
Operation of vehicles	(half is def. or rehab. in case (3))	17,713	17,713	8,857	18,339	18,339	9,170
Transport services	(half is defensive in case (3))	4,917	4,917	2,459	5,033	5,033	2,517
Communications	(half is defensive in case (3))	2,747	2,747	1,374	2,879	2,879	1,440
Recreation and culture		22,675	22,675	22,675	22,921	22,921	22,921
Education services		6,498	6,498	6,498	6,899	6,899	6,899
Hotels, cafes and restaurants	(1/4 is defensive in case (3))	22,768	22,768	17,076	22,286	22,286	16,715
Insurance and other financial services	(half is defensive in case (3))	13,429	13,429	6,715	15,386	15,386	7,693
Other goods and services		16,696	16,696	16,696	17,256	17,256	17,256
Total household final consumption expenditure		261,035	219,901	173,884	264,068	222,455	174,984
Total government final consumption expenditure	(1/4 def. in cases (2) (3); 1/4 rehab. in case (3))	86,055	64,541	43,028	88,481	66,361	44,241
Consumption expenditure (private + public)		**347,090**	**284,442**	**216,912**	**352,549**	**288,815**	**219,225**
Investment (INV)							
Total private gross fixed capital formation				64,825			64,526
Total public gross fixed capital formation				23,611			23,622
Total fixed capital formation (INV)				**88,436**			**88,148**
Consumption of fixed capital (DEP)				**57,464**			**59,953**
Consumer durables							
Expenditure on consumer durables (ECD)				**37,124**			**34,753**

Note: All values are in millions of 2002–2003 dollars

Table 9.2 (Continued): Items *a*, *b*, *c*, *d*, *rr*, and *tt*: Consumption expenditure, expenditure on consumer durables (ECD), investment in producer goods (INV) and depreciation of producer goods (DEP) – Australia, 1986–2003

AUSTRALIA

Year	1991(1)	1991(2)	1991(3)	1992(1)	1992(2)	1992(3)	1993(1)	1993(2)	1993(3)
Components of consumption expenditure (CON)									
Food	37,804	37,804	18,902	38,628	38,628	19,314	38,951	38,951	19,476
Cigarettes and tobacco	12,977	0	0	12,103	0	0	11,277	0	0
Alcoholic beverages	7,231	3,616	3,616	7,141	3,571	3,571	7,041	3,521	3,521
Clothing and footwear	12,500	12,500	12,500	12,867	12,867	12,867	12,668	12,668	12,668
Rent and other dwelling services	55,758	27,879	27,879	57,453	28,727	28,727	59,077	29,539	29,539
Electricity, gas and other fuel	6,633	6,633	3,317	6,717	6,717	3,359	6,963	6,963	3,482
Furnishings and household equipment	16,186	16,186	16,186	16,685	16,685	16,685	17,243	17,243	17,243
Health	16,075	8,038	8,038	16,814	8,407	8,407	17,369	8,685	8,685
Purchase of vehicles	9,022	9,022	9,022	8,542	8,542	8,542	9,009	9,009	9,009
Operation of vehicles	19,559	19,559	9,780	20,141	20,141	10,071	20,709	20,709	10,355
Transport services	6,498	6,498	3,249	7,231	7,231	3,616	7,401	7,401	3,701
Communications	3,716	3,716	1,858	4,070	4,070	2,035	4,638	4,638	2,319
Recreation and culture	28,243	28,243	28,243	29,152	29,152	29,152	30,110	30,110	30,110
Education services	8,025	8,025	8,025	8,065	8,065	8,065	8,090	8,090	8,090
Hotels, cafes and restaurants	23,881	23,881	17,911	23,993	23,993	17,995	23,441	23,441	17,581
Insurance and other financial services	20,782	20,782	10,391	19,539	19,539	9,770	19,044	19,044	9,522
Other goods and services	20,924	20,924	20,924	21,993	21,993	21,993	23,197	23,197	23,197
Total household final consumption expenditure	301,129	253,305	199,839	306,892	258,327	204,166	312,586	263,208	208,494
Total government final consumption expenditure	99,463	74,597	49,732	101,327	75,995	50,664	102,799	77,099	51,400
Consumption expenditure (private + public)	**400,592**	**327,902**	**249,570**	**408,219**	**334,322**	**254,829**	**415,385**	**340,307**	**259,894**
Investment (INV)									
Total private gross fixed capital formation			72,220			67,736			74,259
Total public gross fixed capital formation			23,257			22,954			22,420
Total fixed capital formation (INV)			**95,477**			**90,690**			**96,679**
Consumption of fixed capital (DEP)			**71,678**			**74,530**			**76,811**
Consumer durables									
Expenditure on consumer durables (ECD)			**37,708**			**38,094**			**38,920**

Note: All values are in millions of 2002–2003 dollars

Table 9.2 (Continued): Items *a*, *b*, *c*, *d*, *rr*, and *tt*: Consumption expenditure, expenditure on consumer durables (ECD), investment in producer goods (INV) and depreciation of producer goods (DEP) – Australia, 1986-2003

AUSTRALIA

Year	1994(1)	1994(2)	1994(3)	1995(1)	1995(2)	1995(3)	1996(1)	1996(2)	1996(3)
Components of consumption expenditure (CON)									
Food	39,053	39,053	19,527	40,286	40,286	20,143	41,792	41,792	20,896
Cigarettes and tobacco	10,388	0	0	9,772	0	0	9,716	0	0
Alcoholic beverages	6,794	3,397	3,397	6,825	3,413	3,413	6,797	3,399	3,399
Clothing and footwear	12,782	12,782	12,782	13,198	13,198	13,198	13,597	13,597	13,597
Rent and other dwelling services	61,096	30,548	30,548	63,298	31,649	31,649	65,560	32,780	32,780
Electricity, gas and other fuel	6,966	6,966	3,483	7,304	7,304	3,652	7,493	7,493	3,747
Furnishings and household equipment	17,884	17,884	17,884	18,402	18,402	18,402	18,866	18,866	18,866
Health	18,110	9,055	9,055	18,247	9,124	9,124	18,024	9,012	9,012
Purchase of vehicles	9,047	9,047	9,047	10,184	10,184	10,184	10,427	10,427	10,427
Operation of vehicles	21,395	21,395	10,698	21,844	21,844	10,922	22,102	22,102	11,051
Transport services	7,300	7,300	3,650	7,663	7,663	3,832	8,218	8,218	4,109
Communications	5,232	5,232	2,616	5,725	5,725	2,863	6,531	6,531	3,266
Recreation and culture	32,373	32,373	32,373	35,082	35,082	35,082	38,009	38,009	38,009
Education services	8,286	8,286	8,286	8,434	8,434	8,434	8,746	8,746	8,746
Hotels, cafes and restaurants	24,652	24,652	18,489	26,756	26,756	20,067	27,640	27,640	20,730
Insurance and other financial services	18,325	18,325	9,163	19,416	19,416	9,708	19,860	19,860	9,930
Other goods and services	23,887	23,887	23,887	25,213	25,213	25,213	26,820	26,820	26,820
Total household final consumption expenditure	320,369	270,182	214,884	335,371	283,692	225,884	348,380	295,292	235,384
Total government final consumption expenditure	104,032	78,024	52,016	106,974	80,231	53,487	111,845	83,884	55,923
Consumption expenditure (private + public)	**424,401**	**348,206**	**266,900**	**442,345**	**363,923**	**279,371**	**460,225**	**379,175**	**291,306**
Investment (INV)									
Total private gross fixed capital formation			81,317			89,896			93,085
Total public gross fixed capital formation			21,725			24,510			23,588
Total fixed capital formation (INV)			**103,042**			**114,406**			**116,673**
Consumption of fixed capital (DEP)			**79,880**			**82,520**			**85,124**
Consumer durables									
Expenditure on consumer durables (ECD)			**39,713**			**41,784**			**42,890**

Note: All values are in millions of 2002-2003 dollars

Table 9.2 (Continued): Items *a*, *b*, *c*, *d*, *rr*, and *tt*: Consumption expenditure, expenditure on consumer durables (ECD), investment in producer goods (INV) and depreciation of producer goods (DEP) – Australia, 1986-2003

AUSTRALIA

Year	1997(1)	1997(2)	1997(3)	1998(1)	1998(2)	1998(3)	1999(1)	1999(2)	1999(3)
Components of consumption expenditure (CON)									
Food	41,566	41,566	20,783	42,686	42,686	21,343	43,338	43,338	21,669
Cigarettes and tobacco	9,789	0	0	9,946	0	0	10,042	0	0
Alcoholic beverages	6,974	3,487	3,487	7,251	3,626	3,626	7,749	3,875	3,875
Clothing and footwear	13,501	13,501	13,501	14,079	14,079	14,079	15,429	15,429	15,429
Rent and other dwelling services	67,605	33,803	33,803	69,703	34,852	34,852	72,127	36,064	36,064
Electricity, gas and other fuel	7,669	7,669	3,835	8,112	8,112	4,056	8,503	8,503	4,252
Furnishings and household equipment	19,256	19,256	19,256	19,655	19,655	19,655	20,013	20,013	20,013
Health	17,445	8,723	8,723	16,640	8,320	8,320	17,962	8,981	8,981
Purchase of vehicles	11,363	11,363	11,363	13,665	13,665	13,665	14,404	14,404	14,404
Operation of vehicles	22,398	22,398	11,199	22,914	22,914	11,457	23,670	23,670	11,835
Transport services	8,860	8,860	4,430	9,275	9,275	4,638	10,125	10,125	5,063
Communications	7,289	7,289	3,645	7,912	7,912	3,956	8,981	8,981	4,491
Recreation and culture	40,052	40,052	40,052	42,987	42,987	42,987	45,430	45,430	45,430
Education services	9,220	9,220	9,220	9,664	9,664	9,664	9,934	9,934	9,934
Hotels, cafes and restaurants	27,131	27,131	20,348	28,371	28,371	21,278	31,276	31,276	23,457
Insurance and other financial services	21,588	21,588	10,794	23,007	23,007	11,504	24,567	24,567	12,284
Other goods and services	28,169	28,169	28,169	30,133	30,133	30,133	30,631	30,631	30,631
Total household final consumption expenditure	358,796	304,074	242,606	375,713	319,257	255,211	393,853	335,220	267,809
Total government final consumption expenditure	113,315	84,986	56,658	117,569	88,177	58,785	121,990	91,493	60,995
Consumption expenditure (private + public)	472,111	389,060	299,264	493,282	407,434	313,996	515,843	426,713	328,804
Investment (INV)									
Total private gross fixed capital formation			102,820			116,761			120,872
Total public gross fixed capital formation			23,004			21,115			25,330
Total fixed capital formation (INV)			125,824			137,876			146,202
Consumption of fixed capital (DEP)			88,950			93,773			97,990
Consumer durables									
Expenditure on consumer durables (ECD)			44,120			47,399			49,846

Note: All values are in millions of 2002-2003 dollars

Table 9.2 (Continued): Items *a, b, c, d, rr,* and *tt:* Consumption expenditure, expenditure on consumer durables (ECD), investment in producer goods (INV) and depreciation of producer goods (DEP) – Australia, 1986-2003

AUSTRALIA

Year	2000(1)	2000(2)	2000(3)	2001(1)	2001(2)	2001(3)	2002(1)	2002(2)	2002(3)
Components of consumption expenditure (CON)									
Food	44,837	44,837	22,419	45,792	45,792	22,896	46,563	46,563	23,282
Cigarettes and tobacco	9,985	0	0	9,911	0	0	9,910	0	0
Alcoholic beverages	8,176	4,088	4,088	8,450	4,225	4,225	8,655	4,328	4,328
Clothing and footwear	16,317	16,317	16,317	15,604	15,604	15,604	16,520	16,520	16,520
Rent and other dwelling services	74,448	37,224	37,224	76,942	38,471	38,471	79,405	39,703	39,703
Electricity, gas and other fuel	8,741	8,741	4,371	9,040	9,040	4,520	9,100	9,100	4,550
Furnishings and household equipment	21,695	21,695	21,695	22,096	22,096	22,096	23,673	23,673	23,673
Health	18,622	9,311	9,311	20,648	10,324	10,324	23,021	11,511	11,511
Purchase of vehicles	13,804	13,804	13,804	14,645	14,645	14,645	14,350	14,350	14,350
Operation of vehicles	24,330	24,330	12,165	24,145	24,145	12,073	25,270	25,270	12,635
Transport services	10,577	10,577	5,289	11,371	11,371	5,686	11,178	11,178	5,589
Communications	10,120	10,120	5,060	11,299	11,299	5,650	12,083	12,083	6,042
Recreation and culture	48,190	48,190	48,190	49,947	49,947	49,947	51,742	51,742	51,742
Education services	10,102	10,102	10,102	10,273	10,273	10,273	10,527	10,527	10,527
Hotels, cafes and restaurants	32,991	32,991	24,743	32,906	32,906	24,680	33,051	33,051	24,788
Insurance and other financial services	26,187	26,187	13,094	27,245	27,245	13,623	28,410	28,410	14,205
Other goods and services	30,995	30,995	30,995	31,177	31,177	31,177	32,107	32,107	32,107
Total household final consumption expenditure	409,955	349,509	278,865	421,383	358,560	285,888	435,506	370,115	295,550
Total government final consumption expenditure	125,939	94,454	62,970	128,422	96,317	64,211	131,047	98,285	65,524
Consumption expenditure (private + public)	**535,894**	**443,963**	**341,835**	**549,805**	**454,877**	**350,099**	**566,553**	**468,400**	**361,073**
Investment (INV)									
Total private gross fixed capital formation			133,238			122,144			135,273
Total public gross fixed capital formation			25,111			25,103			27,280
Total fixed capital formation (INV)			**158,349**			**147,247**			**162,553**
Consumption of fixed capital (DEP)			**103,794**			**107,713**			**114,217**
Consumer durables									
Expenditure on consumer durables (ECD)			**51,816**			**52,345**			**54,543**

Note: All values are in millions of 2002-2003 dollars

Table 9.2 (Continued): Items *a*, *b*, *c*, *d*, *rr*, and *tt*: Consumption expenditure, expenditure on consumer durables (ECD), investment in producer goods (INV) and depreciation of producer goods (DEP) – Australia, 1986–2003

AUSTRALIA

Year	2003(1)	2003(2)	2003(3)
Components of consumption expenditure (CON)			
Food	47,569	47,569	23,785
Cigarettes and tobacco	9,910	0	0
Alcoholic beverages	8,901	4,451	4,451
Clothing and footwear	17,553	17,553	17,553
Rent and other dwelling services	82,499	41,250	41,250
Electricity, gas and other fuel	9,455	9,455	4,728
Furnishings and household equipment	25,362	25,362	25,362
Health	24,562	12,281	12,281
Purchase of vehicles	15,568	15,568	15,568
Operation of vehicles	25,714	25,714	12,857
Transport services	11,279	11,279	5,640
Communications	12,678	12,678	6,339
Recreation and culture	53,884	53,884	53,884
Education services	10,702	10,702	10,702
Hotels, cafes and restaurants	34,059	34,059	25,544
Insurance and other financial services	29,314	29,314	14,657
Other goods and services	33,224	33,224	33,224
Total household final consumption expenditure	452,238	384,342	307,823
Total government final consumption expenditure	136,829	102,622	68,415
Consumption expenditure (private + public)	**589,067**	**486,964**	**376,237**
Investment (INV)			
Total private gross fixed capital formation			156,671
Total public gross fixed capital formation			28,131
Total fixed capital formation (INV)			**184,802**
Consumption of fixed capital (DEP)			**119,407**
Consumer durables			
Expenditure on consumer durables (ECD)			**58,483**

Note: All values are in millions of 2002–2003 dollars

Table 9.3: Items *a*, *b*, *c*, *d*, *rr*, and *tt*: Consumption expenditure, expenditure on consumer durables (ECD), investment in producer goods (INV) and depreciation of producer goods (DEP) – Victoria, 1986-2003

VICTORIA

Year		1986(1)	1986(2)	1986(3)	1987(1)	1987(2)	1987(3)
Components of consumption expenditure (CON)							
Food	(half is defensive in case (3))	9,593	9,593	4,797	9,682	9,682	4,841
Cigarettes and tobacco	(none adds to welfare in cases (2) and (3))	3,534	0	0	3,523	0	0
Alcoholic beverages	(half adds to welfare in cases (2) and (3))	1,549	775	775	1,545	773	773
Clothing and footwear	(consumer durables)	3,659	3,659	3,659	3,751	3,751	3,751
Rent and other dwelling services	(half is defensive in cases (2) and (3))	11,484	5,742	5,742	11,817	5,909	5,909
Electricity, gas and other fuel	(half is defensive in case (3))	1,834	1,834	917	1,918	1,918	959
Furnishings and household equipment	(consumer durables)	4,118	4,118	4,118	4,103	4,103	4,103
Health	(half is def. or rehab. in cases (2) and (3))	3,872	1,936	1,936	3,990	1,995	1,995
Purchase of vehicles	(consumer durables)	2,367	2,367	2,367	1,847	1,847	1,847
Operation of vehicles	(half is def. or rehab. in case (3))	4,420	4,420	2,210	4,565	4,565	2,283
Transport services	(half is defensive in case (3))	1,275	1,275	638	1,328	1,328	664
Communications	(half is defensive in case (3))	702	702	351	722	722	361
Recreation and culture		5,776	5,776	5,776	5,873	5,873	5,873
Education services		2,178	2,178	2,178	2,246	2,246	2,246
Hotels, cafes and restaurants	(1/4 is defensive in case (3))	5,469	5,469	4,102	5,357	5,357	4,018
Insurance and other financial services	(half is defensive in case (3))	3,647	3,647	1,824	4,205	4,205	2,103
Other goods and services		4,365	4,365	4,365	4,584	4,584	4,584
Net expenditure interstate	(1/4 def. in cases (2) (3); 1/4 rehab. in case (3))	1,063	532	532	988	494	494
Total household final consumption expenditure		69,044	58,387	46,284	70,119	59,351	46,802
Total government final consumption expenditure		22,637	16,978	11,319	23,191	17,393	11,596
Consumption expenditure (private + public)		**91,681**	**75,365**	**57,603**	**93,310**	**76,744**	**58,397**
Investment (INV)							
Total private gross fixed capital formation				15,445	16,277		
Total public gross fixed capital formation				5,341	4,999		
Total fixed capital formation (INV)				**20,786**	**21,276**		
Consumption of fixed capital (DEP)				**13,441**	**14,344**		
Consumer durables							
Expenditure on consumer durables (ECD)				**10,144**	**9,701**		

Note: All values are in millions of 2002-2003 dollars

Table 9.3 (Continued): Items *a*, *b*, *c*, *d*, *rr*, and *tt*: Consumption expenditure, expenditure on consumer durables (ECD), investment in producer goods (INV) and depreciation of producer goods (DEP) – Victoria, 1986-2003

VICTORIA

Year	1988(1)	1988(2)	1988(3)	1989(1)	1989(2)	1989(3)	1990(1)	1990(2)	1990(3)
Components of consumption expenditure (CON)									
Food	9,718	9,718	4,859	9,984	9,984	4,992	9,969	9,969	4,985
Cigarettes and tobacco	3,460	0	0	3,491	0	0	3,517	0	0
Alcoholic beverages	1,594	797	797	1,684	842	842	1,683	842	842
Clothing and footwear	3,855	3,855	3,855	3,783	3,783	3,783	3,494	3,494	3,494
Rent and other dwelling services	12,170	6,085	6,085	12,605	6,303	6,303	13,027	6,514	6,514
Electricity, gas and other fuel	1,900	1,900	950	1,967	1,967	984	2,100	2,100	1,050
Furnishings and household equipment	4,148	4,148	4,148	4,254	4,254	4,254	4,186	4,186	4,186
Health	3,889	1,945	1,945	4,145	2,073	2,073	4,333	2,167	2,167
Purchase of vehicles	1,725	1,725	1,725	2,028	2,028	2,028	2,529	2,529	2,529
Operation of vehicles	4,710	4,710	2,355	4,800	4,800	2,400	4,981	4,981	2,491
Transport services	1,398	1,398	699	1,489	1,489	745	1,519	1,519	760
Communications	759	759	380	818	818	409	886	886	443
Recreation and culture	6,103	6,103	6,103	6,630	6,630	6,630	7,154	7,154	7,154
Education services	2,205	2,205	2,205	2,358	2,358	2,358	2,510	2,510	2,510
Hotels, cafes and restaurants	5,510	5,510	4,133	5,872	5,872	4,404	5,993	5,993	4,495
Insurance and other financial services	4,504	4,504	2,252	4,872	4,872	2,436	5,499	5,499	2,750
Other goods and services	4,809	4,809	4,809	5,087	5,087	5,087	5,200	5,200	5,200
Net expenditure interstate	1,188	594	594	1,213	607	607	975	488	488
Total household final consumption expenditure	71,818	60,765	47,893	75,308	63,766	50,333	77,958	66,029	52,054
Total government final consumption expenditure	24,094	18,071	12,047	24,605	18,454	12,303	24,719	18,539	12,360
Consumption expenditure (private + public)	95,912	78,835	59,940	99,913	82,219	62,635	102,677	84,568	64,413
Investment (INV)									
Total private gross fixed capital formation			17,648			20,207			18,978
Total public gross fixed capital formation			4,620			4,665			5,743
Total fixed capital formation (INV)			22,268			24,872			24,721
Consumption of fixed capital (DEP)			14,831			15,776			15,802
Consumer durables									
Expenditure on consumer durables (ECD)			9,728			10,065			10,209

Note: All values are in millions of 2002-2003 dollars

Table 9.3 (Continued): Items *a, b, c, d, rr,* and *tt*: Consumption expenditure, expenditure on consumer durables (ECD), investment in producer goods (INV) and depreciation of producer goods (DEP) – Victoria, 1986-2003

VICTORIA

Year	1991(1)	1991(2)	1991(3)	1992(1)	1992(2)	1992(3)	1993(1)	1993(2)	1993(3)
Components of consumption expenditure (CON)									
Food	9,884	9,884	4,942	10,089	10,089	5,045	9,944	9,944	4,972
Cigarettes and tobacco	3,385	0	0	3,167	0	0	2,948	0	0
Alcoholic beverages	1,661	831	831	1,721	861	861	1,687	844	844
Clothing and footwear	*3,332*	*3,332*	*3,332*	*3,416*	*3,416*	*3,416*	*3,375*	*3,375*	*3,375*
Rent and other dwelling services	13,458	6,729	6,729	13,861	6,931	6,931	14,177	7,089	7,089
Electricity, gas and other fuel	2,104	2,104	1,052	2,162	2,162	1,081	2,232	2,232	1,116
Furnishings and household equipment	*3,804*	*3,804*	*3,804*	*3,873*	*3,873*	*3,873*	*4,084*	*4,084*	*4,084*
Health	4,367	2,184	2,184	4,632	2,316	2,316	5,253	2,627	2,627
Purchase of vehicles	*2,153*	*2,153*	*2,153*	*1,916*	*1,916*	*1,916*	*2,123*	*2,123*	*2,123*
Operation of vehicles	4,834	4,834	2,417	4,934	4,934	2,467	5,088	5,088	2,544
Transport services	1,686	1,686	843	1,871	1,871	936	1,945	1,945	973
Communications	930	930	465	1,022	1,022	511	1,175	1,175	588
Recreation and culture	6,776	6,776	6,776	6,759	6,759	6,759	7,008	7,008	7,008
Education services	2,254	2,254	2,254	2,319	2,319	2,319	2,387	2,387	2,387
Hotels, cafes and restaurants	5,787	5,787	4,340	5,951	5,951	4,463	5,587	5,587	4,190
Insurance and other financial services	5,578	5,578	2,789	5,186	5,186	2,593	5,042	5,042	2,521
Other goods and services	5,182	5,182	5,182	5,389	5,389	5,389	5,697	5,697	5,697
Net expenditure interstate	1,104	552	552	1,085	543	543	1,098	549	549
Total household final consumption expenditure	*76,681*	*64,599*	*50,644*	*77,766*	*65,537*	*51,417*	*79,408*	*66,795*	*52,685*
Total government final consumption expenditure	*25,308*	*18,981*	*12,654*	*25,783*	*19,337*	*12,892*	*25,143*	*18,857*	*12,572*
Consumption expenditure (private + public)	**101,989**	**83,580**	**63,298**	**103,549**	**84,874**	**64,308**	**104,551**	**85,652**	**65,256**
Investment (INV)									
Total private gross fixed capital formation			*15,304*			*14,030*			*16,440*
Total public gross fixed capital formation			*4,855*			*4,730*			*4,031*
Total fixed capital formation (INV)			**20,159**			**18,760**			**20,471**
Consumption of fixed capital (DEP)			**15,042**			**15,337**			**16,217**
Consumer durables									
Expenditure on consumer durables (ECD)			**9,289**			**9,205**			**9,582**

Note: All values are in millions of 2002-2003 dollars

Table 9.3 (Continued): Items *a*, *b*, *c*, *d*, *rr*, and *tt*: Consumption expenditure, expenditure on consumer durables (ECD), investment in producer goods (INV) and depreciation of producer goods (DEP) – Victoria, 1986-2003

VICTORIA

Year	1994(1)	1994(2)	1994(3)	1995(1)	1995(2)	1995(3)	1996(1)	1996(2)	1996(3)
Components of consumption expenditure (CON)									
Food	9,929	9,929	4,965	10,238	10,238	5,119	10,537	10,537	5,269
Cigarettes and tobacco	2,738	0	0	2,561	0	0	2,515	0	0
Alcoholic beverages	1,663	832	832	1,739	870	870	1,738	869	869
Clothing and footwear	*3,205*	*3,205*	*3,205*	*3,174*	*3,174*	*3,174*	*3,117*	*3,117*	*3,117*
Rent and other dwelling services	14,575	7,288	7,288	14,970	7,485	7,485	15,373	7,687	7,687
Electricity, gas and other fuel	2,181	2,181	1,091	2,303	2,303	1,152	2,412	2,412	1,206
Furnishings and household equipment	*4,079*	*4,079*	*4,079*	*4,114*	*4,114*	*4,114*	*4,288*	*4,288*	*4,288*
Health	5,601	2,801	2,801	5,543	2,772	2,772	5,439	2,720	2,720
Purchase of vehicles	*2,152*	*2,152*	*2,152*	*2,401*	*2,401*	*2,401*	*2,438*	*2,438*	*2,438*
Operation of vehicles	5,202	5,202	2,601	5,338	5,338	2,669	5,403	5,403	2,702
Transport services	1,883	1,883	942	1,991	1,991	996	2,189	2,189	1,095
Communications	1,316	1,316	658	1,447	1,447	724	1,645	1,645	823
Recreation and culture	7,663	7,663	7,663	8,973	8,973	8,973	9,780	9,780	9,780
Education services	2,443	2,443	2,443	2,450	2,450	2,450	2,540	2,540	2,540
Hotels, cafes and restaurants	5,641	5,641	4,231	5,972	5,972	4,479	5,628	5,628	4,221
Insurance and other financial services	4,805	4,805	2,403	5,106	5,106	2,553	5,159	5,159	2,580
Other goods and services	5,690	5,690	5,690	6,058	6,058	6,058	6,297	6,297	6,297
Net expenditure interstate	1,111	556	556	1,182	591	591	1,261	631	631
Total household final consumption expenditure	80,512	67,664	53,596	84,523	71,282	56,578	86,925	73,339	58,259
Total government final consumption expenditure	24,544	18,408	12,272	25,328	18,996	12,664	26,410	19,808	13,205
Consumption expenditure (private + public)	**105,056**	**86,072**	**65,868**	**109,851**	**90,278**	**69,242**	**113,335**	**93,146**	**71,464**
Investment (INV)									
Total private gross fixed capital formation			17,887			18,407			21,103
Total public gross fixed capital formation			4,619			5,482			4,754
Total fixed capital formation (INV)			**22,506**			**23,889**			**25,857**
Consumption of fixed capital (DEP)			**17,388**			**17,067**			**18,729**
Consumer durables									
Expenditure on consumer durables (ECD)			**9,436**			**9,689**			**9,843**

Note: All values are in millions of 2002-2003 dollars

Table 9.3 (Continued): Items *a*, *b*, *c*, *d*, *rr*, and *tt*: Consumption expenditure, expenditure on consumer durables (ECD), investment in producer goods (INV) and depreciation of producer goods (DEP) – Victoria, 1986-2003

VICTORIA

Year	1997(1)	1997(2)	1997(3)	1998(1)	1998(2)	1998(3)	1999(1)	1999(2)	1999(3)
Components of consumption expenditure (CON)									
Food	10,596	10,596	5,298	10,837	10,837	5,419	11,173	11,173	5,587
Cigarettes and tobacco	2,520	0	0	2,538	0	0	2,568	0	0
Alcoholic beverages	1,757	879	879	1,797	899	899	1,949	975	975
Clothing and footwear	*3,103*	*3,103*	*3,103*	*3,390*	*3,390*	*3,390*	*3,955*	*3,955*	*3,955*
Rent and other dwelling services	15,760	7,880	7,880	16,225	8,113	8,113	16,805	8,403	8,403
Electricity, gas and other fuel	2,442	2,442	1,221	2,610	2,610	1,305	2,701	2,701	1,351
Furnishings and household equipment	*4,584*	*4,584*	*4,584*	*4,829*	*4,829*	*4,829*	*4,993*	*4,993*	*4,993*
Health	5,335	2,668	2,668	5,091	2,546	2,546	5,440	2,720	2,720
Purchase of vehicles	*2,731*	*2,731*	*2,731*	*3,351*	*3,351*	*3,351*	*3,714*	*3,714*	*3,714*
Operation of vehicles	5,516	5,516	2,758	5,670	5,670	2,835	5,852	5,852	2,926
Transport services	2,315	2,315	1,158	2,394	2,394	1,197	2,630	2,630	1,315
Communications	1,848	1,848	924	1,989	1,989	995	2,261	2,261	1,131
Recreation and culture	10,458	10,458	10,458	11,239	11,239	11,239	11,922	11,922	11,922
Education services	2,654	2,654	2,654	2,798	2,798	2,798	2,930	2,930	2,930
Hotels, cafes and restaurants	5,465	5,465	4,099	5,558	5,558	4,169	6,251	6,251	4,688
Insurance and other financial services	5,603	5,603	2,802	5,896	5,896	2,948	6,274	6,274	3,137
Other goods and services	6,476	6,476	6,476	7,567	7,567	7,567	7,127	7,127	7,127
Net expenditure interstate	1,337	669	669	1,275	638	638	1,152	576	576
Total household final consumption expenditure	89,917	75,886	60,359	94,753	80,322	64,235	99,492	84,456	67,448
Total government final consumption expenditure	26,500	19,875	13,250	26,850	20,138	13,425	27,943	20,957	13,972
Consumption expenditure (private + public)	**116,417**	**95,761**	**73,609**	**121,603**	**100,460**	**77,660**	**127,435**	**105,413**	**81,419**
Investment (INV)									
Total private gross fixed capital formation			26,467			27,302			31,008
Total public gross fixed capital formation			3,416			4,269			5,243
Total fixed capital formation (INV)			**29,883**			**31,571**			**36,251**
Consumption of fixed capital (DEP)	**21,202**			**21,765**			**24,259**		
Consumer durables									
Expenditure on consumer durables (ECD)			**10,418**			**11,570**			**12,662**

Note: All values are in millions of 2002-2003 dollars

Table 9.3 (Continued): Items *a, b, c, d, rr,* and *tt*: Consumption expenditure, expenditure on consumer durables (ECD), investment in producer goods (INV) and depreciation of producer goods (DEP) – Victoria, 1986–2003

VICTORIA

Year	2000(1)	2000(2)	2000(3)	2001(1)	2001(2)	2001(3)	2002(1)	2002(2)	2002(3)
Components of consumption expenditure (CON)									
Food	11,438	11,438	5,719	11,725	11,725	5,863	11,714	11,714	5,857
Cigarettes and tobacco	2,566	0	0	2,557	0	0	2,573	0	0
Alcoholic beverages	2,019	1,010	1,010	2,067	1,034	1,034	2,076	1,038	1,038
Clothing and footwear	4,493	4,493	4,493	3,994	3,994	3,994	4,314	4,314	4,314
Rent and other dwelling services	17,348	8,674	8,674	17,937	8,969	8,969	18,505	9,253	9,253
Electricity, gas and other fuel	2,779	2,779	1,390	2,938	2,938	1,469	2,855	2,855	1,428
Furnishings and household equipment	5,412	5,412	5,412	5,384	5,384	5,384	6,214	6,214	6,214
Health	5,620	2,810	2,810	6,034	3,017	3,017	6,548	3,274	3,274
Purchase of vehicles	3,469	3,469	3,469	4,093	4,093	4,093	3,984	3,984	3,984
Operation of vehicles	5,962	5,962	2,981	5,982	5,982	2,991	6,231	6,231	3,116
Transport services	2,813	2,813	1,407	3,030	3,030	1,515	3,033	3,033	1,517
Communications	2,540	2,540	1,270	2,863	2,863	1,432	3,049	3,049	1,525
Recreation and culture	12,602	12,602	12,602	12,914	12,914	12,914	13,998	13,998	13,998
Education services	2,972	2,972	2,972	3,070	3,070	3,070	3,167	3,167	3,167
Hotels, cafes and restaurants	7,110	7,110	5,333	6,816	6,816	5,112	7,111	7,111	5,333
Insurance and other financial services	6,640	6,640	3,320	6,845	6,845	3,423	7,020	7,020	3,510
Other goods and services	7,211	7,211	7,211	7,231	7,231	7,231	7,618	7,618	7,618
Net expenditure interstate	1,161	581	581	1,273	637	637	1,246	623	623
Total household final consumption expenditure	103,983	88,515	70,652	106,601	90,541	72,145	111,154	94,496	75,767
Total government final consumption expenditure	28,685	21,514	14,343	29,676	22,257	14,838	30,139	22,604	15,070
Consumption expenditure (private + public)	132,668	110,029	84,994	136,277	112,798	86,983	141,293	117,100	90,836
Investment (INV)									
Total private gross fixed capital formation			34,154			33,350			36,676
Total public gross fixed capital formation			5,329			4,815			5,477
Total fixed capital formation (INV)			39,483			38,165			42,153
Consumption of fixed capital (DEP)			26,358			27,731			29,626
Consumer durables									
Expenditure on consumer durables (ECD)			13,374			13,471			14,512

Note: All values are in millions of 2002–2003 dollars

Table 9.3 (Continued): Items *a*, *b*, *c*, *d*, *rr*, and *tt*: Consumption expenditure, expenditure on consumer durables (ECD), investment in producer goods (INV) and depreciation of producer goods (DEP) - Victoria, 1986-2003

VICTORIA

Year	2003(1)	2003(2)	2003(3)
Components of consumption expenditure (CON)			
Food	11,964	11,964	5,982
Cigarettes and tobacco	2,563	0	0
Alcoholic beverages	2,054	1,027	1,027
Clothing and footwear	4,638	4,638	4,638
Rent and other dwelling services	19,223	9,612	9,612
Electricity, gas and other fuel	3,180	3,180	1,590
Furnishings and household equipment	6,527	6,527	6,527
Health	6,725	3,363	3,363
Purchase of vehicles	4,213	4,213	4,213
Operation of vehicles	6,350	6,350	3,175
Transport services	3,117	3,117	1,559
Communications	3,199	3,199	1,600
Recreation and culture	14,467	14,467	14,467
Education services	3,205	3,205	3,205
Hotels, cafes and restaurants	6,905	6,905	5,179
Insurance and other financial services	7,332	7,332	3,666
Other goods and services	7,964	7,964	7,964
Net expenditure interstate	1,222	611	611
Total household final consumption expenditure	114,847	97,673	78,376
Total government final consumption expenditure	31,635	23,726	15,818
Consumption expenditure (private + public)	**146,482**	**121,399**	**94,193**
Investment (INV)			
Total private gross fixed capital formation			41,527
Total public gross fixed capital formation			6,329
Total fixed capital formation (INV)			**47,856**
Consumption of fixed capital (DEP)			**31,120**
Consumer durables			
Expenditure on consumer durables (ECD)			**15,378**

Note: All values are in millions of 2002-2003 dollars

Table 9.4: Items *a*, *b*, *c*, *d*, *rr*, and *tt*: Consumption expenditure, expenditure on consumer durables (ECD), investment in producer goods (INV) and depreciation of producer goods (DEP) – Rest-of-Australia, 1986–2003

REST-of-AUSTRALIA

Year		1986(1)	1986(2)	1986(3)	1987(1)	1987(2)	1987(3)
Components of consumption expenditure (CON)							
Food	(half is defensive in case (3))	26,541	26,541	13,271	26,512	26,512	13,256
Cigarettes and tobacco	(none adds to welfare in cases (2) and (3))	9,945	0	0	9,940	0	0
Alcoholic beverages	(half adds to welfare in cases (2) and (3))	5,528	2,764	2,764	5,322	2,661	2,661
Clothing and footwear	(consumer durables)	9,146	9,146	9,146	8,942	8,942	8,942
Rent and other dwelling services	(half is defensive in cases (2) and (3))	35,473	17,737	17,737	36,724	18,362	18,362
Electricity, gas and other fuel	(half is defensive in case (3))	3,875	3,875	1,938	4,049	4,049	2,025
Furnishings and household equipment	(consumer durables)	11,306	11,306	11,306	11,093	11,093	11,093
Health	(half is def. or rehab. in cases (2) and (3))	9,075	4,538	4,538	9,685	4,843	4,843
Purchase of vehicles	(consumer durables)	6,528	6,528	6,528	5,017	5,017	5,017
Operation of vehicles	(half is def. or rehab. in case (3))	13,293	13,293	6,647	13,774	13,774	6,887
Transport services	(half is defensive in case (3))	3,642	3,642	1,821	3,705	3,705	1,853
Communications	(half is defensive in case (3))	2,045	2,045	1,023	2,157	2,157	1,079
Recreation and culture		16,899	16,899	16,899	17,048	17,048	17,048
Education services		4,320	4,320	4,320	4,653	4,653	4,653
Hotels, cafes and restaurants	(1/4 is defensive in case (3))	17,299	17,299	12,974	16,929	16,929	12,697
Insurance and other financial services	(half is defensive in case (3))	9,782	9,782	4,891	11,181	11,181	5,591
Other goods and services		12,331	12,331	12,331	12,672	12,672	12,672
Net expenditure interstate		-1,063	-532	-532	-988	-494	-494
Total household final consumption expenditure		191,991	161,514	127,600	193,949	163,104	128,182
Total government final consumption expenditure		63,418	47,564	31,709	65,290	48,968	32,645
Consumption expenditure (private + public)	(1/4 def. in cases (2) (3); 1/4 rehab. in case (3))	255,409	209,077	159,309	259,239	212,071	160,827
Investment (INV)							
Total private gross fixed capital formation				-			-
Total public gross fixed capital formation				-			-
Total fixed capital formation (INV)				68,079			67,651
Consumption of fixed capital (DEP)				44,023			45,609
Consumer durables							
Expenditure on consumer durables (ECD)				26,980			25,052

Note: All values are in millions of 2002-2003 dollars

Table 9.4 (Continued): Items *a*, *b*, *c*, *d*, *rr*, and *tt*: Consumption expenditure, expenditure on consumer durables (ECD), investment in producer goods (INV) and depreciation of producer goods (DEP) - Rest-of-Australia, 1986-2003

REST-of-AUSTRALIA

Year	1988(1)	1988(2)	1988(3)	1989(1)	1989(2)	1989(3)	1990(1)	1990(2)	1990(3)
Components of consumption expenditure (CON)									
Food	27,001	27,001	13,501	26,576	26,576	13,288	27,339	27,339	13,670
Cigarettes and tobacco	9,930	0	0	9,892	0	0	9,871	0	0
Alcoholic beverages	5,358	2,679	2,679	5,354	2,677	2,677	5,601	5,601	2,801
Clothing and footwear	9,116	9,116	9,116	9,218	9,218	9,218	9,407	9,407	9,407
Rent and other dwelling services	37,966	18,983	18,983	39,452	19,726	19,726	40,919	20,460	20,460
Electricity, gas and other fuel	4,069	4,069	2,035	4,182	4,182	2,091	4,421	4,421	2,211
Furnishings and household equipment	*11,625*	*11,625*	*11,625*	*12,030*	*12,030*	*12,030*	*12,534*	*12,534*	*12,534*
Health	10,052	5,026	5,026	10,751	5,376	5,376	11,081	5,541	5,541
Purchase of vehicles	*5,024*	*5,024*	*5,024*	*6,257*	*6,257*	*6,257*	*7,094*	*7,094*	*7,094*
Operation of vehicles	14,023	14,023	7,012	14,294	14,294	7,147	14,735	14,735	7,368
Transport services	3,875	3,875	1,938	4,143	4,143	2,072	4,403	4,403	2,202
Communications	2,278	2,278	1,139	2,441	2,441	1,221	2,651	2,651	1,326
Recreation and culture	18,183	18,183	18,183	19,464	19,464	19,464	20,750	20,750	20,750
Education services	4,583	4,583	4,583	5,047	5,047	5,047	5,461	5,461	5,461
Hotels, cafes and restaurants	17,326	17,326	12,995	17,757	17,757	13,318	18,455	18,455	13,841
Insurance and other financial services	12,082	12,082	6,041	13,320	13,320	6,660	14,877	14,877	7,439
Other goods and services	13,510	13,510	13,510	14,521	14,521	14,521	15,380	15,380	15,380
Net expenditure interstate	-1,188	-594	-594	-1,213	-607	-607	-975	-488	-488
Total household final consumption expenditure	*200,695*	*168,789*	*132,794*	*209,860*	*176,422*	*139,505*	*220,938*	*185,820*	*146,993*
Total government final consumption expenditure	*67,403*	*50,552*	*33,702*	*68,717*	*51,538*	*34,359*	*71,437*	*53,578*	*35,719*
Consumption expenditure (private + public)	**268,098**	**219,341**	**166,495**	**278,577**	**227,960**	**173,863**	**292,375**	**239,398**	**182,712**
Investment (INV)									
Total private gross fixed capital formation			-			-			-
Total public gross fixed capital formation			-			-			-
Total fixed capital formation (INV)			**73,275**			**81,407**			**82,357**
Consumption of fixed capital (DEP)			48,802			51,636			52,642
Consumer durables									
Expenditure on consumer durables (ECD)			**25,765**			**27,505**			**29,035**

Note: All values are in millions of 2002-2003 dollars

Table 9.4 (Continued): Items *a, b, c, d, rr*, and *tt*: Consumption expenditure, expenditure on consumer durables (ECD), investment in producer goods (INV) and depreciation of producer goods (DEP) – Rest-of-Australia, 1986-2003

REST-of-AUSTRALIA

Year	1991(1)	1991(2)	1991(3)	1992(1)	1992(2)	1992(3)	1993(1)	1993(2)	1993(3)
Components of consumption expenditure (CON)									
Food	27,920	27,920	13,960	28,539	28,539	14,270	29,007	29,007	14,504
Cigarettes and tobacco	9,592	0	0	8,936	0	0	8,329	0	0
Alcoholic beverages	5,570	2,785	2,785	5,420	2,710	2,710	5,354	2,677	2,677
Clothing and footwear	9,168	9,168	9,168	9,451	9,451	9,451	9,293	9,293	9,293
Rent and other dwelling services	42,300	21,150	21,150	43,592	21,796	21,796	44,900	22,450	22,450
Electricity, gas and other fuel	4,529	4,529	2,265	4,555	4,555	2,278	4,731	4,731	2,366
Furnishings and household equipment	12,382	12,382	12,382	12,812	12,812	12,812	13,159	13,159	13,159
Health	11,708	5,854	5,854	12,182	6,091	6,091	12,116	6,058	6,058
Purchase of vehicles	6,869	6,869	6,869	6,626	6,626	6,626	6,886	6,886	6,886
Operation of vehicles	14,725	14,725	7,363	15,207	15,207	7,604	15,621	15,621	7,811
Transport services	4,812	4,812	2,406	5,360	5,360	2,680	5,456	5,456	2,728
Communications	2,786	2,786	1,393	3,048	3,048	1,524	3,463	3,463	1,732
Recreation and culture	21,467	21,467	21,467	22,393	22,393	22,393	23,102	23,102	23,102
Education services	5,771	5,771	5,771	5,746	5,746	5,746	5,703	5,703	5,703
Hotels, cafes and restaurants	18,094	18,094	13,571	18,042	18,042	13,532	17,854	17,854	13,391
Insurance and other financial services	15,204	15,204	7,602	14,353	14,353	7,177	14,002	14,002	7,001
Other goods and services	15,742	15,742	15,742	16,604	16,604	16,604	17,500	17,500	17,500
Net expenditure interstate	-1,104	-552	-552	-1,085	-543	-543	-1,098	-549	-549
Total household final consumption expenditure	224,448	188,706	149,195	229,126	192,791	152,749	233,178	196,413	155,810
Total government final consumption expenditure	74,155	55,616	37,078	75,544	56,658	37,772	77,656	58,242	38,828
Consumption expenditure (private + public)	298,603	244,322	186,272	304,670	249,449	190,521	310,834	254,655	194,638
Investment (INV)									
Total private gross fixed capital formation			-			-			-
Total public gross fixed capital formation			-			-			-
Total fixed capital formation (INV)			75,902			72,405			76,486
Consumption of fixed capital (DEP)			56,636			59,193			60,594
Consumer durables									
Expenditure on consumer durables (ECD)			28,419			28,889			29,338

Note: All values are in millions of 2002-2003 dollars

Table 9.4 (Continued): Items *a*, *b*, *c*, *d*, *rr*, and *tt*: Consumption expenditure, expenditure on consumer durables (ECD), investment in producer goods (INV) and depreciation of producer goods (DEP) - Rest-of-Australia, 1986-2003

REST-of-AUSTRALIA

Year	1994(1)	1994(2)	1994(3)	1995(1)	1995(2)	1995(3)	1996(1)	1996(2)	1996(3)
Components of consumption expenditure (CON)									
Food	29,124	29,124	14,562	30,048	30,048	15,024	31,255	31,255	15,628
Cigarettes and tobacco	7,650	0	0	7,211	0	0	7,201	0	0
Alcoholic beverages	5,131	2,566	2,566	5,086	2,543	2,543	5,059	2,530	2,530
Clothing and footwear	9,577	9,577	9,577	10,024	10,024	10,024	10,480	10,480	10,480
Rent and other dwelling services	46,521	23,261	23,261	48,328	24,164	24,164	50,187	25,094	25,094
Electricity, gas and other fuel	4,785	4,785	2,393	5,001	5,001	2,501	5,081	5,081	2,541
Furnishings and household equipment	13,805	13,805	13,805	14,288	14,288	14,288	14,578	14,578	14,578
Health	12,509	6,255	6,255	12,704	6,352	6,352	12,585	6,293	6,293
Purchase of vehicles	6,895	6,895	6,895	7,783	7,783	7,783	7,989	7,989	7,989
Operation of vehicles	16,193	16,193	8,097	16,506	16,506	8,253	16,699	16,699	8,350
Transport services	5,417	5,417	2,709	5,672	5,672	2,836	6,029	6,029	3,015
Communications	3,916	3,916	1,958	4,278	4,278	2,139	4,886	4,886	2,443
Recreation and culture	24,710	24,710	24,710	26,109	26,109	26,109	28,229	28,229	28,229
Education services	5,843	5,843	5,843	5,984	5,984	5,984	6,206	6,206	6,206
Hotels, cafes and restaurants	19,011	19,011	14,258	20,784	20,784	15,588	22,012	22,012	16,509
Insurance and other financial services	13,520	13,520	6,760	14,310	14,310	7,155	14,701	14,701	7,351
Other goods and services	18,197	18,197	18,197	19,155	19,155	19,155	20,523	20,523	20,523
Net expenditure interstate	-1,111	-556	-556	-1,182	-591	-591	-1,261	-631	-631
Total household final consumption expenditure	239,857	202,518	161,288	250,848	212,410	169,307	261,455	221,953	177,125
Total government final consumption expenditure	79,488	59,616	39,744	81,646	61,235	40,823	85,435	64,076	42,718
Consumption expenditure (private + public)	319,345	262,134	201,032	332,494	273,645	210,130	346,890	286,029	219,842
Investment (INV)									
Total private gross fixed capital formation			-			-			-
Total public gross fixed capital formation			-			-			-
Total fixed capital formation (INV)			80,884			91,616			91,663
Consumption of fixed capital (DEP)			62,492			65,453			66,395
Consumer durables									
Expenditure on consumer durables (ECD)			30,277			32,095			33,047

Note: All values are in millions of 2002–2003 dollars

Table 9.4 (Continued): Items *a*, *b*, *c*, *d*, *rr*, and *tt*: Consumption expenditure, expenditure on consumer durables (ECD), investment in producer goods (INV) and depreciation of producer goods (DEP) – Rest-of-Australia, 1986-2003

REST-of-AUSTRALIA

Year	1997(1)	1997(2)	1997(3)	1998(1)	1998(2)	1998(3)	1999(1)	1999(2)	1999(3)
Components of consumption expenditure (CON)									
Food	30,970	30,970	15,485	31,849	31,849	15,925	32,165	32,165	16,083
Cigarettes and tobacco	7,269	0	0	7,408	0	0	7,474	0	0
Alcoholic beverages	5,217	2,609	2,609	5,454	2,727	2,727	5,800	2,900	2,900
Clothing and footwear	10,398	10,398	10,398	10,689	10,689	10,689	11,474	11,474	11,474
Rent and other dwelling services	51,845	25,923	25,923	53,478	26,739	26,739	55,322	27,661	27,661
Electricity, gas and other fuel	5,227	5,227	2,614	5,502	5,502	2,751	5,802	5,802	2,901
Furnishings and household equipment	14,672	14,672	14,672	14,826	14,826	14,826	15,020	15,020	15,020
Health	12,110	6,055	6,055	11,549	5,775	5,775	12,522	6,261	6,261
Purchase of vehicles	8,632	8,632	8,632	10,314	10,314	10,314	10,690	10,690	10,690
Operation of vehicles	16,882	16,882	8,441	17,244	17,244	8,622	17,818	17,818	8,909
Transport services	6,545	6,545	3,273	6,881	6,881	3,441	7,495	7,495	3,748
Communications	5,441	5,441	2,721	5,923	5,923	2,962	6,720	6,720	3,360
Recreation and culture	29,594	29,594	29,594	31,748	31,748	31,748	33,508	33,508	33,508
Education services	6,566	6,566	6,566	6,866	6,866	6,866	7,004	7,004	7,004
Hotels, cafes and restaurants	21,666	21,666	16,250	22,813	22,813	17,110	25,025	25,025	18,769
Insurance and other financial services	15,985	15,985	7,993	17,111	17,111	8,556	18,293	18,293	9,147
Other goods and services	21,693	21,693	21,693	22,566	22,566	22,566	23,504	23,504	23,504
Net expenditure interstate	-1,337	-669	-669	-1,275	-638	-638	-1,152	-576	-576
Total household final consumption expenditure	268,879	228,189	182,247	280,960	238,935	190,977	294,361	250,764	200,361
Total government final consumption expenditure	86,815	65,111	43,408	90,719	68,039	45,360	94,047	70,535	47,024
Consumption expenditure (private + public)	355,694	293,300	225,655	371,679	306,974	236,336	388,408	321,299	247,385
Investment (INV)									
Total private gross fixed capital formation			-			-			-
Total public gross fixed capital formation			-			-			-
Total fixed capital formation (INV)			95,489			104,448			110,177
Consumption of fixed capital (DEP)			67,748			72,008			73,731
Consumer durables									
Expenditure on consumer durables (ECD)			33,702			35,829			37,184

Note: All values are in millions of 2002-2003 dollars

Table 9.4 (Continued): Items *a*, *b*, *c*, *d*, *rr*, and *tt*: Consumption expenditure, expenditure on consumer durables (ECD), investment in producer goods (INV) and depreciation of producer goods (DEP) – Rest-of-Australia, 1986–2003

REST-of-AUSTRALIA

Year	2000(1)	2000(2)	2000(3)	2001(1)	2001(2)	2001(3)	2002(1)	2002(2)	2002(3)
Components of consumption expenditure (CON)									
Food	33,399	33,399	16,700	34,067	34,067	17,034	34,849	34,849	17,425
Cigarettes and tobacco	7,419	0	0	7,354	0	0	7,337	0	0
Alcoholic beverages	6,157	3,079	3,079	6,383	3,192	3,192	6,579	3,290	3,290
Clothing and footwear	*11,824*	*11,824*	*11,824*	*11,610*	*11,610*	*11,610*	*12,206*	*12,206*	*12,206*
Rent and other dwelling services	57,100	28,550	28,550	59,005	29,503	29,503	60,900	30,450	30,450
Electricity, gas and other fuel	5,962	5,962	2,981	6,102	6,102	3,051	6,245	6,245	3,123
Furnishings and household equipment	*16,283*	*16,283*	*16,283*	*16,712*	*16,712*	*16,712*	*17,459*	*17,459*	*17,459*
Health	13,002	6,501	6,501	14,614	7,307	7,307	16,473	8,237	8,237
Purchase of vehicles	*10,335*	*10,335*	*10,335*	*10,552*	*10,552*	*10,552*	*10,366*	*10,366*	*10,366*
Operation of vehicles	18,368	18,368	9,184	18,163	18,163	9,082	19,039	19,039	9,520
Transport services	7,764	7,764	3,882	8,341	8,341	4,171	8,145	8,145	4,073
Communications	7,580	7,580	3,790	8,436	8,436	4,218	9,034	9,034	4,517
Recreation and culture	35,588	35,588	35,588	37,033	37,033	37,033	37,744	37,744	37,744
Education services	7,130	7,130	7,130	7,203	7,203	7,203	7,360	7,360	7,360
Hotels, cafes and restaurants	25,881	25,881	19,411	26,090	26,090	19,568	25,940	25,940	19,455
Insurance and other financial services	19,547	19,547	9,774	20,400	20,400	10,200	21,390	21,390	10,695
Other goods and services	23,784	23,784	23,784	23,946	23,946	23,946	24,489	24,489	24,489
Net expenditure interstate	-1,161	-581	-581	-1,273	-637	-637	-1,246	-623	-623
Total household final consumption expenditure	305,972	260,994	208,214	314,782	268,020	213,743	324,352	275,619	219,783
Total government final consumption expenditure	97,254	72,941	48,627	98,746	74,060	49,373	100,908	75,681	50,454
Consumption expenditure (private + public)	**403,226**	**333,935**	**256,841**	**413,528**	**342,079**	**263,116**	**425,260**	**351,300**	**270,237**
Investment (INV)									
Total private gross fixed capital formation			-			-			-
Total public gross fixed capital formation			-			-			-
Total fixed capital formation (INV)			115,998			110,076			120,357
Consumption of fixed capital (DEP)			77,436			75,804			84,591
Consumer durables									
Expenditure on consumer durables (ECD)			38,442			38,874			40,031

Note: All values are in millions of 2002-2003 dollars

Table 9.4 (Continued): Items *a*, *b*, *c*, *d*, *rr*, and *tt*: Consumption expenditure, expenditure on consumer durables (ECD), investment in producer goods (INV) and depreciation of producer goods (DEP) – Rest-of-Australia, 1986-2003

REST-of-AUSTRALIA Year	2003(1)	2003(2)	2003(3)
Components of consumption expenditure (CON)			
Food	35,605	35,605	17,803
Cigarettes and tobacco	7,347	0	0
Alcoholic beverages	6,847	3,424	3,424
Clothing and footwear	*12,915*	*12,915*	*12,915*
Rent and other dwelling services	63,276	31,638	31,638
Electricity, gas and other fuel	6,275	6,275	3,138
Furnishings and household equipment	*18,835*	*18,835*	*18,835*
Health	17,837	8,919	8,919
Purchase of vehicles	*11,355*	*11,355*	*11,355*
Operation of vehicles	19,364	19,364	9,682
Transport services	8,162	8,162	4,081
Communications	9,479	9,479	4,740
Recreation and culture	39,417	39,417	39,417
Education services	7,497	7,497	7,497
Hotels, cafes and restaurants	27,154	27,154	20,366
Insurance and other financial services	21,982	21,982	10,991
Other goods and services	25,260	25,260	25,260
Net expenditure interstate	-1,222	-611	-611
Total household final consumption expenditure	337,391	286,669	229,447
Total government final consumption expenditure	105,194	78,896	52,597
Consumption expenditure (private + public)	**442,585**	**365,565**	**282,044**
Investment (INV)			
Total private gross fixed capital formation			-
Total public gross fixed capital formation			-
Total fixed capital formation (INV)			**135,769**
Consumption of fixed capital (DEP)			**88,287**
Consumer durables			
Expenditure on consumer durables (ECD)			**43,105**

Note: All values are in millions of 2002-2003 dollars

Table 9.5: Items *e* and *f*: Service from consumer durables (SCD) – Australia, Victoria, and Rest-of-Australia, 1986-2003

	AUSTRALIA			VICTORIA						REST-of-AUST	
	ECD ($)	Consumer durables ($)	SCD ($)	ECD ($)	Consumer durables ($)	SCD ($)	Vic. Pop. (000s)	Per capita ECD (single $)	Per capita SCD (single $)	ECD ($)	SCD ($)
Year	*a*	*b*	*c*	*d*	*e*	*f*	*g*	*h*	*i*	*j = a - d*	*k = c - f*
1976	-30,321.3	-	-	-8,233.2	-	-	-	-	-	-	-
1977	-30,282.7	-	-	-8,188.1	-	-	-	-	-	-	-
1978	-29,562.5	-	-	-7,954.7	-	-	-	-	-	-	-
1979	-30,435.1	-	-	-8,148.5	-	-	-	-	-	-	-
1980	-30,825.8	-	-	-8,211.0	-	-	-	-	-	-	-
1981	-32,850.0	-	-	-8,688.4	-	-	-	-	-	-	-
1982	-33,936.2	-	-	-8,924.1	-	-	-	-	-	-	-
1983	-33,386.7	-	-	-8,752.7	-	-	-	-	-	-	-
1984	-34,116.6	-	-	-8,002.9	-	-	-	-	-	-	-
1985	-36,158.0	321,874.8	-	-8,853.8	83,957.4	-	-	-	-	-	-
1986	-37,124.0	328,677.5	32,187.5	-10,144.0	85,868.1	8,395.7	4,160.9	-2,438.0	2,017.8	-26,980.0	23,791.7
1987	-34,753.0	333,147.8	32,867.7	-9,701.0	87,381.0	8,586.8	4,210.1	-2,304.2	2,039.6	-25,052.0	24,280.9
1988	-35,493.0	339,078.4	33,314.8	-9,728.0	89,154.3	8,738.1	4,262.6	-2,282.2	2,050.0	-25,765.0	24,576.7
1989	-37,570.0	346,213.3	33,907.8	-10,065.0	91,070.8	8,915.4	4,320.2	-2,329.8	2,063.7	-27,505.0	24,992.4
1990	-39,244.0	354,631.5	34,621.3	-10,209.0	93,068.8	9,107.1	4,378.6	-2,331.6	2,079.9	-29,035.0	25,514.2
1991	-37,708.0	359,489.5	35,463.2	-9,289.0	93,669.4	9,306.9	4,420.4	-2,101.4	2,105.5	-28,419.0	26,156.3
1992	-38,094.0	363,647.3	35,949.0	-9,205.0	93,950.4	9,366.9	4,455.0	-2,066.2	2,102.6	-28,889.0	26,582.0
1993	-38,920.0	369,180.6	36,364.7	-9,582.0	94,779.7	9,395.0	4,472.4	-2,142.5	2,100.7	-29,338.0	26,969.7
1994	-39,713.0	374,777.0	36,918.1	-9,436.0	96,212.8	9,478.0	4,487.6	-2,102.7	2,112.0	-30,277.0	27,440.1
1995	-41,784.0	380,403.0	37,477.7	-9,689.0	97,048.0	9,621.3	4,517.4	-2,144.8	2,129.8	-32,095.0	27,856.4
1996	-42,890.0	386,169.0	38,040.3	-9,843.0	96,747.0	9,704.8	4,560.2	-2,158.5	2,128.2	-33,047.0	28,335.5
1997	-44,120.0	395,536.0	38,616.9	-10,418.0	97,464.0	9,674.7	4,597.2	-2,266.2	2,104.5	-33,702.0	28,942.2
1998	-47,399.0	407,442.0	39,553.6	-11,570.0	99,306.0	9,746.4	4,637.8	-2,494.7	2,101.5	-35,829.0	29,807.2
1999	-49,846.0	419,718.0	40,744.2	-12,662.0	101,903.0	9,930.6	4,686.4	-2,701.9	2,119.0	-37,184.0	30,813.6
2000	-51,816.0	432,290.0	41,971.8	-13,374.0	105,068.0	10,190.3	4,741.3	-2,820.7	2,149.2	-38,442.0	31,781.5
2001	-52,345.0	446,927.0	43,229.0	-13,471.0	109,250.0	10,506.8	4,804.7	-2,803.7	2,186.8	-38,874.0	32,722.2
2002	-54,543.0	463,376.0	44,692.7	-14,512.0	114,557.0	10,925.0	4,857.2	-2,987.7	2,249.2	-40,031.0	33,767.7
2003	-58,483.0	482,939.0	46,337.6	-15,378.0	120,353.0	11,455.7	4,911.4	-3,131.1	2,332.5	-43,105.0	34,881.9

Note: All values are in millions of 2002-2003 dollars except where indicated

9.2.5. Items g, h, and i: Adjusted CON(1), CON(2), and CON(3)

The values for adjusted CON(1), CON(2), and CON(3) were derived by following equation (3.1).

9.2.6. Item j: Distribution Index (DI)

As explained in Chapter 3, the DI we used to weight adjusted CON(1), CON(2), and CON(3) was constructed on the basis that a fall in the ratio of the median annual income to per capita GDP or GSP represents a growing gap between the income of the rich and the poor.

To construct the DI for Australia, we began by obtaining the median weekly incomes for the census years of 1986, 1991, 1996, and 2001. We then multiplied the weekly incomes by 52 to obtain annual values for each of these four years. For the intervening years, we used straight-line interpolation and subsequently altered the nominal values to acquire the real median annual incomes for each year at 2002-03 prices.

Having done this, we then calculated the ratio of real median annual incomes to per capita real GDP and set the ratio for 1986 at an index value of 100.0. The DI for each year after 1986 was obtained by: (a) multiplying the *previous* year's index value by the *previous* year's ratio of real median annual incomes to per capita real GDP; and (b) dividing the result for (a) by the *current* year's ratio of real median annual incomes to per capita real GDP (Table 9.6).

We applied the same method for Victoria except, naturally, we used Victorian values (Table 9.7). As for the Rest-of-Australia, it was first necessary to calculate the median weekly incomes for 1986, 1991, 1996, and 2001. To do this, we determined the ratio of Victoria's population to that of the Rest-of-Australia and then used the ratio in the following equation:

$$\text{Rest-of-Australia med. income} = \frac{\left[\text{Aust med. income} - \left[\text{Vic med. income} \times \left(\text{Vic pop/ROA pop}\right)\right]\right]}{\left[1 - \left(\text{Vic pop/ROA pop}\right)\right]} \quad (9.1)$$

To calculate the annual DI values for the Rest-of-Australia, we followed the same procedure used to calculate the DI for Australia and Victoria (Table 9.8).

Data sources:

ABS, *Census of Population and Housing (various),* AGPS, Canberra.
ABS, Catalogue No. 5204.0.
ABS, Catalogue No. 5220.0.
ABS, Catalogue No. 3101.0.
ABS, Catalogue No. 3105.0.65.001.
ABS, Catalogue No. 3311.2.55.001.

Table 9.6: Item *j*: Distribution Index (DI) – Australia, 1986-2003

AUSTRALIA

Year	Median weekly income (single $)	Nominal median annual income (single $) (a x 52)	Deflator (2003 = 100.00)	Real median annual income (single $) (b/c x 100)	Per capita real GDP ($)	Ratio of real med. annual income to per cap. real GDP ($) (d/e)	Distribution Index (1986 = 100.0)
	a	b	c	d	e	f	g
1986	184	9,568.0	58.1	16,471.1	26,718.7	0.616	100.0
1987	-	10,441.6	62.2	16,791.7	26,938.9	0.623	98.9
1988	-	11,315.2	67.3	16,825.2	27,924.0	0.603	102.3
1989	-	12,188.8	73.3	16,629.9	28,559.3	0.582	105.9
1990	-	13,062.4	77.3	16,900.4	29,189.7	0.579	106.5
1991	268	13,936.0	79.9	17,437.0	28,792.2	0.606	101.8
1992	-	14,185.6	81.5	17,409.6	28,521.9	0.610	101.0
1993	-	14,435.2	82.4	17,527.2	29,277.8	0.599	103.0
1994	-	14,684.8	83.1	17,663.1	30,097.3	0.587	105.0
1995	-	14,934.4	84.1	17,755.1	30,993.8	0.573	107.6
1996	292	15,184.0	86.2	17,623.1	31,889.6	0.553	111.6
1997	-	16,047.2	87.4	18,355.0	32,716.1	0.561	109.9
1998	-	16,910.4	88.7	19,066.0	33,821.4	0.564	109.4
1999	-	17,773.6	88.8	20,017.2	35,213.1	0.568	108.4
2000	-	18,636.8	90.5	20,582.7	36,101.5	0.570	108.1
2001	375	19,500.0	95.1	20,499.0	36,346.4	0.564	109.3
2002	-	20,363.2	97.5	20,892.6	37,317.1	0.560	110.1
2003	-	21,226.4	100.0	21,226.4	37,906.3	0.560	110.1

Note: All values are in millions of 2002-2003 dollars except where indicated

Table 9.7: Item *j*: Distribution Index (DI) – Victoria, 1986-2003

VICTORIA							
Year	Median weekly income (single $)	Nominal median annual income (single $)	Deflator	Real median annual income (single $)	Per capita real GSP ($)	Ratio of real med. annual income to per cap. real GDP ($)	Distribution Index
	a	*b*	*c*	*d*	*e*	*f*	*g*
		(*a x 52*)	(2003 = 100.00)	(*b/c x 100*)		(*d/e*)	(1986 = 100.0)
1986	*184*	*9,568.0*	58.1	16,471.1	26,743.9	0.616	**100.0**
1987	-	10,493.6	62.2	16,875.3	27,057.2	0.624	**98.7**
1988	-	11,419.2	67.3	16,979.9	28,158.5	0.603	**102.1**
1989	-	12,344.8	73.3	16,842.8	28,900.3	0.583	**105.7**
1990	-	13,270.4	77.3	17,169.5	30,086.6	0.571	**107.9**
1991	*273*	*14,196.0*	79.9	17,762.3	29,156.6	0.609	**101.1**
1992	-	14,372.8	81.5	17,639.3	28,242.9	0.625	**98.6**
1993	-	14,549.6	82.4	17,666.1	29,340.9	0.602	**102.3**
1994	-	14,726.4	83.1	17,713.1	30,269.3	0.585	**105.2**
1995	-	14,903.2	84.1	17,718.1	31,125.6	0.569	**108.2**
1996	*290*	*15,080.0*	86.2	17,502.4	32,205.2	0.543	**113.3**
1997	-	16,016.0	87.4	18,319.3	32,858.4	0.558	**110.5**
1998	-	16,952.0	88.7	19,112.9	34,179.1	0.559	**110.1**
1999	-	17,888.0	88.8	20,146.1	36,211.0	0.556	**110.7**
2000	-	18,824.0	90.5	20,789.5	36,957.0	0.563	**109.5**
2001	*380*	*19,760.0*	95.1	20,772.3	37,544.6	0.553	**111.3**
2002	-	20,696.0	97.5	21,234.1	38,512.6	0.551	**111.7**
2003	-	21,632.0	100.0	21,632.0	39,067.1	0.554	**111.2**

Note: All values are in millions of 2002-2003 dollars except where indicated

Table 9.8: Item *j*: Distribution Index (DI) – Rest-of-Australia, 1986-2003

	REST-of-AUST										
	Australian population	Victorian population	Rest-of-Aus population	Ratio of Victorian to Rest-of-Aus population	Median weekly income	Nominal median annual income	Deflator	Real median annual income	Per capita real GDP of Rest-of-Aus	Ratio of real med. annual income to per cap. real GDP	Distribution Index
	(000s)	(000s)	(000s)	(ratio)	(single $)	(single $)	2003 = 100.00	(single $)	($)	($)	1986 = 100.0
			(a - b)	(b/c)		(e x 52)		(f/g x 100)		(h/i)	
Year	a	b	c	d	e	f	g	h	i	j	k
1986	16,018.4	4,160.9	11,857.5	0.351	184	9,568.0	58.1	16,471.1	26,709.9	0.617	**100.0**
1987	16,263.9	4,210.1	12,053.8	0.349	-	10,423.7	62.2	16,762.9	26,897.5	0.623	**98.9**
1988	16,532.2	4,262.6	12,269.6	0.347	-	11,279.5	67.3	16,772.1	27,842.6	0.602	**102.4**
1989	16,814.4	4,320.2	12,494.3	0.346	-	12,135.2	73.3	16,556.8	28,441.4	0.582	**105.9**
1990	17,065.1	4,378.6	12,686.5	0.345	-	12,990.9	77.3	16,807.9	28,880.2	0.582	**106.0**
1991	17,284.0	4,420.4	12,863.7	0.344	266	13,846.7	79.9	17,325.2	28,666.9	0.604	**102.0**
1992	17,494.7	4,455.0	13,039.7	0.342	-	14,121.0	81.5	17,330.3	28,617.2	0.606	**101.8**
1993	17,667.1	4,472.4	13,194.7	0.339	-	14,395.4	82.4	17,478.9	29,256.3	0.597	**103.2**
1994	17,854.7	4,487.6	13,367.2	0.336	-	14,669.8	83.1	17,645.0	30,039.6	0.587	**105.0**
1995	18,071.8	4,517.4	13,554.4	0.333	-	14,944.1	84.1	17,766.7	30,949.8	0.574	**107.4**
1996	18,310.7	4,560.2	13,750.6	0.332	293	15,218.5	86.2	17,663.1	31,785.0	0.556	**111.0**
1997	18,517.6	4,597.2	13,920.4	0.330	-	16,057.7	87.4	18,367.0	32,669.1	0.562	**109.7**
1998	18,711.3	4,637.8	14,073.5	0.330	-	16,896.9	88.7	19,050.8	33,703.6	0.565	**109.1**
1999	18,925.9	4,686.4	14,239.5	0.329	-	17,736.1	88.8	19,975.0	34,884.7	0.573	**107.7**
2000	19,153.4	4,741.3	14,412.0	0.329	-	18,575.3	90.5	20,514.8	35,820.1	0.573	**107.7**
2001	19,413.2	4,804.7	14,608.5	0.329	373	19,414.5	95.1	20,409.1	35,952.3	0.568	**108.6**
2002	19,641.0	4,857.2	14,783.8	0.329	-	20,253.7	97.5	20,780.3	36,924.3	0.563	**109.6**
2003	19,872.6	4,911.4	14,961.2	0.328	-	21,092.9	100.0	21,092.9	37,525.2	0.562	**109.7**

Note: All values are in millions of 2002-2003 dollars except where indicated

9.2.7. Items k, l, and m: Weighted CON(1), CON(2), and CON(3)

The annual values of weighted CON(1), CON(2), and CON(3) were calculated by applying the Distribution Index to the adjusted measures of CON(1), CON(2), and CON(3) as per equation (3.2).

9.2.8. Item n: Welfare from Publicly-provided Service Capital (WPPSC)

The welfare generated by publicly-provided service capital (WPPSC) is equal to the consumption or depreciation value of government-provided service capital (e.g., roads, bridges, schools, hospitals, and museums). This value is not provided by the ABS national and state accounts.

To calculate WPPSC for Australia and Victoria, we first estimated the public sector share of the consumption of fixed capital (DEP). To do this, we multiplied the total consumption of fixed capital by the ratio of public to private sector investment. This gave us an estimated value of the consumption of publicly-provided fixed capital. We then multiplied this value by 0.75 on the assumption that 75% of all government investment spending is on service capital rather than producer goods. The annual values of WPPSC for Australia, Victoria, and the Rest-of-Australia, and the steps involved in their calculation appear in Table 9.9. The Rest-of-Australia values were the difference between the Australian and Victorian values.

Data sources:

ABS, Catalogue No. 5204.0.
ABS, Catalogue No. 5220.0.

9.2.9. Item o: Value of Non-paid Household Labour

The estimated number of unpaid household labour hours in Australia in 1997 was 17.669 billion (ABS, 2000, Catalogue No. 5240.0). Given there were 6.998 million households in 1997, this amounts to 2,524.7 hours of unpaid household work per Australian household. To estimate the number of unpaid household labour hours in other years during the study period, we assumed that labour-reducing technological progress embodied in household appliances increased at a rate of 1% per annum. We therefore adjusted the hours of unpaid household work per Australian household upwards by 1% per annum in the years prior to 1997, and downwards by the same percentage in the years following 1997. We then multiplied the estimated hours of unpaid household work per Australian household per year by the changing number of households in Australia. This provided us with the total number of household labour hours for each year over the study period.

In a 1997 ABS study on unpaid household labour, a range of valuation methods were used to determine the value of unpaid household work. One of the methods used — and the one we employed — was the net opportunity cost method. The net opportunity cost of one household labour hour was $13.47 in 1997. This is equivalent to $15.41 per hour in 2002-03 prices. Based on the assumption that the real value of one household labour hour remained unchanged over the study period, we finally calculated the total value of Australia's unpaid household labour by multiplying the total number of household labour hours for each year by $15.41 per hour (Table 9.10). We adopted the same approach for Victoria and assumed that the values for the Rest-of-Australia were equal to the values calculated for Australia less the Victorian values (see also Table 9.10).

Data sources:

ABS (1994), *Catalogue* No. 5240.0.
ABS (2000), *Catalogue* No. 5240.0.

9.2.10. Item p: Value of Volunteer Labour

The value of volunteer labour was calculated along similar lines to non-paid household labour. The net opportunity cost method was again used, while it was also assumed that the net opportunity cost of one volunteer hour in 1997 was equivalent to $15.41 per hour in 2002-03 prices. We also assumed that the net opportunity cost of one volunteer hour remained unchanged over the study period.

There were two major studies conducted by the ABS to determine the value of volunteer work in Australia — one in 1992; the other in 1997. The ABS estimated that the number of volunteer hours of labour undertaken by Australians was 1.47 billion in 1992 and 1.78 billion in 1997. To determine the number of volunteer hours undertaken in other years during the study period, we used a straight line interpolation technique. As revealed in Table 9.11, the total value of Australia's volunteer labour was calculated by multiplying the total number of volunteer labour hours by $15.41 per hour.

To determine the value of volunteer labour in Victoria, we used a 1995 and 2000 time survey to ascertain Victoria's share of Australian volunteer labour. We again used a straight line interpolation technique to ascertain the number of volunteer labour hours in each year and multiplied the annual values by $15.41. The values for the Rest-of-Australia were calculated by subtracting the Victorian from the Australian values (see also Table 9.11).

Data sources:

ABS (2001), *Catalogue* No. 4441.0.
ABS (2000), *Catalogue* No. 5240.0.

9.2.11. Item q: Cost of Unemployment, Underemployment, and Labour Underutilisation

The cost of unemployment (broadly defined) was calculated using comprehensive hours-based measures of labour underutilisation developed by the Centre of Full Employment and Equity (CofFEE). We began our estimation exercise by determining the ratio of the official unemployment rate to CofFEE's CU8 rate of unemployment. The CU8 rate equals the official unemployment rate plus CofFEE's estimates of hidden unemployment and underemployment.

Table 9.9: Item *n*: Welfare from publicly-provided service capital (WPPSC) – Australia, Victoria, and Rest-of-Australia, 1986–2003

	AUSTRALIA						VICTORIA						REST-of-AUST
	Cons. of fixed capital (DEP) ($)	Public sector investment ($)	Private sector investment ($)	Ratio of public to private inv. (%)	Cons. of pub-provided fixed capital ($)	SPPSC ($)	Cons. of fixed capital (DEP) ($)	Public sector investment ($)	Private sector investment ($)	Ratio of public to private inv. (%)	Cons. of pub-provided fixed capital ($)	SPPSC ($)	SPPSC ($)
Year	a	b	c	(b/c) d	$(a \times d)$ e	$(e \times 0.75)$ f	g	h	i	(h/i) j	$(g \times j)$ k	$(k \times 0.75)$ l	$m = f - l$
1986	57,464.0	23,611.0	64,825.0	0.36	20,929.9	15,697.4	13,441.1	5,341.0	15,445.0	0.35	4,648.0	3,486.0	12,211.4
1987	59,953.0	23,622.0	64,526.0	0.37	21,947.9	16,460.9	14,343.9	4,999.0	16,277.0	0.31	4,405.3	3,304.0	13,156.9
1988	63,633.0	21,001.0	74,256.0	0.28	17,996.6	13,497.5	14,830.8	4,620.0	17,648.0	0.26	3,882.5	2,911.9	10,585.6
1989	67,412.0	21,059.0	84,219.0	0.25	16,856.4	12,642.3	15,776.1	4,665.0	20,207.0	0.23	3,642.1	2,731.6	9,910.7
1990	68,444.0	24,638.0	81,367.0	0.30	20,724.9	15,543.7	15,801.6	5,743.0	18,978.0	0.30	4,781.8	3,586.3	11,957.3
1991	71,678.0	23,257.0	72,220.0	0.32	23,082.5	17,311.8	15,042.1	4,855.0	15,304.0	0.32	4,771.9	3,578.9	13,732.9
1992	74,530.0	22,954.0	67,736.0	0.34	25,256.3	18,942.2	15,336.8	4,730.0	14,030.0	0.34	5,170.6	3,877.9	15,064.3
1993	76,811.0	22,420.0	74,259.0	0.30	23,190.5	17,392.9	16,217.5	4,031.0	16,440.0	0.25	3,976.4	2,982.3	14,410.5
1994	79,880.0	21,725.0	81,317.0	0.27	21,341.1	16,005.8	17,388.3	4,619.0	17,887.0	0.26	4,490.2	3,367.7	12,638.1
1995	82,520.0	24,510.0	89,896.0	0.27	22,498.9	16,874.2	17,067.0	5,482.0	18,407.0	0.30	5,082.9	3,812.2	13,062.0
1996	85,124.0	23,588.0	93,085.0	0.25	21,570.7	16,178.0	18,729.2	4,754.0	21,103.0	0.23	4,219.2	3,164.4	13,013.6
1997	88,950.0	23,004.0	102,820.0	0.22	19,900.9	14,925.6	21,201.6	3,416.0	26,467.0	0.13	2,736.4	2,052.3	12,873.3
1998	93,773.0	21,115.0	116,761.0	0.18	16,957.9	12,718.4	21,765.4	4,269.0	27,302.0	0.16	3,403.3	2,552.5	10,165.9
1999	97,990.0	25,330.0	120,872.0	0.21	20,534.8	15,401.1	24,259.3	5,243.0	31,008.0	0.17	4,101.9	3,076.4	12,324.7
2000	103,794.0	25,111.0	133,238.0	0.19	19,561.8	14,671.3	26,357.6	5,329.0	34,154.0	0.16	4,112.5	3,084.4	11,586.9
2001	107,713.0	25,103.0	122,144.0	0.21	22,137.1	16,602.9	27,731.0	4,815.0	33,350.0	0.14	4,003.7	3,002.8	13,600.1
2002	114,217.0	27,280.0	135,273.0	0.20	23,033.7	17,275.3	29,626.4	5,477.0	36,676.0	0.15	4,424.3	3,318.2	13,957.1
2003	119,407.0	28,131.0	156,671.0	0.18	21,440.1	16,080.1	31,119.6	6,329.0	41,527.0	0.15	4,742.8	3,557.1	12,522.9

Note: All values are in millions of 2002–2003 dollars except where indicated

Table 9.10: Item *o*: Value of unpaid household labour – Australia, Victoria, and Rest-of-Australia, 1986-2003

	AUSTRALIA						VICTORIA				REST-of-AUST
	Annual hours of household labour per household	Number of households	Total number of annual household labour hours	Net opp. Cost per hour in 1997 at 1996-97 prices	Net opp. Cost per hour at 2002-03 prices	Total value of household work	Annual hours of household labour per household	Number of households	Total number of annual household labour hours	Total value of household work	Total value of household work
		(000s)	(millions)	(single $)	(single $)	($)		(000s)	(millions)	($)	($)
			(*a* x *c*)			(*d* x *f*)			(*h* x *j*)	(*f* x *k*)	(*l* - *g*)
Year	*a*	*c*	*d*	*e*	*f*	*g*	*h*	*j*	*k*	*l*	*m*
1986	2,816.8	5,187.4	14,611.7	-	15.41	225,124.2	2,816.8	1,345.6	3,790.3	58,397.9	166,726.3
1987	2,788.9	5,315.0	14,822.9	-	15.41	228,378.9	2,788.9	1,372.8	3,828.4	58,985.4	169,393.4
1988	2,761.3	5,442.6	15,028.5	-	15.41	231,547.0	2,761.3	1,399.9	3,865.5	59,555.6	171,991.4
1989	2,733.9	5,570.3	15,228.6	-	15.41	234,630.1	2,733.9	1,427.0	3,901.4	60,108.8	174,521.3
1990	2,706.9	5,697.9	15,423.3	-	15.41	237,629.4	2,706.9	1,454.1	3,936.2	60,645.1	176,984.3
1991	2,680.1	5,825.5	15,612.6	-	15.41	240,546.3	2,680.1	1,481.3	3,969.9	61,164.9	179,381.4
1992	2,653.5	6,040.0	16,027.2	-	15.41	246,934.1	2,653.5	1,528.6	4,056.0	62,491.9	184,442.2
1993	2,627.2	6,254.5	16,432.1	-	15.41	253,171.8	2,627.2	1,575.8	4,140.1	63,786.7	189,385.1
1994	2,601.2	6,469.0	16,827.4	-	15.41	259,261.8	2,601.2	1,623.1	4,222.0	65,049.6	194,212.2
1995	2,575.5	6,683.5	17,213.2	-	15.41	265,206.4	2,575.5	1,670.4	4,302.0	66,281.3	198,925.0
1996	2,550.0	6,898.0	17,589.7	-	15.41	271,007.8	2,550.0	1,717.6	4,379.9	67,482.3	203,525.5
1997	2,524.7	6,998.3	17,668.9	13.47	15.41	272,227.4	2,524.7	1,746.7	4,410.0	67,945.4	204,282.1
1998	2,499.7	7,098.7	17,744.8	-	15.41	273,396.3	2,499.7	1,775.8	4,439.0	68,392.7	205,003.7
1999	2,475.0	7,199.0	17,817.4	-	15.41	274,515.4	2,475.0	1,804.9	4,467.0	68,824.4	205,690.9
2000	2,450.5	7,299.3	17,886.8	-	15.41	275,585.5	2,450.5	1,834.0	4,494.1	69,241.0	206,344.5
2001	2,426.2	7,399.7	17,953.2	-	15.41	276,607.5	2,426.2	1,863.0	4,520.1	69,642.5	206,965.0
2002	2,402.2	7,500.0	18,016.4	-	15.41	277,582.2	2,402.2	1,892.1	4,545.2	70,029.3	207,552.9
2003	2,378.4	7,600.3	18,076.7	-	15.41	278,510.5	2,378.4	1,921.2	4,569.4	70,401.6	208,108.9

Note: All values are in millions of 2002-2003 dollars except where indicated

Table 9.11: Item *p*: Value of volunteer labour - Australia, Victoria, and Rest-of-Australia, 1986-2003

	AUSTRALIA			VICTORIA			REST-of-AUST
	Total number of annual volunteer labour hours (millions)	Net opp. Cost per hour at 2002-03 prices (single $)	Total value of volunteer labour ($)	Victorian share of Australian vol. labour (%)	Total number of annual volunteer labour hours (millions)	Total value of volunteer labour ($)	Total value of volunteer labour ($)
Year	*a*	*b*	(*a* x *b*) *c*	*d*	(*a* x *d*) *e*	(*b* x *e*) *f*	(*c* - *f*) *g*
1986	1,100.2	15.41	16,950.7	-	144.2	2,222.0	14,728.8
1987	1,162.1	15.41	17,905.4	-	173.2	2,668.7	15,236.6
1988	1,224.1	15.41	18,860.0	-	202.2	3,115.4	15,744.5
1989	1,286.1	15.41	19,814.6	-	231.2	3,562.2	16,252.4
1990	1,348.0	15.41	20,769.2	-	260.2	4,008.9	16,760.3
1991	1,410.0	15.41	21,723.8	-	289.2	4,455.6	17,268.2
1992	1,471.9	15.41	22,678.4	-	318.2	4,902.3	17,776.1
1993	1,533.9	15.41	23,633.0	-	347.2	5,349.1	18,284.0
1994	1,595.9	15.41	24,587.7	-	376.2	5,795.8	18,791.9
1995	1,657.8	15.41	25,542.3	0.244	405.2	6,242.5	19,299.7
1996	1,719.8	15.41	26,496.9	-	434.2	6,689.3	19,807.6
1997	1,781.7	15.41	27,451.5	-	463.2	7,136.0	20,315.5
1998	1,843.7	15.41	28,406.1	-	492.2	7,582.7	20,823.4
1999	1,905.7	15.41	29,360.7	-	521.2	8,029.4	21,331.3
2000	1,967.6	15.41	30,315.4	0.280	550.1	8,476.2	21,839.2
2001	2,029.6	15.41	31,270.0	-	579.1	8,922.9	22,347.1
2002	2,091.5	15.41	32,224.6	-	608.1	9,369.6	22,855.0
2003	2,153.5	15.41	33,179.2	-	637.1	9,816.4	23,362.8

Note: All values are in millions of 2002-2003 dollars except where indicated

Table 9.12: Item q: Cost of unemployment, underemployment, and labour underutilisation - Australia, 1986-2003

AUSTRALIA										
Year	Number of unempl. people (000s)	Official unempl. rate (%)	CofFEE CU8 rate (%)	Ratio of CU8 to official unempl. rate (c/b)	Number of CU8 (000s) (c × d)	Award rates of pay indices 1986 = 100.0	Nominal minimum weekly wage (single $)	Deflator 2003 = 100.0	Real minimum weekly wage (single $)	Weekly direct cost of unempl. ($) (e × i)	Total cost of CU8 ($) (-j × 52)
	a	b	c	d	e	f	g	h	i	j	k
1986	589.6	7.8	12.3	1.58	933.6	100.0	242.5	58.1	417.40	389.67	-20,263.1
1987	616.9	8.0	13.1	1.65	1,016.3	104.9	255.2	62.2	410.33	417.03	-21,685.3
1988	562.9	7.1	12.1	1.71	962.5	109.5	266.4	67.3	396.16	381.32	-19,828.5
1989	484.5	5.9	10.1	1.71	829.9	116.8	285.1	73.3	388.98	322.82	-16,786.6
1990	546.1	6.5	10.7	1.66	904.9	123.5	301.6	77.3	390.28	353.18	-18,365.2
1991	793.2	9.4	16.1	1.72	1,364.5	129.9	318.2	79.9	398.13	543.26	-28,249.5
1992	904.7	10.6	18.7	1.77	1,602.9	134.4	329.8	81.5	404.73	648.72	-33,733.5
1993	912.2	10.6	18.7	1.76	1,606.3	136.1	333.8	82.4	405.30	651.01	-33,852.5
1994	835.3	9.5	17.2	1.80	1,506.2	137.6	337.8	83.1	406.33	612.00	-31,823.9
1995	728.2	8.1	14.8	1.83	1,331.8	139.3	343.0	84.1	407.80	543.13	-28,242.9
1996	745.5	8.2	14.9	1.82	1,357.7	141.6	349.4	86.2	405.53	550.58	-28,630.2
1997	761.7	8.3	15.2	1.83	1,395.3	-	363.1	87.4	415.28	579.44	-30,131.1
1998	728.1	7.8	14.3	1.84	1,336.3	-	376.7	88.7	424.76	567.61	-29,515.8
1999	647.5	6.9	12.9	1.87	1,211.2	-	390.4	88.8	439.68	532.55	-27,692.7
2000	598.0	6.2	11.8	1.90	1,133.7	-	404.1	90.5	446.26	505.93	-26,308.4
2001	675.7	6.9	12.5	1.81	1,221.4	-	417.7	95.1	439.13	536.38	-27,891.7
2002	627.1	6.3	12.0	1.89	1,185.7	-	431.4	97.5	442.62	524.79	-27,289.3
2003	620.7	6.2	11.9	1.93	1,197.6	-	448.4	100.0	448.40	537.00	-27,923.9

Note: All values are in millions of 2002-2003 dollars except where indicated

Table 9.13: Item q: Cost of unemployment, underemployment, and labour underutilisation – Victoria and Rest-of-Australia, 1986–2003

Year	VICTORIA Number of unempl. people (000s) a	Official unempl. rate (%) b	CofFEE CU8 rate (%) c	Ratio of CU8 to official unempl. rate (ratio) d (c/b)	Number of CU8 (000s) e $(c \times d)$	Real minimum weekly wage (single $) i	Weekly direct cost of unempl. ($) j $(e \times i)$	Total cost of CU8 ($) k $(-j \times 52)$	AUSTRALIA Total cost of CU8 ($) l (Table 9.12)	REST-of-AUST Total cost of CU8 ($) m $(-j \times 52)$
1986	125.4	6.3	9.8	1.56	195.1	417.40	81.42	-4,233.9	-20,263.1	-16,029.1
1987	123.0	6.0	10.3	1.72	211.2	410.33	86.64	-4,505.3	-21,685.3	-17,180.0
1988	121.6	5.9	9.3	1.58	191.7	396.16	75.93	-3,948.6	-19,828.5	-15,880.0
1989	99.0	4.6	8.3	1.80	178.6	388.98	69.48	-3,613.1	-16,786.6	-13,173.5
1990	119.8	5.4	7.6	1.41	168.6	390.28	65.80	-3,421.8	-18,365.2	-14,943.4
1991	214.5	9.8	13.8	1.41	302.1	398.13	120.26	-6,253.3	-28,249.5	-21,996.1
1992	250.0	11.4	18.5	1.62	405.7	404.73	164.20	-8,538.4	-33,733.5	-25,195.2
1993	262.4	12.0	20.1	1.68	439.5	405.30	178.14	-9,263.1	-33,852.5	-24,589.4
1994	230.2	10.4	20.0	1.92	442.7	406.33	179.88	-9,353.7	-31,823.9	-22,470.2
1995	190.5	8.4	16.8	2.00	381.0	407.80	155.37	-8,079.4	-28,242.9	-20,163.5
1996	187.1	8.2	15.3	1.87	349.1	405.53	141.57	-7,361.6	-28,630.2	-21,268.6
1997	202.8	8.8	15.8	1.80	364.1	415.28	151.21	-7,863.0	-30,131.1	-22,268.1
1998	187.0	7.9	14.4	1.82	340.9	424.76	144.78	-7,528.7	-29,515.8	-21,987.1
1999	168.8	7.2	13.3	1.85	311.8	439.68	137.10	-7,129.1	-27,692.7	-20,563.7
2000	147.3	6.2	11.5	1.85	273.2	446.26	121.93	-6,340.1	-26,308.4	-19,968.3
2001	156.5	6.4	10.8	1.69	264.1	439.13	115.97	-6,030.6	-27,891.7	-21,861.1
2002	143.5	5.8	11.4	1.97	282.1	442.62	124.84	-6,491.7	-27,289.3	-20,797.6
2003	146.7	5.9	10.7	1.81	266.0	448.40	119.30	-6,203.4	-27,923.9	-21,720.5

Note: All values are in millions of 2002-2003 dollars except where indicated

This ratio was then multiplied by the number of people officially estimated by the ABS to be unemployed to obtain an equivalent number of people unemployed as per the CU8 definition. We then assumed that the cost per unemployed person was equal to the real minimum wage less the sum of the unemployment welfare payment and the average rent assistance allowance (i.e., real minimum wage minus $240.50 at 2002-03 prices). The total cost of CU8 unemployment was calculated by multiplying the number of people unemployed as per the CU8 definition by the cost per unemployed person (Table 9.12).

The one problem we did have in calculating the cost of CU8 unemployment was the difficulty obtaining the nominal minimum weekly wage for years prior to 1996. We therefore used the award rates of pay indices for the years 1986 to 1996 to estimate the change in the nominal minimum weekly wage between 1986 and 1995.

The cost of CU8 unemployment for Victoria was calculated using the same approach as that used for Australia (Table 9.13). The Rest-of-Australia cost of CU8 unemployment was determined by subtracting the Victorian cost from the Australian cost (see also Table 9.13).

Data sources:

ABS, Catalogue No. 6105.0.
ABS, Catalogue No. 6202.2.
ABS, Catalogue No. 6203.0.
ABS, Catalogue No. 6265.0.
ABS, Catalogue No. 6302.0.
CLMI (CofFEE) (2004), *An Alternative View of the Labour Market*, May 2004 (http://e1.newcastle.edu.au/coffee).
National Coalition Against Poverty (NCAP) (2003), *Poverty Scorecard for Australia: 2003*.
Salvation Army (2003), *Poverty in Australia: Fact Sheet*, The Salvation Army of Australia.

9.2.12. Item r: Cost of Crime

As mentioned in Chapter 3, the calculation of the total cost of the crime involved aggregating the cost of six categories of crime — namely, homicide, assault, robbery, break and entry, motor vehicle theft, and other theft. We established separate crime indexes for each crime category based on the number of reported cases for each year of the study period. We did this for both Australia and Victoria.

The individual crime indexes were then multiplied by the estimated cost of each category of crime for the years 1988 (Walker, 1992), 1996 (Walker, 1997), and 2001 (Mayhew, 2003) (Table 9.14). We adopted the same approach for Victoria and assumed the real cost per each crime category was the same in Victoria as it was for Australia (Table 9.15). The cost of crime for the Rest-of-Australia was assumed to equal the difference between the Australian and the Victorian cost of crime (also Table 9.15 and Figure 9.1).

Sources:

ABS, Catalogue No. 1301.0 (various).
ABS, Catalogue No. 1301.2 (various).
ABS (2003), *Catalogue* No. 4102.0.

ABS (2002), *Catalogue* No. 4509.0.

ABS (2004), *Catalogue* No. 4510.0.

Australian Institute of Criminology (2003), *Australian Crime: Facts and Figures, 2003*, AIC, Canberra.

Mayhew, P. (2003), 'Counting the costs of crime in Australia', *Australian Institute of Criminology: Trends and Issues*, No. 247, AIC, Canberra.

Walker, J. (1992), 'Estimates of the cost of crime in Australia in 1988', *Australian Institute of Criminology: Trends and Issues*, No. 39, AIC, Canberra.

Walker, J. (1997), 'Estimates of the cost of crime in Australia in 1996', *Australian Institute of Criminology: Trends and Issues*, No. 72, AIC, Canberra.

9.2.13. Item s: Cost of Family Breakdown

We calculated the cost of family breakdown by using the number of divorces as a proxy for family disunity and dysfunctionality. Based on evidence provided in a Report of the House of Representatives Standing Committee on Legal and Constitutional Affairs (1998), we assumed that the cost per divorce was around $20,000 in 1990 (legal fees, counselling costs, disruption to children, psychological impact). This equated to $27,287 per divorce at 2002-03 prices. We assumed that this cost remained constant throughout the study period.

Based again on evidence from the above Report that the average duration of a marriage that ends in divorce is around ten years, we assumed that number of dysfunctional families in any one year was equal to four times the number of divorces for that year. We assumed that the cost per dysfunctional family was half that of a divorce (i.e., $13,644 at 2002-03 prices).

The total cost of family breakdown was then calculated by summing the cost of divorce and the estimated cost of family dysfunction (Table 9.16 for Australia; Table 9.17 for Victoria and the Rest-of-Australia).

Sources:

ABS, Catalogue No. 1301.0 and 1301.2 (various).

ABS, Catalogue No. 3101.0, 3310.0 and 3307.0.55.001.

ABS, Catalogue No. 3311.2.55.001.

ABS (2003), *Catalogue* No. 4102.0.

Report of the House of Representatives Standing Committee on Legal and Constitutional Affairs (1998), *To Have and to Hold: Strategies to Strengthen Marriage and Relationships*, Commonwealth of Australia, Canberra.

9.2.14. Item t: Change in Foreign Debt Position

The change in Australia's foreign debt position (net foreign liabilities) was drawn straight from ABS national accounting data. Since it is provided only in current prices, we used the GDP deflator to adjust the annual change in foreign debt to 2002-03 prices (see Table 9.18).

Table 9.14: Item r: Cost of crime – Australia, 1986-2003

	AUSTRALIA					Assault						
	Homicide											
	Number of homicides	Nominal cost of homicide ($)	Real cost of homicide ($)	Real cost per homicide ($)	Total cost of homicide ($)	Number of assaults	Number of sexual assaults	Total number of assaults	Nominal cost of assault ($)	Real cost of assault ($)	Real cost per assault ($)	Total cost of assault ($)
				(c/a)	(a x d)			(f + g)			(j/h)	(h x k)
Year	a	b	c	d	e	f	g	h	i	j	k	l
1986	310	-	-	1.29	-400.7	77,847	7,050	84,897	-	-	0.0047	-402.3
1987	300	-	-	1.28	-382.6	78,157	7,450	85,607	-	-	0.0052	-444.2
1988	325	275	408.9	1.26	-408.9	78,337	8,950	87,287	331	492.2	0.0056	-492.2
1989	325	-	-	1.24	-403.3	81,037	8,900	89,937	-	-	0.0061	-547.6
1990	327	-	-	1.22	-400.2	82,860	9,722	92,581	-	-	0.0065	-605.3
1991	329	-	-	1.21	-397.0	84,682	10,543	95,225	-	-	0.0070	-665.4
1992	331	-	-	1.19	-393.7	86,505	11,365	97,869	-	-	0.0074	-727.9
1993	333	-	-	1.17	-390.3	88,327	12,186	100,513	-	-	0.0079	-792.8
1994	320	-	-	1.15	-369.6	90,150	12,722	102,872	-	-	0.0083	-857.6
1995	356	-	-	1.14	-405.0	101,710	13,099	114,809	-	-	0.0088	-1,008.8
1996	350	323	392.2	1.12	-392.2	114,156	14,542	128,698	979	1,188.7	0.0092	-1,188.7
1997	360	-	-	1.27	-456.5	124,500	14,353	138,853	-	-	0.0096	-1,336.5
1998	332	-	-	1.42	-470.0	130,903	14,336	145,239	-	-	0.0100	-1,454.5
1999	386	-	-	1.56	-603.4	134,271	14,104	148,375	-	-	0.0104	-1,543.7
2000	363	-	-	1.71	-621.0	138,708	15,759	154,467	-	-	0.0108	-1,667.2
2001	346	554	643.0	1.86	-643.0	152,283	16,897	169,180	1,630	1,891.8	0.0112	-1,891.8
2002	363	-	-	1.97	-716.2	159,548	17,850	177,398	-	-	0.0116	-2,054.9
2003	358	-	-	2.12	-759.1	166,813	18,803	185,616	-	-	0.0120	-2,222.4

Note: All values are in millions of 2002-2003 dollars except where indicated

Table 9.14 (Continued): Item r: Cost of crime - Australia, 1986-2003

AUSTRALIA	Robbery					Break & entry				
	Number of robberies	Nominal cost of robberies ($)	Real cost of robberies ($)	Real cost per robbery ($)	Total cost of robberies ($)	Number of B & E	Nominal cost of B & E ($)	Real cost of B & E ($)	Real cost per B & E ($)	Total cost of B & E ($)
Year	m	n	o	p (o/m)	q (m x p)	r	s	t	u (t/r)	v (r x u)
1986	8,350	-	-	0.047	-391.6	124,000	-	-	0.009	-1,106.2
1987	8,100	-	-	0.046	-368.8	159,000	-	-	0.008	-1,333.8
1988	8,500	253	376.2	0.044	-376.2	169,000	893	1,327.9	0.008	-1,327.9
1989	9,353	-	-	0.043	-401.0	181,000	-	-	0.007	-1,325.9
1990	10,206	-	-	0.041	-423.3	231,196	-	-	0.007	-1,570.6
1991	11,059	-	-	0.040	-443.3	281,392	-	-	0.006	-1,762.0
1992	11,912	-	-	0.039	-461.0	331,587	-	-	0.006	-1,900.0
1993	12,765	-	-	0.037	-476.2	381,783	-	-	0.005	-1,984.5
1994	13,967	-	-	0.036	-501.7	379,505	-	-	0.005	-1,770.9
1995	14,564	-	-	0.035	-502.9	385,162	-	-	0.004	-1,592.4
1996	16,372	-	-	0.034	-558.8	402,079	1,193	1,448.5	0.004	-1,448.5
1997	21,305	-	-	0.033	-697.6	421,569	-	-	0.004	-1,760.7
1998	23,801	-	-	0.031	-746.2	434,376	-	-	0.005	-2,063.5
1999	22,606	-	-	0.030	-677.3	415,735	-	-	0.005	-2,213.6
2000	23,336	-	-	0.029	-666.7	436,968	-	-	0.006	-2,577.4
2001	26,591	600	696.4	0.026	-696.4	435,754	2,430	2,820.3	0.006	-2,820.3
2002	20,961	-	-	0.025	-519.8	394,374	-	-	0.007	-2,691.6
2003	23,459	-	-	0.023	-544.5	423,441	-	-	0.007	-3,133.1

Note: All values are in millions of 2002-2003 dollars except where indicated

Table 9.14 (Continued): Item r: Cost of crime - Australia, 1986-2003

AUSTRALIA

Year	M veh. theft					Other theft					Total cost of crime ($)	Total cost of crime-related incidents ($)
	Number of MVT	Nominal cost of MVT ($)	Real cost of MVT ($)	Real cost per MVT ($)	Total cost of MVT ($)	Number of other thefts	Nominal cost of other thefts ($)	Real cost of other thefts ($)	Real cost per other theft ($)	Total cost of other thefts ($)		
	w	x	y	z (y/w)	aa $(w \times z)$	bb	cc	dd	ee (dd/bb)	ff $(bb \times ee)$	gg $e+l+q+v+aa+ff$	hh $(2 \times gg)$
1986	124,500	-	-	0.009	-1,074.5	382,000	-	-	0.005	-2,016.0	-5,391.4	-10,782.7
1987	132,000	-	-	0.008	-1,110.6	439,000	-	-	0.005	-2,312.3	-5,952.4	-11,904.7
1988	121,000	667	991.8	0.008	-991.8	437,000	1,545	2,297.3	0.005	-2,297.3	-5,894.3	-11,788.6
1989	127,000	-	-	0.008	-1,013.4	438,000	-	-	0.005	-2,298.1	-5,989.3	-11,978.6
1990	123,368	-	-	0.008	-957.7	446,753	-	-	0.005	-2,339.5	-6,296.6	-12,593.2
1991	119,736	-	-	0.008	-903.5	455,506	-	-	0.005	-2,380.7	-6,551.9	-13,103.8
1992	116,104	-	-	0.007	-850.9	464,259	-	-	0.005	-2,421.7	-6,755.1	-13,510.2
1993	112,472	-	-	0.007	-799.9	473,012	-	-	0.005	-2,462.5	-6,906.3	-13,812.6
1994	119,469	-	-	0.007	-823.7	481,765	-	-	0.005	-2,503.2	-6,826.7	-13,653.3
1995	127,094	-	-	0.007	-848.7	490,518	-	-	0.005	-2,543.7	-6,901.5	-13,803.0
1996	122,914	654	794.1	0.006	-794.1	521,762	2,224	2,700.4	0.005	-2,700.4	-7,082.7	-14,165.4
1997	130,138	-	-	0.007	-862.6	530,881	-	-	0.005	-2,546.6	-7,660.5	-15,321.0
1998	131,587	-	-	0.007	-894.4	563,482	-	-	0.004	-2,489.6	-8,118.2	-16,236.4
1999	129,552	-	-	0.007	-902.3	612,559	-	-	0.004	-2,474.5	-8,414.7	-16,829.5
2000	138,912	-	-	0.007	-990.8	681,268	-	-	0.004	-2,494.1	-9,017.3	-18,034.5
2001	139,894	880	1,021.4	0.007	-1,021.4	700,137	1,980	2,298.1	0.003	-2,298.1	-9,371.0	-18,741.9
2002	113,389	-	-	0.007	-838.2	679,460	-	-	0.003	-2,023.0	-8,843.7	-17,687.4
2003	130,667	-	-	0.008	-987.9	658,783	-	-	0.003	-1,712.0	-9,358.9	-18,717.8

Note: All values are in millions of 2002-2003 dollars except where indicated

Table 9.15: Item r: Cost of crime – Victoria and Rest-of-Australia, 1986-2003

	VICTORIA			Assault						Robbery		
	Homicide											
Year	Number of homicides	Real cost per homicide ($)	Total cost of homicide ($)	Number of assaults	Number of sexual assaults	Total number of assaults	Real cost per assualt ($)	Total cost of assault ($)	Number of robberies	Real cost per robbery ($)	Total cost of robberies ($)
	a	b	c	e	f	g	h	i	j	k	l
			(a x b)			(e + f)		(g x h)			(j x k)
1986	109	1.29	-140.9	10,375	2,292	12,667	0.0047	-60.0	1,666	0.047	-78.1
1987	132	1.28	-168.4	10,920	2,348	13,269	0.0052	-68.8	2,090	0.046	-95.1
1988	145	1.26	-182.4	13,014	2,405	15,419	0.0056	-86.9	1,811	0.044	-80.2
1989	168	1.24	-208.5	15,671	2,461	18,132	0.0061	-110.4	1,818	0.043	-77.9
1990	143	1.22	-175.0	13,738	2,517	16,255	0.0065	-106.3	1,776	0.041	-73.7
1991	155	1.21	-187.0	14,702	2,574	17,276	0.0070	-120.7	1,995	0.040	-80.0
1992	124	1.19	-147.5	14,979	2,630	17,609	0.0074	-131.0	1,933	0.039	-74.8
1993	113	1.17	-132.7	15,255	2,686	17,941	0.0079	-141.5	1,904	0.037	-71.0
1994	122	1.15	-140.8	15,531	2,743	18,274	0.0083	-152.3	1,637	0.036	-58.8
1995	135	1.14	-153.6	15,807	2,799	18,606	0.0088	-163.5	1,705	0.035	-58.9
1996	109	1.12	-122.1	16,220	2,767	18,987	0.0092	-175.4	1,911	0.034	-65.2
1997	132	1.27	-167.4	16,632	2,832	19,464	0.0096	-187.4	2,463	0.033	-80.6
1998	145	1.42	-205.3	17,571	2,967	20,538	0.0100	-205.7	2,996	0.031	-93.9
1999	158	1.56	-247.0	18,510	3,135	21,645	0.0104	-225.2	3,404	0.030	-102.0
2000	171	1.71	-292.5	19,449	3,302	22,751	0.0108	-245.6	3,326	0.029	-95.0
2001	184	1.86	-341.9	20,388	3,470	23,858	0.0112	-266.8	3,248	0.026	-85.1
2002	197	1.97	-388.7	21,327	3,638	24,965	0.0116	-289.2	3,170	0.025	-78.6
2003	210	2.12	-445.3	22,266	3,805	26,071	0.0120	-312.1	3,092	0.023	-71.8

Note: All values are in millions of 2002-2003 dollars except where indicated

Table 9.15 (Continued): Item r: Cost of crime - Victoria and Rest-of-Australia, 1986-2003

	VICTORIA											AUSTRALIA	REST-of-AUST
	Break & entry			M/V theft			Other theft			VICTORIA			
Year	Number of B & E	Real cost per B & E ($)	Total cost of B & E ($)	Number of MVT	Real cost per MVT ($)	Total cost of MVT ($)	Number of OT	Real cost per OT ($)	Total cost of OT ($)	Total cost of crime ($)	Total cost of crime-related incidents ($)	Total cost of crime-related incidents ($)	Total cost of crime-related incidents ($)
	m	n	o $(m \times n)$	p	q	r $(p \times q)$	s	t	u $(s \times t)$	v $c+i+t+o+r+tu$	w $(2 \times v)$	x (Table 9.14)	y $(x - w)$
1986	76,372	0.009	-681.3	26,334	0.009	-227.3	105,460	0.005	-556.6	-1,744.2	-3,488.4	-10,782.7	-7,294.3
1987	87,045	0.008	-730.2	32,598	0.008	-274.3	115,809	0.005	-610.0	-1,946.8	-3,893.7	-11,904.7	-8,011.1
1988	90,569	0.008	-711.6	32,777	0.008	-268.7	118,416	0.005	-622.5	-1,952.3	-3,904.7	-11,788.6	-7,883.9
1989	88,527	0.007	-648.5	35,574	0.008	-283.9	118,954	0.005	-624.1	-1,953.3	-3,906.6	-11,978.6	-8,071.9
1990	87,128	0.007	-591.9	34,951	0.008	-271.3	117,060	0.005	-613.0	-1,831.2	-3,662.3	-12,593.2	-8,930.9
1991	94,201	0.006	-589.9	35,721	0.008	-269.5	133,049	0.005	-695.4	-1,942.5	-3,885.0	-13,103.8	-9,218.8
1992	87,834	0.006	-503.3	31,368	0.007	-229.9	132,237	0.005	-689.8	-1,776.2	-3,552.4	-13,510.2	-9,957.8
1993	80,463	0.005	-418.3	27,578	0.007	-196.1	125,388	0.005	-652.8	-1,612.4	-3,224.8	-13,812.6	-10,587.7
1994	72,260	0.005	-337.2	27,701	0.007	-191.0	118,538	0.005	-615.9	-1,496.1	-2,992.1	-13,653.3	-10,661.2
1995	70,923	0.004	-293.2	29,259	0.007	-195.4	111,689	0.005	-579.2	-1,443.7	-2,887.5	-13,803.0	-10,915.5
1996	70,667	0.004	-254.6	28,737	0.006	-185.7	119,278	0.005	-617.3	-1,420.3	-2,840.6	-14,165.4	-11,324.8
1997	74,081	0.004	-309.4	30,442	0.007	-201.8	119,570	0.005	-573.6	-1,520.1	-3,040.3	-15,321.0	-12,280.8
1998	70,589	0.005	-335.3	29,563	0.007	-200.9	125,569	0.004	-554.8	-1,595.9	-3,191.9	-16,236.4	-13,044.5
1999	76,275	0.005	-406.1	32,075	0.007	-223.4	133,609	0.004	-539.7	-1,743.4	-3,486.8	-16,829.5	-13,342.7
2000	78,774	0.006	-464.6	36,591	0.007	-261.0	141,219	0.004	-517.0	-1,875.8	-3,751.5	-18,034.5	-14,283.0
2001	81,273	0.006	-526.0	41,107	0.007	-300.1	148,829	0.003	-488.5	-2,008.4	-4,016.9	-18,741.9	-14,725.0
2002	83,772	0.007	-571.8	45,623	0.007	-337.2	156,439	0.003	-465.8	-2,131.2	-4,262.5	-17,687.4	-13,424.9
2003	86,271	0.007	-638.3	50,139	0.008	-379.1	164,049	0.003	-426.3	-2,272.9	-4,545.8	-18,717.8	-14,171.9

Note: All values are in millions of 2002-2003 dollars except where indicated

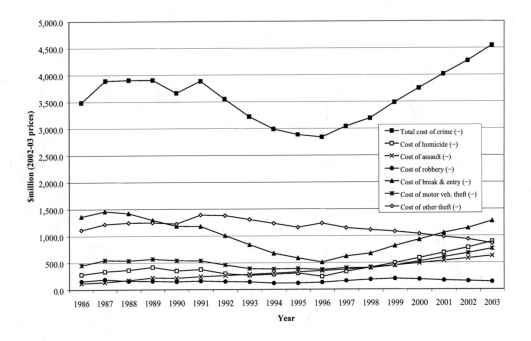

Figure 9.1. Cost of crime in Victoria, 1986-2003

To determine Victoria's share of the change in Australia's foreign debt, we assumed that it depended on two factors: (a) Victoria's share of consumption (CON) spending, and (b) Victoria's GSP as a percentage of Australia's GDP. We reasoned that the first factor was a proxy for import spending over export earnings and the second factor reflected Victoria's ability to service its debt. Hence, Victoria's share of the change in foreign debt was estimated by use of equation (9.2) below:

$$\text{Vic. share of } \Delta \text{ in o/s debt} =$$
$$\text{Aus. share of } \Delta \text{ in o/s debt} \times \frac{\text{Vic CON}}{\text{Aus CON}} \times \frac{\text{Vic CON/Vic GSP}}{\text{Aus CON/Aus GDP}} \qquad (9.2)$$

The values for the Rest-of-Australia was assumed to be the difference between the Australian and Victorian values (see also Table 9.18).

Data sources:

ABS, Catalogue No. 5204.0.
ABS, Catalogue No. 5220.0.
ABS, Catalogue No. 5302.0.

Table 9.16: Item s: Cost of family breakdown – Australia, 1986-2003

	AUSTRALIA							
	Number of divorces	Cost per divorce (1989-90 prices) (single $)	Cost per divorce (2002-03 prices) (single $)	Total cost of divorce ($)	Number of dysfunctional families	Cost per dysfunctional family (single $)	Total cost of family dysfunction ($)	Total cost of family b/down ($)
Year	a	b	c	(a x c) d	(a x 4) e	(c/2) f	(e x f) g	(d + g) h
1986	39,417	-	27,287	1,075.6	157,668	13,644	2,151.2	-3,226.7
1987	40,469	-	27,287	1,104.3	161,876	13,644	2,208.6	-3,312.9
1988	41,521	-	27,287	1,133.0	166,084	13,644	2,266.0	-3,399.0
1989	42,573	-	27,287	1,161.7	170,292	13,644	2,323.4	-3,485.1
1990	43,625	20,000	27,287	1,190.4	174,500	13,644	2,380.8	-3,571.2
1991	44,677	-	27,287	1,219.1	178,708	13,644	2,438.2	-3,657.3
1992	45,729	-	27,287	1,247.8	182,916	13,644	2,495.6	-3,743.5
1993	48,363	-	27,287	1,319.7	193,452	13,644	2,639.4	-3,959.1
1994	48,312	-	27,287	1,318.3	193,248	13,644	2,636.6	-3,954.9
1995	49,712	-	27,287	1,356.5	198,848	13,644	2,713.0	-4,069.5
1996	52,466	-	27,287	1,431.7	209,864	13,644	2,863.3	-4,295.0
1997	51,288	-	27,287	1,399.5	205,152	13,644	2,799.0	-4,198.5
1998	51,370	-	27,287	1,401.7	205,480	13,644	2,803.5	-4,205.2
1999	52,566	-	27,287	1,434.4	210,264	13,644	2,868.8	-4,303.1
2000	49,906	-	27,287	1,361.8	199,624	13,644	2,723.6	-4,085.4
2001	55,330	-	27,287	1,509.8	221,320	13,644	3,019.6	-4,529.4
2002	54,004	-	27,287	1,473.6	216,016	13,644	2,947.2	-4,420.9
2003	55,045	-	27,287	1,502.0	220,180	13,644	3,004.1	-4,506.1

Note: All values are in millions of 2002-2003 dollars except where indicated

Table 9.17: Item s: Cost of family breakdown – Victoria and Rest-of-Australia, 1986-2003

	VICTORIA								AUSTRALIA	REST-of-AUST
	Number of divorces	Cost per divorce (1989-90 prices) (single $)	Cost per divorce (2002-03 prices) (single $)	Total cost of divorce ($)	Number of dysfunctional families	Cost per dysfunctional family (single $)	Total cost of family dysfunction ($)	Total cost of family b/down ($)	Total cost of family b/down (Aus) ($) (Table 9.16)	Total cost of family b/down (ROA) ($)
Year	a	b	c	d (a x c)	e (a x 4)	f (c/2)	g (e x f)	h (d + g)	i	j (i - h)
1986	10,452	-	27,287	285.2	41,808	13,644	570.4	-855.6	-3,226.7	-2,371.1
1987	10,588	-	27,287	288.9	42,352	13,644	577.8	-866.8	-3,312.9	-2,446.1
1988	10,725	-	27,287	292.7	42,900	13,644	585.3	-878.0	-3,399.0	-2,521.0
1989	10,861	-	27,287	296.4	43,444	13,644	592.7	-889.1	-3,485.1	-2,596.0
1990	10,998	20,000	27,287	300.1	43,992	13,644	600.2	-900.3	-3,571.2	-2,670.9
1991	11,134	-	27,287	303.8	44,536	13,644	607.6	-911.4	-3,657.3	-2,745.9
1992	10,523	-	27,287	287.1	42,092	13,644	574.3	-861.4	-3,743.5	-2,882.0
1993	10,935	-	27,287	298.4	43,740	13,644	596.8	-895.2	-3,959.1	-3,063.9
1994	11,228	-	27,287	306.4	44,912	13,644	612.8	-919.1	-3,954.9	-3,035.8
1995	11,838	-	27,287	323.0	47,352	13,644	646.1	-969.1	-4,069.5	-3,100.4
1996	12,491	-	27,287	340.8	49,964	13,644	681.7	-1,022.5	-4,295.0	-3,272.4
1997	12,463	-	27,287	340.1	49,852	13,644	680.2	-1,020.2	-4,198.5	-3,178.3
1998	12,307	-	27,287	335.8	49,228	13,644	671.6	-1,007.5	-4,205.2	-3,197.8
1999	12,742	-	27,287	347.7	50,968	13,644	695.4	-1,043.1	-4,303.1	-3,260.1
2000	12,002	-	27,287	327.5	48,008	13,644	655.0	-982.5	-4,085.4	-3,102.9
2001	13,306	-	27,287	363.1	53,224	13,644	726.2	-1,089.3	-4,529.4	-3,440.2
2002	12,987	-	27,287	354.4	51,948	13,644	708.8	-1,063.1	-4,420.9	-3,357.7
2003	13,237	-	27,287	361.2	52,948	13,644	722.4	-1,083.6	-4,506.1	-3,422.5

Note: All values are in millions of 2002-2003 dollars except where indicated

Table 9.18: Item *t*: Change in overseas debt position – Australia, Victoria, and Rest-of-Australia, 1986-2003

	AUSTRALIA				VICTORIA								REST-of-AUST
	Nominal o/s debt position	Change in nominal o/s debt	Deflator	Real o/s debt position	Victorian CON	Australian CON	Ratio of Vic/Aus CON	Victorian GSP	Australian GDP	Ratio of GSP to GDP	Vic. share of o/s debt	Vic. share of o/s debt	ROA share of overseas debt
	($)	($)	(%)	($)	($)	($)	(ratio)	($)	($)	(ratio)	(%)	($)	($)
				$(b/c \times 100)$			(e/f)			(h/i)	$(g \times e/h \times i/f)$	$(d \times k)$	$(d-h)$
Year	a	b	c	d	e	f	g	h	i	j	k	l	m
1985	53,055												
1986	78,396	-25,341	58.09	-43,623.9	91,681.0	347,090.0	0.264	111,277.3	427,989.7	0.260	0.268	-11,706.5	-31,917.5
1987	87,971	-9,575	62.18	-15,398.0	93,310.0	352,549.0	0.265	113,913.9	438,130.5	0.260	0.269	-4,148.7	-11,249.4
1988	96,502	-8,531	67.25	-12,685.2	95,912.0	364,010.0	0.263	120,027.6	461,644.7	0.260	0.267	-3,387.2	-9,298.0
1989	113,989	-17,487	73.29	-23,858.6	99,913.0	378,490.0	0.264	124,854.1	480,208.1	0.260	0.268	-6,394.5	-17,464.1
1990	130,809	-16,820	77.29	-21,762.1	102,677.0	395,052.0	0.260	131,737.0	498,126.1	0.264	0.255	-5,558.7	-16,203.4
1991	143,153	-12,344	79.92	-15,445.1	101,989.0	400,592.0	0.255	128,882.9	497,644.9	0.259	0.250	-3,865.6	-11,579.5
1992	162,466	-19,313	81.48	-23,702.3	103,549.0	408,219.0	0.254	125,822.0	498,980.7	0.252	0.255	-6,048.2	-17,654.2
1993	177,453	-14,987	82.36	-18,197.2	104,551.0	415,385.0	0.252	131,224.1	517,252.8	0.254	0.250	-4,544.1	-13,653.1
1994	171,313	6,140	83.14	7,385.3	105,056.0	424,401.0	0.248	135,835.7	537,379.8	0.253	0.242	1,790.3	5,595.0
1995	190,790	-19,477	84.11	-23,155.7	109,851.0	442,345.0	0.248	140,606.5	560,111.9	0.251	0.246	-5,688.7	-17,467.0
1996	193,872	-3,082	86.16	-3,577.1	113,335.0	460,225.0	0.246	146,860.5	583,922.3	0.252	0.241	-862.5	-2,714.6
1997	208,628	-14,756	87.43	-16,878.1	116,417.0	472,111.0	0.247	151,056.9	605,823.2	0.249	0.244	-4,116.0	-12,762.1
1998	227,782	-19,154	88.69	-21,595.6	121,603.0	493,282.0	0.247	158,516.3	632,841.9	0.250	0.243	-5,239.4	-16,356.2
1999	230,689	-2,907	88.79	-3,274.0	127,435.0	515,843.0	0.247	169,699.3	666,438.3	0.255	0.240	-784.7	-2,489.3
2000	272,639	-41,950	90.55	-46,330.1	132,668.0	535,894.0	0.248	175,225.5	691,466.5	0.253	0.242	-11,205.0	-35,125.1
2001	302,573	-29,934	95.13	-31,467.5	136,277.0	549,805.0	0.248	180,391.3	705,600.7	0.256	0.240	-7,561.9	-23,905.6
2002	323,199	-20,626	97.47	-21,162.3	141,293.0	566,553.0	0.249	187,064.4	732,943.6	0.255	0.244	-5,157.1	-16,005.2
2003	357,190	-33,991	100.00	-33,991.0	146,482.0	589,067.0	0.249	191,875.1	753,298.4	0.255	0.243	-8,251.9	-25,739.1

Note: All values are in millions of 2002-2003 dollars except where indicated

9.2.15. Item u: Cost of Non-renewable Resource Depletion

As outlined in Chapters 6 and 7, the method we have employed to calculate the cost of non-renewable resource depletion is a variation on El Serafy's user cost approach that is expressed in equation (6.1) (El Serafy, 1989; Lawn, 1998). To identify the income (X) and capital ($R - X$) components of non-renewable resource depletion — the latter of which constitutes the true user cost — we used a discount rate of 2% on the assumption that it approximates the regeneration rate of most renewable resources. We also assumed that the average mine life of non-renewable resources is forty years. This means that a set-aside ratio of 44.4% is required on the part of the resource liquidator — in other words, for every dollar of net receipts received, approximately 56 cents constitutes genuine income while 44 cents is equal to the user cost of the resource.

We felt it was necessary to make two further adjustments to finally calculate the user cost of non-renewable resource depletion. The first was necessary because the setting aside of 44.4% of the net receipts from non-renewable resource depletion assumes that non-renewable resource prices will remain constant over time. This is unlikely. Indeed, we assumed that increased resource scarcity will probably lead to a doubling of non-renewable resource prices over a forty year period. This makes it necessary to set aside 88.8% of the net receipts from non-renewable resource depletion.

Second, we opted to treat resource receipts in the same manner as Daly and Cobb (1989). Daly and Cobb argue that the value of the net receipts from resource depletion understates the figure that ought to be used in the calculation of user costs. Their argument is based on the belief that non-renewable resource availability is not only a function of the relative and absolute scarcity of resources, but is also a function of the cost of exploration and extraction activities. Thus, according to Daly and Cobb, the cost of exploration and extraction should also be included in the calculation of user costs because they both constitute a great deal more than the "regrettable necessities" associated with the depletion of non-renewable resources.

In order to incorporate the cost of exploration and extraction activities in the user cost of non-renewable resources, it was assumed that the user cost equated to 88.8% of the *total dollar value* of all mining production (Table 9.19). Once again, the user cost for the Rest-of-Australia was assumed to be the Australian cost less the Victorian cost (Table 9.19).

Data sources:

ABS, Catalogue No. 1301.0 (various).
ABS, Catalogue No. 1301.2 (various).
ABS, Catalogue No. 4608.0.
ABS, Catalogue No. 8415.0 (various).

9.2.16. Item v: Cost of Lost Agricultural Land

The annual cost of land degradation in Australia between 1991 and 2001 has been estimated by the ABS (2003, Catalogue No. 4617.0). We adjusted the ABS values so they were measured in 2003-03 prices. For the period 1986-1990, we assumed the annual cost was the same as it was in 1991; while we assumed the yearly cost in 2002 and 2003 was the same as it was in 2001 (Table 9.20).

Since the cost of lost agricultural land was calculated on a cumulative basis to reflect the amount required to compensate citizens for the cumulative impact of land degradation over time, we were forced to make an estimation of the cumulative cost up to 1986. We assumed this to be $30 billion at 2002-03 prices. We made this assumption on the basis that a great deal of Australia's land degradation had already occurred prior to 1986.

The Victorian cost of land degradation was calculated by multiplying the cumulative Australian cost by Victoria's share of Australia's total area of agricultural land (Table 9.20).

The cost of land degradation for the Rest-of-Australia was assumed to be the difference between the Australian and Victorian cost (also Table 9.20).

Data sources:

ABS, Catalogue No. 1301.0 (various).
ABS, Catalogue No. 1301.2 (various).
ABS (2003), *Catalogue* No. 4617.0, pp. 170-171 (Figure 25.10).
ABS (2002), *Catalogue* No. 5206.0.
ABS, Catalogue No. 7113.0.

9.2.17. Item w: Cost of Excessive Irrigation Water Use

It has been computed that excessive irrigation occurs within the Murray-Darling Basin if diversions and extractions exceed 7,500 gigalitres per year (Hamilton et al., 1997). It has also been estimated that the value of water to irrigators in the Murray-Darling Basin was $56.40 per megalitre in 1988 (M-DBC, 1989). This equates to $83.86 per megalitre at 2002-03 prices. We assumed that this value remained steady over the study period.

We ascertained the environmental damage of excessive irrigation by subtracting 7,500 gigalitres from the total quantity of water diverted from the Murray-Darling Basin in each year. The excess quantity was then multiplied by the value of the water to determine the annual cost of excessive water use.

Because of the non-substitutable nature of water, the cost of excessive irrigation water use was calculated to reflect the fund that is required to compensate citizens for the cumulative impact of excessive irrigation water use over time. We assumed that the cumulative cost up to 1986 was already $10 billion at 2002-03 prices.

Since the water extracted from the Murray-Darling Basin is approximately 75% of all irrigation water used in Australia (Hamilton and Denniss, 2000), we increased the cost applicable to the Murray-Darling Basin by 33% to obtain the total Australian cost of excessive irrigation water use (Table 9.21).

We adopted the same approach to Victoria except: (a) we assumed that Victoria's share of the Australian cumulative cost up to 1986 was equal to the ratio of Victoria's cost in 1986 to that of Australia in the same year (34.26%); and (b) Victoria uses 10% of non-Murray-Darling Basin water. We based this final assumption on the fact that most of Victoria's irrigation water comes from the Murray-Darling Basin and, secondly, all other major irrigation regions in Australia lie outside of Victoria (Table 9.21).

Table 9.19: Item *u*: Cost of non-renewable resource depletion – Australia, Victoria, and Rest-of-Australia, 1986-2003

	AUSTRALIA			VICTORIA			REST-of-AUST
	Real value of non-ren. resource depletion ($)	User cost or "set aside" quotient	User cost of non-ren. resource depletion ($) (a x b)	Real value of non-ren. resource depletion ($)	User cost or "set aside" quotient	User cost of non-ren. resource depletion ($) (d x e)	User cost of non-ren. resource depletion ($) (c - f)
Year	a	b	c	d	e	f	g
1986	17,274	0.89	-15,339.4	3,399	0.89	-3,018.7	-12,320.8
1987	16,313	0.89	-14,486.6	3,210	0.89	-2,850.9	-11,635.8
1988	19,177	0.89	-17,029.5	3,774	0.89	-3,351.3	-13,678.3
1989	20,137	0.89	-17,882.3	3,963	0.89	-3,519.1	-14,363.2
1990	22,306	0.89	-19,808.4	4,243	0.89	-3,767.6	-16,040.8
1991	23,723	0.89	-21,066.7	4,898	0.89	-4,349.6	-16,717.1
1992	24,884	0.89	-22,097.1	4,912	0.89	-4,362.3	-17,734.8
1993	25,032	0.89	-22,229.2	5,001	0.89	-4,441.2	-17,788.0
1994	25,476	0.89	-22,622.8	4,842	0.89	-4,300.2	-18,322.6
1995	27,229	0.89	-24,179.9	4,408	0.89	-3,914.6	-20,265.3
1996	29,325	0.89	-26,041.3	4,157	0.89	-3,691.2	-22,350.1
1997	29,806	0.89	-26,468.6	3,813	0.89	-3,385.8	-23,082.8
1998	30,790	0.89	-27,342.4	3,668	0.89	-3,257.5	-24,084.9
1999	30,661	0.89	-27,227.6	2,638	0.89	-2,342.5	-24,885.1
2000	32,393	0.89	-28,765.5	3,618	0.89	-3,212.7	-25,552.8
2001	34,805	0.89	-30,907.5	3,348	0.89	-2,973.4	-27,934.2
2002	34,701	0.89	-30,815.5	2,839	0.89	-2,521.0	-28,294.5
2003	34,827	0.89	-30,926.7	2,878	0.89	-2,556.1	-28,370.6

Note: All values are in millions of 2002-2003 dollars except where indicated

Table 9.20: Item *v*: Cost of lost agricultural land - Australia, Victoria, and Rest-of-Australia, 1986-2003

Year	AUSTRALIA Area of agricultural land used (mill. of ha)	Annual cost of lost agric. land at 1996-97 prices ($)	Cumul. cost of lost agric. land at 1996-97 prices ($)	Cumul. cost of lost agric. land at 2002-03 prices ($)	VICTORIA Area of agricultural land used (mill. of ha)	Percentage of Aust. agric land	Annual cost of lost agric. land at 2002-03 prices ($)	Cumul. cost of lost agric. land at 2002-03 prices ($)	REST-of-AUST Cumul. cost of lost agric. land at 2002-03 prices ($)
	a	*b*	*c* $(b + c)$	*d*	*e*	*f* (e/a)	*g* $(f \times (d1 - d0))$	*h* $(h + g)$	*l* $(d - h)$
Up to 1986	488.0	-	-30,000.0	-34,314.4	14.2	0.0291	-	-998.5	-
1986	468.3	-269.0	-30,269.0	-34,622.1	13.2	0.0282	-8.7	-1,007.2	-33,614.9
1987	471.0	-274.0	-30,543.0	-34,935.5	13.1	0.0278	-8.7	-1,015.9	-33,919.6
1988	472.0	-279.0	-30,822.0	-35,254.6	13.1	0.0278	-8.9	-1,024.7	-34,229.9
1989	466.9	-284.0	-31,106.0	-35,579.4	13.1	0.0281	-9.1	-1,033.9	-34,545.6
1990	464.3	-289.0	-31,395.0	-35,910.0	13.1	0.0282	-9.3	-1,043.2	-34,866.8
1991	462.8	-294.0	-31,689.0	-36,246.3	12.7	0.0274	-9.2	-1,052.4	-35,193.9
1992	466.0	-299.0	-31,988.0	-36,588.3	12.4	0.0266	-9.1	-1,061.5	-35,526.8
1993	460.1	-303.0	-32,291.0	-36,934.9	12.3	0.0267	-9.3	-1,070.8	-35,864.1
1994	469.1	-305.0	-32,596.0	-37,283.7	13.0	0.0277	-9.7	-1,080.4	-36,203.3
1995	463.3	-309.0	-32,905.0	-37,637.2	12.7	0.0274	-9.7	-1,090.1	-36,547.0
1996	465.2	-314.0	-33,219.0	-37,996.3	12.8	0.0275	-9.9	-1,100.0	-36,896.3
1997	462.2	-319.0	-33,538.0	-38,361.2	12.7	0.0275	-10.0	-1,110.0	-37,251.2
1998	463.8	-322.0	-33,860.0	-38,729.5	12.7	0.0274	-10.1	-1,120.1	-37,609.4
1999	453.7	-321.0	-34,181.0	-39,096.7	12.8	0.0282	-10.4	-1,130.5	-37,966.2
2000	455.5	-326.0	-34,507.0	-39,469.5	13.3	0.0292	-10.9	-1,141.4	-38,328.2
2001	455.7	-339.0	-34,846.0	-39,857.3	13.2	0.0290	-11.2	-1,152.6	-38,704.7
2002	447.0	-352.0	-35,198.0	-40,259.9	12.8	0.0286	-11.5	-1,164.1	-39,095.8
2003	455.1	-365.0	-35,563.0	-40,677.4	13.0	0.0285	-11.9	-1,176.0	-39,501.4

Note: All values are in millions of 2002-2003 dollars except where indicated

Table 9.21: Item *w*: Cost of irrigation water use – Victoria, Australia, and Rest-of-Australia, 1986-2003

	AUSTRALIA						
	Total diversions from M-DB (GL)	$/ML in 1988 at 1988 prices ($)	$/ML at 2003 prices ($)	Env-damaging water div. from M-DB (000s ha)	Annual cost of excessive water use ($)	Cumul. cost of excessive water use ($)	Total cost of irrigation water use ($)
Year	a	b	c	$(a - 7,500GL)$ d	$(c \times d/1,000)$ e	$(e - f)$ f	$(f \times 1.33)$ g
Up to 1986						-10,000.0	
1986	10,800	-	83.86	3,300	276.8	-10,276.8	-13,702.3
1987	10,200	-	83.86	2,700	226.4	-10,503.2	-14,004.2
1988	12,000	56.40	83.86	4,500	377.4	-10,880.6	-14,507.4
1989	10,000	-	83.86	2,500	209.7	-11,090.2	-14,787.0
1990	10,800	-	83.86	3,300	276.8	-11,367.0	-15,156.0
1991	12,000	-	83.86	4,500	377.4	-11,744.4	-15,659.2
1992	12,200	-	83.86	4,700	394.2	-12,138.5	-16,184.7
1993	9,200	-	83.86	1,700	142.6	-12,281.1	-16,374.8
1994	10,500	-	83.86	3,000	251.6	-12,532.7	-16,710.3
1995	12,131	-	83.86	4,631	388.4	-12,921.1	-17,228.1
1996	11,785	-	83.86	4,285	359.4	-13,280.4	-17,707.3
1997	12,298	-	83.86	4,798	402.4	-13,682.8	-18,243.8
1998	11,924	-	83.86	4,424	371.0	-14,053.8	-18,738.4
1999	11,381	-	83.86	3,881	325.5	-14,379.3	-19,172.4
2000	9,542	-	83.86	2,042	171.3	-14,550.6	-19,400.8
2001	12,023	-	83.86	4,523	379.3	-14,929.9	-19,906.5
2002	11,567	-	83.86	4,067	341.1	-15,271.0	-20,361.3
2003	11,266	-	83.86	3,766	315.8	-15,586.8	-20,782.4

Note: All values are in millions of 2002-2003 dollars except where indicated

Table 9.21 (Continued): Item *w*: Cost of irrigation water use – Victoria, Australia, and Rest-of-Australia, 1986-2003

	VICTORIA			Total cost of irrigation water use ($)	REST-of-AUST Total cost of irrigation water use ($)
	Total diversions from M-DB (GL)	Annual cost of excessive water use ($)	Cumul. cost of excessive water use ($)		
Year	*h*	(*h/a* x *e*) *i*	(*i - j*) *j*	(*j* + (0.1 x (*g - f*)) *k*	(*g - k*) *l*
Up to 1986			-3,425.9		
1986	3,700	94.8	-3,520.7	-3,863.3	-9,839.0
1987	3,500	77.7	-3,598.4	-3,948.5	-10,055.7
1988	4,100	128.9	-3,727.4	-4,090.1	-10,417.4
1989	3,200	67.1	-3,794.5	-4,164.1	-10,622.8
1990	3,900	99.9	-3,894.4	-4,273.3	-10,882.7
1991	4,200	132.1	-4,026.5	-4,418.0	-11,241.2
1992	4,100	132.5	-4,159.0	-4,563.6	-11,621.1
1993	2,800	43.4	-4,202.3	-4,611.7	-11,763.1
1994	3,700	88.7	-4,291.0	-4,708.8	-12,001.5
1995	4,823	154.4	-4,445.4	-4,876.1	-12,352.0
1996	4,130	125.9	-4,571.4	-5,014.0	-12,693.2
1997	4,106	134.3	-4,705.7	-5,161.8	-13,082.0
1998	3,930	122.3	-4,828.0	-5,296.4	-13,442.0
1999	3,370	96.4	-4,924.4	-5,403.7	-13,768.8
2000	3,317	59.5	-4,983.9	-5,468.9	-13,931.8
2001	3,491	110.1	-5,094.0	-5,591.7	-14,314.8
2002	3,834	113.1	-5,207.1	-5,716.1	-14,645.2
2003	3,567	100.0	-5,307.1	-5,826.6	-14,955.8

Note: All values are in millions of 2002-2003 dollars except where indicated

The cost of excessive irrigation water use for the Rest-of-Australia was assumed to be the difference between the Australian cost and the Victorian cost (also Table 9.21).

Sources:

Hamilton, C. and Denniss, R. (2000), *Tracking Well-being in Australia: The Genuine Progress Indicator 2000*, Australia Institute Discussion Paper, Number 35, December 2000.

Murray-Darling Basin Commission (M-DBC) (1989), *Basis for Economic Analysis Using the Murray-Darling Basin Commission's Computer Models*, M-DBC Technical Report, 89/6.

Murray-Darling Basin Commission (M-DBC) (various), *Water Audit Monitoring Report*, M-DBC.

9.2.18. Item x: Cost of Timber Depletion

Unlike a non-renewable resource, the exploitation of timber resources results in a 'user cost' only if there is a decline in stocks — that is, if the rate at which timber stocks are harvested (h) exceeds its natural regeneration rate (y). Should this occur, the proceeds from the portion of all extracted timber that exceeds the sustainable harvest rate must be treated the same way as the proceeds from non-renewable resources. Since this requires the El Serafy (1989) user cost formula to be applied (equation 7.1), a discount rate must again be chosen as well as the approximate life of an unsustainably harvested forest/plantation.

As in the case of non-renewable resource depletion, we chose a 2% discount rate to reflect the regeneration rate of the timber stocks that would need to be cultivated to keep timber stocks intact. Second, we assumed that, on average, a forest or timber plantation that was continuously harvested at an unsustainable rate would be depleted in fifty years. Finally, it was assumed that the market prices of timber resources ought to double if they are harvested unsustainably. Based on these assumptions, the set-aside rate or the user cost of timber resource depletion — should it occur — equals 72.9% of net receipts. In addition, it was decided that, in a similar manner to non-renewable resources, the cost of timber extraction activities should not be excluded when calculating the user cost of timber resources. The user cost was therefore calculated by multiplying the *total production value* in the years where timber stocks declined by 0.729.

Of course, one of the major differences between renewable and non-renewable resources is that the stocks of the former can be augmented. In the years where this occurred, the value of the expansion must be counted as a positive figure (i.e., as a benefit). The reason for this is as follows. The annual benefit of any increase in the source function of renewable natural capital is equal to the value of the maximum amount of timber that can be sustainably harvested from the increased portion of the stock. Thus, the annual benefit (B) equals the value of the increase in the stock of timber resources (ΔS) multiplied by the annual regeneration rate (y). This is given by the following:

$$B = \Delta S \times y \tag{9.3}$$

If timber resources are being harvested sustainably (i.e., $h \leq y$), the benefits from increasing the stock of timber can be enjoyed indefinitely. Consequently, the net present value (NPV) of an infinite series of benefits is equal to the benefits enjoyed each year divided by the discount rate (r). That is:

$$\text{Net present value (NPV) of benefits} = \frac{B}{r} \tag{9.4}$$

$$= \frac{\Delta S \times y}{r} \tag{9.5}$$

If, in order to satisfy the strong sustainability condition, the discount rate is assumed to equal to the regeneration rate of timber stocks (i.e., $y = r$), the NPV of the benefits equals the value of the increased stock of timber. In other words:

$$\text{Net present value (NPV) of benefits} = \Delta S \tag{9.6}$$

To go the next step and calculate the user cost or otherwise of timber resources, we classified all timber stocks into the following categories: (a) native forest timber; (b) hardwood timber; and (c) softwood timber (broadleaved and coniferous). The respective monetary values of each category of timber in 2002-03 prices were derived from the national balance sheet estimates produced by the ABS. We assumed that the value of each category of timber was the same across Australia. They were:

- native forest timber: \$81.19 per hectare;
- hardwood timber: \$2,656.89 per hectare;
- softwood timber: \$4,157.66 per hectare.

The values for the cost of timber depletion (or benefit of timber augmentation) are revealed in Tables 9.22 (Australia) and 9.23 (Victoria and Rest-of-Australia).

Sources:

Australian Bureau of Agricultural and Resource Economics (ABARE) (various), *Australian Forest and Wood Product Statistics*, AGPS, Canberra.

ABS, Catalogue No. 1301.0 (various) and 1301.2 (various).

ABS, Catalogue No. 5241.0.

ABS, Catalogue No. 5241.0.40.001.

Bureau of Resource Sciences (1998), *Australia's State of the Forests Report: 1998*, AGPS, Canberra.

Bureau of Resource Sciences (2003), *Australia's State of the Forests Report: 2003*, AGPS, Canberra.

Table 9.22: Item *x*: Cost of timber depletion – Australia, 1986-2003

	AUSTRALIA							Hardwood			
	Native										
	Old and new definition of timber (000s ha)	Adjustment of old to new definition (000s ha)	Area of native timber (000s ha)	Change in native timber (000s ha)	Value per hectare ($)	Value of change in stocks ($)	User cost of native timber depletion ($)	Area of h/wood timber (000s ha)	Change in h/wood timber (000s ha)	Value per hectare ($)	Value of change in stocks ($)
						(*d* x *e*)					(*i* x *j*)
Year	*a*	*b*	*c*	*d*	*e*	*f*	*g*	*h*	*i*	*j*	*k*
1986	41,282	153,680	153,680	-845	17.10	-14.45	-10.53	40	6	2,926.89	17.56
1987	41,055	152,835	152,835	-845	17.10	-14.45	-10.53	46	6	2,926.89	17.56
1988	40,828	151,990	151,990	-845	17.10	-14.45	-10.53	52	6	2,926.89	17.56
1989	40,971	152,522	152,522	532	17.10	9.10	9.10	60	8	2,926.89	23.42
1990	40,819	151,956	151,956	-566	17.10	-9.68	-7.05	96	36	2,926.89	105.37
1991	40,818	151,953	151,953	-4	17.10	-0.06	-0.05	106	10	2,926.89	29.27
1992	41,057	152,842	152,842	890	17.10	15.21	15.21	116	10	2,926.89	29.27
1993	40,719	151,584	151,584	-1,258	17.10	-21.52	-15.67	154	38	2,926.89	111.22
1994	40,719	151,584	151,584	0	17.10	0.00	0.00	155	1	2,926.89	2.93
1995	40,709	151,547	151,547	-37	17.10	-0.64	-0.46	156	1	2,926.89	2.93
1996	127,056	153,691	153,691	2,144	17.10	36.66	36.66	157	1	2,926.89	2.93
1997	155,835	-	155,835	2,144	17.10	36.66	36.66	158	1	2,926.89	2.93
1998	157,979	-	157,979	2,144	17.10	36.66	36.66	266	108	2,926.89	314.64
1999	160,123	-	160,123	2,144	17.10	36.66	36.66	373	108	2,926.89	314.64
2000	162,267	-	162,267	2,144	17.10	36.66	36.66	481	108	2,926.89	314.64
2001	164,411	-	164,411	2,144	17.10	36.66	36.66	588	108	2,926.89	314.64
2002	162,680	-	162,680	-1,731	17.10	-29.60	-21.56	638	50	2,926.89	146.34
2003	164,824	-	164,824	2,144	17.10	36.66	36.66	746	108	2,926.89	314.64

Note: All values are in millions of 2002-2003 dollars except where indicated

Table 9.22 (Continued): Item x: Cost of timber depletion – Australia, 1986-2003

	AUSTRALIA					All timber
	Softwood					
Year	Area of s/wood timber (000s ha)	Change in s/wood timber (000s ha)	Value per hectare ($)	Value of change in stocks ($) (m x n)	User cost of s/wood timber depletion ($)	User cost of all timber depletion ($) (g + k + p)
	l	m	n	o	p	q
1986	832	29	4,640.16	134.56	134.56	**141.6**
1987	861	29	4,640.16	132.24	132.24	**139.3**
1988	889	29	4,640.16	132.24	132.24	**139.3**
1989	913	24	4,640.16	111.36	111.36	**143.9**
1990	943	30	4,640.16	139.20	139.20	**237.5**
1991	939	-4	4,640.16	-18.56	-13.52	**15.7**
1992	956	17	4,640.16	78.88	78.88	**123.4**
1993	963	7	4,640.16	32.48	32.48	**128.0**
1994	943	-20	4,640.16	-92.80	-67.61	**-64.7**
1995	923	-20	4,640.16	-92.80	-67.61	**-65.1**
1996	903	-20	4,640.16	-92.80	-67.61	**-28.0**
1997	883	-20	4,640.16	-92.80	-67.61	**-28.0**
1998	907	24	4,640.16	112.52	112.52	**463.8**
1999	932	24	4,640.16	112.52	112.52	**463.8**
2000	956	24	4,640.16	112.52	112.52	**463.8**
2001	980	24	4,640.16	112.52	112.52	**463.8**
2002	988	8	4,640.16	37.12	37.12	**161.9**
2003	1,012	24	4,640.16	112.52	112.52	**463.8**

Note: All values are in millions of 2002-2003 dollars except where indicated

Table 9.23: Item x: Cost of timber depletion – Victoria and Rest-of-Australia, 1986-2003

	VICTORIA					Hardwood				
	Native									
	Area of native timber	Change in native timber	Value per hectare	Value of change in stocks	User cost of native timber depletion	Area of h/wood timber	Change in h/wood timber	Value per hectare	Value of change in stocks	User cost of h/wood timber depletion
	(000s ha)	(000s ha)	($)	($)	($)	(000s ha)	(000s ha)	($)	($)	($)
				(b x c)					(g x h)	
Year	a	b	c	d	e	f	g	h	i	j
1986	6,180	-13	81.19	-1.06	-0.77	14	0	2,656.89	0.00	0.00
1987	6,167	-13	81.19	-1.06	-0.77	14	0	2,656.89	0.00	0.00
1988	6,155	-12	81.19	-0.97	-0.71	14	0	2,656.89	0.00	0.00
1989	6,322	167	81.19	13.56	13.56	15	1	2,656.89	2.66	2.66
1990	6,285	-37	81.19	-3.00	-2.19	17	2	2,656.89	5.31	5.31
1991	6,285	0	81.19	0.00	0.00	18	1	2,656.89	2.66	2.66
1992	6,355	70	81.19	5.68	5.68	20	2	2,656.89	5.31	5.31
1993	6,361	6	81.19	0.49	0.49	18	-2	2,656.89	-5.31	-3.87
1994	6,361	0	81.19	0.00	0.00	18	0	2,656.89	0.66	0.66
1995	6,359	-2	81.19	-0.16	-0.12	19	0	2,656.89	0.66	0.66
1996	6,822	463	81.19	37.59	37.59	19	0	2,656.89	0.66	0.66
1997	7,285	463	81.19	37.59	37.59	19	0	2,656.89	0.66	0.66
1998	7,393	108	81.19	8.77	8.77	47	28	2,656.89	73.06	73.06
1999	7,501	108	81.19	8.77	8.77	74	28	2,656.89	73.06	73.06
2000	7,608	107	81.19	8.69	8.69	102	28	2,656.89	73.06	73.06
2001	7,716	108	81.19	8.77	8.77	129	28	2,656.89	73.06	73.06
2002	7,935	219	81.19	17.78	17.78	143	14	2,656.89	37.20	37.20
2003	8,043	108	81.19	8.77	8.77	171	28	2,656.89	73.06	73.06

Note: All values are in millions of 2002-2003 dollars except where indicated

Table 9.23 (Continued): Item x: Cost of timber depletion - Victoria and Rest-of-Australia, 1986-2003

	VICTORIA Softwood					All timber	AUSTRALIA All timber	REST-of-AUST All timber
	Area of s/wood timber (000s ha)	Change in s/wood timber (000s ha)	Value per hectare ($)	Value of change in stocks ($)	User cost of s/wood timber depletion ($)	User cost of all timber depletion ($)	User cost of all timber depletion ($)	User cost of all timber depletion ($)
Year	k	l	m	n (l x m)	o	p (e + j + o)	q (Table 9.22)	r (q − p)
1986	190	7	4,157.66	29.10	29.10	28.3	141.6	113.3
1987	197	7	4,157.66	27.02	27.02	26.3	139.3	113.0
1988	203	7	4,157.66	27.02	27.02	26.3	139.3	113.0
1989	207	4	4,157.66	16.63	16.63	32.8	143.9	111.0
1990	209	2	4,157.66	8.32	8.32	11.4	237.5	226.1
1991	210	1	4,157.66	4.16	4.16	6.8	15.7	8.9
1992	216	6	4,157.66	24.95	24.95	35.9	123.4	87.4
1993	216	0	4,157.66	0.00	0.00	-3.4	128.0	131.4
1994	211	-5	4,157.66	-20.79	-15.14	-14.5	-64.7	-50.2
1995	206	-5	4,157.66	-20.79	-15.14	-14.6	-65.1	-50.5
1996	201	-5	4,157.66	-20.79	-15.14	23.1	-28.0	-51.1
1997	196	-5	4,157.66	-20.79	-15.14	23.1	-28.0	-51.1
1998	201	5	4,157.66	20.79	20.79	102.6	463.8	361.2
1999	206	5	4,157.66	20.79	20.79	102.6	463.8	361.2
2000	211	5	4,157.66	20.79	20.79	102.5	463.8	361.3
2001	216	5	4,157.66	20.79	20.79	102.6	463.8	361.2
2002	217	1	4,157.66	4.16	4.16	59.1	161.9	102.8
2003	222	5	4,157.66	20.79	20.79	102.6	463.8	361.2

Note: All values are in millions of 2002-2003 dollars except where indicated

9.2.19. Item y: Cost of Air Pollution

There has, unfortunately, been very little previous work conducted on the cost of air pollution in Australia. Even data on air pollution emissions is limited in both specificity and scope. Hence, to estimate the total cost of air pollution in Australia, we constructed an air pollution index on the basis that: (a) air pollution is very much a function of production and therefore closely related to the rate of increase in GDP (or GSP in the case of a state or province); and (b) air pollution abatement technology constantly reduces the impact of a per unit of production on air quality.

To construct air pollution indexes for Australia and Victoria, we set the value of real GDP (Australia) and real GSP (Victoria) at 100.0 for the year 1992. We did this because 1992 was the year of our point estimate of the cost of pollution. We then assumed that air pollution abatement technology improved at the rate of 1% per annum (equivalent to halving the impact of real GDP on air quality every seventy years). We then calculated the respective air pollution indexes by adjusting the real GDP and real GSP indexes upwards by 1% per annum in the years prior to 1992, and downwards by the same percentage in the years following 1992. This was achieved by multiplying the real GDP/GSP indexes by the air pollution technology index.

In 1992, the ABS estimated air pollution control costs — in other words, the amount Australians spent defending themselves against air pollution — at $652.6 million in 1992 at 2002-03 prices. Based on estimates of the ratio of air pollution control to damage costs by Zolotas (1981), the air pollution damage cost was assumed to be ten times the control cost. As a consequence, we conservatively estimated the total cost of air pollution in Australia at $6.53 billion in 1992 at 2002-03 prices. To calculate the Australian cost of air pollution in other years, the 1992 value of $6.53 billion was weighted by the Australian air pollution index (Table 9.24).

As for the cost of air pollution in Victoria, we assumed that, in 1992, Victoria's share of the Australian $6.53 billion cost was equal to the ratio of Victoria's GSP to Australia's GDP. We then weighted the 1992 Victorian point estimate by Victoria's air pollution index (Table 9.24).

The cost of air pollution for the Rest-of-Australia was assumed to be the cost to Australia less the cost to Victoria (also Table 9.24).

Sources:

ABS, Catalogue No. 4603.0
ABS, Catalogue No. 5204.0
ABS, Catalogue No. 5220.0

9.2.20. Item z: Cost of urban waste-water pollution

To calculate the cost of urban waste-water pollution in Australia, we made use of a Department of Environment, Sport, and Tourism (DEST) cost estimate of $3.58 billion in 1994 at 1989-90 prices. This equated to $4.31 billion at 2002-03 prices.

Table 9.24: Item *y*: Cost of air pollution - Australia, Victoria, and Rest-of-Australia, 1986-2003

	AUSTRALIA					VICTORIA				REST-of-AUST
Year	Australian real GDP ($)	Real GDP index (1992 = 100.0)	Air pollution technology (1992 = 1.00)	Air pollution index Australia (1992 = 100.0)	Cost of air pollution ($)	Victorian real GSP ($)	Real GSP index (1992 = 100.0)	Air pollution index Victoria (1992 = 100.0)	Cost of air pollution ($)	Cost of air pollution ($)
	a	*b*	*c*	*d* (*b* x *c*)	*e* (*d* x -$6,526)	*f*	*g*	*h*	*i* (*h* x -$6,526)	*j* (*e* - *i*)
1986	427,989.7	85.8	1.062	91.0	-5,941.9	111,277	88.4	93.9	-1,544.9	-4,397.0
1987	438,130.5	87.8	1.051	92.3	-6,022.5	113,914	90.5	95.2	-1,565.8	-4,456.6
1988	461,644.7	92.5	1.041	96.3	-6,282.8	120,028	95.4	99.3	-1,633.5	-4,649.3
1989	480,208.1	96.2	1.030	99.2	-6,470.8	124,854	99.2	102.2	-1,682.4	-4,788.4
1990	498,126.1	99.8	1.020	101.8	-6,645.8	131,737	104.7	106.8	-1,757.6	-4,888.2
1991	497,644.9	99.7	1.010	100.7	-6,573.6	128,883	102.4	103.5	-1,702.5	-4,871.1
1992	498,980.7	100.0	1.000	100.0	-6,526.0	125,822	100.0	100.0	-1,645.6	-4,880.4
1993	517,252.8	103.7	0.990	102.6	-6,698.0	131,224	104.3	103.3	-1,699.2	-4,998.8
1994	537,379.8	107.7	0.980	105.6	-6,889.7	135,836	108.0	105.8	-1,741.5	-5,148.2
1995	560,111.9	112.3	0.971	108.9	-7,110.1	140,607	111.8	108.5	-1,784.9	-5,325.2
1996	583,922.3	117.0	0.961	112.5	-7,338.9	146,861	116.7	112.2	-1,845.8	-5,493.1
1997	605,823.2	121.4	0.951	115.5	-7,538.8	151,057	120.1	114.2	-1,879.7	-5,659.1
1998	632,841.9	126.8	0.942	119.5	-7,797.0	158,516	126.0	118.7	-1,953.0	-5,844.0
1999	666,438.3	133.6	0.933	124.6	-8,129.7	169,699	134.9	125.8	-2,070.1	-6,059.6
2000	691,466.5	138.6	0.923	128.0	-8,351.5	175,226	139.3	128.6	-2,116.4	-6,235.1
2001	705,600.7	141.4	0.914	129.3	-8,437.8	180,391	143.4	131.1	-2,157.2	-6,280.6
2002	732,943.6	146.9	0.905	133.0	-8,678.0	187,064	148.7	134.6	-2,214.8	-6,463.2
2003	753,298.4	151.0	0.896	135.3	-8,830.7	191,875	152.5	136.7	-2,249.3	-6,581.4

Note: All values are in millions of 2002-2003 dollars except where indicated

Table 9.25: Item z: Cost of urban waste-water pollution – Victoria, Australia, and Rest-of-Australia, 1986–2003

	AUSTRALIA					VICTORIA		REST-of-AUST
	Cost of urban w/water poll. in 1994 at 1989-90 prices ($)	Cost of urban w/water poll. in 1994 at 2002-03 prices ($)	Population of major Aust urban centres (000s)	Cost of urban w/water poll. per urban Australian (single $)	Total cost of urban waste-water pollution ($)	Population of major Vic urban centres (000s)	Total cost of urban waste-water pollution ($)	Total cost of urban waste-water pollution ($)
Year	a	b	d	d	e ($)\n(c x d)	f	g ($)\n(d x f)	h ($)\n(e - g)
1986	-	-	13,031.1	321.27	-4,186.5	3,433.5	-1,103.1	-3,083.4
1987	-	-	13,160.5	318.09	-4,186.2	3,446.4	-1,096.3	-3,089.9
1988	-	-	13,391.2	314.94	-4,217.4	3,488.7	-1,098.7	-3,118.7
1989	-	-	13,625.5	311.82	-4,248.8	3,534.4	-1,102.1	-3,146.6
1990	-	-	13,825.1	308.74	-4,268.3	3,580.2	-1,105.3	-3,163.0
1991	-	-	14,021.5	305.68	-4,286.1	3,617.4	-1,105.8	-3,180.3
1992	-	-	14,201.2	302.65	-4,298.0	3,645.2	-1,103.2	-3,194.8
1993	-	-	14,352.5	299.66	-4,300.8	3,660.2	-1,096.8	-3,204.0
1994	3,580	4,306.1	14,513.8	296.69	-4,306.1	3,675.1	-1,090.4	-3,215.7
1995	-	-	14,716.0	293.75	-4,322.9	3,705.6	-1,088.5	-3,234.3
1996	-	-	14,929.8	290.84	-4,342.2	3,746.6	-1,089.7	-3,252.6
1997	-	-	15,101.5	287.96	-4,348.7	3,776.6	-1,087.5	-3,261.2
1998	-	-	15,268.9	285.11	-4,353.4	3,813.0	-1,087.1	-3,266.2
1999	-	-	15,457.6	282.29	-4,363.5	3,855.6	-1,088.4	-3,275.1
2000	-	-	15,657.8	279.49	-4,376.3	3,904.4	-1,091.3	-3,285.0
2001	-	-	15,777.3	276.73	-4,366.0	3,959.5	-1,095.7	-3,270.3
2002	-	-	16,088.7	273.99	-4,408.1	4,005.8	-1,097.5	-3,310.6
2003	-	-	16,299.5	271.27	-4,421.6	4,057.7	-1,100.7	-3,320.9

Note: All values are in millions of 2002-2003 dollars except where indicated

We subsequently ascertained the waste-water pollution cost by dividing the total cost in 1994 by the Australian population in that year. This provided us with a cost value of $241.17 per Australian in 1994. We then assumed that pollution abatement technology had advanced over the study period and had thus reduced the cost per Australian at the rate of 1% per annum. Hence, we adjusted the waste-water cost per Australian upwards by 1% per annum in the years prior to 1994, and downwards by the same percentage in the years following 1994.

To calculate the total cost of urban waste-water pollution over the study period, we multiplied the cost per Australian in each year by the change in Australia's population numbers (Table 9.25). We did likewise for Victoria by assuming that the cost per Victorian was the same as the cost per Australian (also Table 9.25). The cost of urban waste-water pollution for the Rest-of-Australia was determined by subtracting the Victorian cost from the Australian cost (also Table 9.25).

Sources:

Department of Environment, Sport, and Tourism (DEST) (1996), *Subsidies to the Use of Natural Resources*, Environmental Economics Research Paper No. 2, AGPS, Canberra.
ABS, Catalogue No. 3101.0.
ABS, Catalogue No. 3105.0.65.001

9.2.21. Item aa: Cost of Long-term Environmental Damage

Over time, humankind has extracted resources, disrupted ecological systems, and generated highly durable and toxic wastes. However, much of the cost of previous actions has yet to fully materialise. Hence, the long-term cost will be inevitably borne by future generations. To gain an approximate measure of the cost of long-term environmental damage, we adopted the method used by Daly and Cobb (1989). Daly and Cobb assumed that the long-term damage of ecological disruption is directly proportional to the consumption of energy resources.

To ascertain the cost of long-term environmental damage, the annual consumption of energy for Australia and Victoria (total energy consumption) was converted to a crude oil barrel equivalent and then multiplied by $2.50 per barrel (2002-03 prices). As with the cost of lost agricultural land, the eventual cost represents the amount that needs to be accumulated to compensate future generations for the long-term impact of environmental damage.

Since the long-term environmental damage of human activity is a cumulative process, two additional steps were required. First, it was necessary to add the annual environmental impact cost to the cost previously incurred in order to compile a cumulative running total. Second, it was necessary to make an assumption regarding the quantity of energy consumed up to 1985. We conservatively estimated this to be the equivalent of 16 billion barrels of crude oil. This equated to a cumulative cost of $40 billion up to 1985 (Table 9.26). This assumption compares favourably with the estimated per capita consumption of energy in the USA by Daly and Cobb (1989).

To calculate the cost of long-term environmental cost for Victoria, we applied the same method for the years 1993 to 2003. However, energy consumption data for Victoria does not exist prior to 1993. To estimate Victoria's share of Australia's energy consumption between

1986 and 1992, we firstly calculated the average ratio of Victoria's energy consumption to that of Australia between 1993 and 2003. We then calculated the average ratio of Victoria's GSP to Australia's GDP for the same period. Having done that, we divided the first ratio by the second ratio to obtain a value to represent the energy efficiency advantage/disadvantage of Victoria. As it turned out, the value we obtained was 1.054. This indicates that Victoria did not use its energy resources as efficiently as the Rest-of-Australia between 1993 and 2003 (i.e., a value of 1.00 would indicate a neutral position). We assumed that this average value of 1.054 was maintained through the period 1986 to 1992.

Finally, to estimate the annual energy consumption of Victoria between 1986 and 1992, we used the following equation:

$$\text{Vic energy consumption} = 1.054 \times \frac{\text{Aus energy consump.} \times \text{Vic GSP}}{\text{Aus GDP}} \qquad (9.7)$$

The cost of long-term environmental damage for the Rest-of-Australia was calculated by subtracting Victoria's cost from that of Australia (Table 9.26).

Sources:

ABS, Catalogue No. 4604.0, 5204.0, and 5220.0.
Daly, H. and Cobb, J. (1989), *For the Common Good: Redirecting the Economy Toward Community, the Environment, and a Sustainable Future,* Beacon Press, Boston.

9.2.22. Item bb: Cost of Lost Natural Capital Services (LNCS)

The annual values for the cost of lost natural capital services (LNCS) were calculated by summing all the environmental costs — that is, Items *u, v, w, x, y, z,* and *aa.*

9.2.23. Item cc: Ecosystem Health Index (EHI)

The life-support function of natural capital and, thus, its overall state of health, is very much a function of the biodiversity found within it. While the environmental items so far calculated capture the loss of the natural environment's source and sink services, they do not capture the impact of the loss of biodiversity on the environment's life-support function. In our attempt to calculate an Ecosystem Health Index (EHI) for Australia, Victoria, and the Rest-of-Australia, we discovered that no inventory of biodiversity levels exists for the years 1986-2003.

To overcome this deficiency, we constructed an EHI on the basis that remnant vegetation loss constitutes the greatest threat to biodiversity (Biodiversity Unit, 1995). Since vegetation thinning also has an effect on biodiversity, it was assumed that the rate of vegetation thinning was the same as that of wholesale clearance. It was also assumed that 500 million hectares of remnant vegetation existed in Australia in 1985 (based on Graetz et al., 1995). The Australian EHI was finally constructed by assigning a base index value of 100.0 for 1986 and adjusting the initial index value in accordance with the annual changes in the area of relatively undisturbed land (Table 9.27).

As for Victoria, we assumed that Victoria's share of Australia's remnant vegetation in 1985 was equivalent to Victoria's share of the total Australian land mass. The EHI of the Rest-of-Australia was calculated by subtracting the various parameters of Victoria (i.e., initial remnant vegetation and annual clearing and thinning rates) from those of Australia (Table 9.28).

Sources:

ABS (2002), *Catalogue* No. 1370.0.
ABS (2003), *Catalogue* No. 4613.0.
ABS (2003), *Catalogue* No. 4617.0.
Biodiversity Unit (1995), *Native Vegetation Clearance, Habitat Loss, and Biodiversity Decline: An Overview of Recent Native Vegetation Clearance in Australia and its Implications for Biodiversity*, Department of Environment, Sports, and Territories, Biodiversity Series Paper No. 6, AGPS, Canberra.
Graetz, R., Wilson, M. and Campbell, S. (1995), *Landcover Disturbance Over the Australian Continent: A Contemporary Assessment*, Department of Environment, Sports, and Territories, Biodiversity Series Paper No. 7.

9.2.24. Item dd: Weighted lost natural capital services (LNCS)

The annual values of weighted lost natural capital services (LNCS) were calculated by applying the Ecosystem Health Index to Item *bb* as per equation (3.3).

9.2.25. Items ee, ff, and gg: GPI(1), GPI(2), and GPI(3)

The calculation of the various GPI figures for Australia, Victoria, and the Rest-of-Australia was achieved by summing the following items:

- GPI(1): Weighted CON(1) and Items *n, o, p, q, r, s, t,* and *dd*.
- GPI(2): Weighted CON(2) and Items *n, o, p, q, r, s, t,* and *dd*.
- GPI(3): Weighted CON(3) and Items *n, o, p, q, r, s, t,* and *dd*.

9.2.26. Item hh: Real GDP and GSP

The real GDP of Australia and the real GSP of Victoria were sourced directly from the national accounts. The Gross Product of the Rest-of-Australia was calculated by subtracting Victoria's GSP from Australia's GDP.

Source:

ABS, Catalogue No. 5204.0 and 5220.0.

Table 9.26: Item *aa*: Cost of long-term environmental damage - Australia, Victoria, and Rest-of-Australia, 1986-2003

	AUSTRALIA				VICTORIA								REST-of-AUST
	Energy consump.	Crude oil barrel equivalent	Annual contrib. to long-term env cost	Cumulative long-term env cost	Energy consump.	Victorian real GSP	Australian real GDP	Ratio of GSP/GDP	Crude oil barrel equivalent	Annual contrib. to long-term env cost	Cumulative long-term env cost		Cumulative long-term env cost
	(Petajoules)	(mill. of barrels)	($)	($)	(Petajoules)	($)	($)	(%)	(mill. of barrels)	($)	($)		($)
	a	(a/6.12)	(b x $2.50)	(d - c)	e	g	h	(g/h)	(e/6.12)	(j x $2.50)	(l + k)		(d - l)
Year	a	b	c	d	e	g	h	i	j	k	l		m
1985	-	-	-	-40,000.0	-	-	-	-	-	-	-10,400.0		-
1986	3,403	556.0	1,390.1	-41,390.1	932	111,277.3	427,989.7	0.260	152.3	380.9	-10,780.9		-30,609.2
1987	3,514	574.2	1,435.5	-42,825.6	963	113,913.9	438,130.5	0.260	157.3	393.3	-11,174.2		-31,651.4
1988	3,622	591.8	1,479.6	-44,305.1	992	120,027.6	461,644.7	0.260	162.2	405.4	-11,579.6		-32,725.6
1989	3,832	626.1	1,565.4	-45,870.5	1,050	124,854.1	480,208.1	0.260	171.6	428.9	-12,008.4		-33,862.1
1990	3,945	644.6	1,611.5	-47,482.0	1,099	131,737.0	498,126.1	0.264	179.6	449.1	-12,457.6		-35,024.5
1991	3,946	644.8	1,611.9	-49,094.0	1,077	128,882.9	497,644.9	0.259	176.0	439.9	-12,897.5		-36,196.5
1992	4,003	654.1	1,635.2	-50,729.2	1,064	125,822.0	498,980.7	0.252	173.8	434.5	-13,332.0		-37,397.2
1993	4,082	667.0	1,667.5	-52,396.7	*1,105*	-	-	-	180.6	451.4	-13,783.4		-38,613.3
1994	4,182	683.3	1,708.3	-54,105.0	1,103	-	-	-	180.2	450.6	-14,234.0		-39,871.0
1995	4,366	713.4	1,783.5	-55,888.5	1,152	-	-	-	188.2	470.6	-14,704.6		-41,183.9
1996	4,506	736.3	1,840.7	-57,729.2	1,185	-	-	-	193.6	484.1	-15,188.6		-42,540.5
1997	4,611	753.4	1,883.6	-59,612.7	1,203	-	-	-	196.6	491.4	-15,680.0		-43,932.7
1998	4,778	780.7	1,951.8	-61,564.5	1,280	-	-	-	209.2	522.9	-16,202.9		-45,361.6
1999	4,970	812.2	2,030.4	-63,594.9	1,324	-	-	-	216.4	540.9	-16,743.9		-46,851.1
2000	5,099	833.2	2,082.9	-65,677.9	1,364	-	-	-	222.8	557.0	-17,300.9		-48,377.0
2001	5,144	840.5	2,101.3	-67,779.2	1,381	-	-	-	225.6	564.0	-17,864.9		-49,914.3
2002	5,282	863.0	2,157.6	-69,936.7	1,423	-	-	-	232.5	581.3	-18,446.2		-51,490.5
2003	5,365	876.7	2,191.6	-72,128.4	1,451	-	-	-	237.1	592.7	-19,038.9		-53,089.5

Note: All values are in millions of 2002-2003 dollars except where indicated

Table 9.27: Item cc: Ecosystem Health Index (EHI) -- Australia and Victoria, 1986-2003

	AUSTRALIA					VICTORIA					
	Cleared vegetation	Significantly thinned vegetation	Significantly disturbed vegetation	Area of remnant vegetation	Ecosystem health index (EHI)	Cleared vegetation	Significantly thinned vegetation	Significantly disturbed vegetation	Area of remnant vegetation	Ecosystem health index (EHI)	
	(hectares)	(hectares)	(hectares)	(hectares)	1986 = 100.0	(hectares)	(hectares)	(hectares)	(hectares)	1986 = 100.0	
			(a + b)	(d - c)				(f + g)	(i - h)		
Year	a	b	c	d	e	f	g	h	i	j	
1985	-	-	-	500,000,000	-	-	-	-	14,609,189	-	
1986	500,000	500,000	1,000,000	499,000,000	100.0	7,776	7,776	15,552	14,593,637	100.0	
1987	500,000	500,000	1,000,000	498,000,000	99.8	7,776	7,776	15,552	14,578,085	99.9	
1988	700,000	700,000	1,400,000	496,600,000	99.5	10,438	10,438	20,876	14,557,209	99.8	
1989	500,000	500,000	1,000,000	495,600,000	99.3	8,298	8,298	16,595	14,540,614	99.6	
1990	650,000	650,000	1,300,000	494,300,000	99.1	6,157	6,157	12,314	14,528,300	99.6	
1991	337,350	337,350	674,700	493,625,300	98.9	2,450	2,450	4,900	14,523,400	99.5	
1992	337,350	337,350	674,700	492,950,600	98.8	2,450	2,450	4,900	14,518,500	99.5	
1993	337,350	337,350	674,700	492,275,900	98.7	2,450	2,450	4,900	14,513,600	99.5	
1994	337,350	337,350	674,700	491,601,200	98.5	2,450	2,450	4,900	14,508,700	99.4	
1995	337,350	337,350	674,700	490,926,500	98.4	2,450	2,450	4,900	14,503,800	99.4	
1996	424,444	424,444	848,888	490,077,612	98.2	2,450	2,450	4,900	14,498,900	99.4	
1997	424,444	424,444	848,888	489,228,724	98.0	2,450	2,450	4,900	14,494,000	99.3	
1998	424,444	424,444	848,888	488,379,836	97.9	2,450	2,450	4,900	14,489,100	99.3	
1999	424,444	424,444	848,888	487,530,948	97.7	2,450	2,450	4,900	14,484,200	99.3	
2000	400,000	400,000	800,000	486,730,948	97.5	2,450	2,450	4,900	14,479,300	99.2	
2001	400,000	400,000	800,000	485,930,948	97.4	2,450	2,450	4,900	14,474,400	99.2	
2002	400,000	400,000	800,000	485,130,948	97.2	2,450	2,450	4,900	14,469,500	99.1	
2003	400,000	400,000	800,000	484,330,948	97.1	2,450	2,450	4,900	14,464,600	99.1	

Table 9.28: Item *cc*: Ecosystem Health Index (EHI) - Rest-of-Australia, 1986-2003

	REST-of-AUST				
	Cleared vegetation (hectares)	Significantly thinned vegetation (hectares)	Significantly disturbed vegetation (hectares)	Area of remnant vegetation (hectares)	Ecosystem health index (EHI) 1986 = 100.0
			(a + b)	*(d - c)*	
Year	*a*	*b*	*c*	*d*	*e*
1985	-	-	-	485,390,811	-
1986	492,224	492,224	984,448	484,406,363	**100.0**
1987	492,224	492,224	984,448	483,421,915	**99.8**
1988	689,562	689,562	1,379,124	482,042,791	**99.5**
1989	491,703	491,703	983,405	481,059,386	**99.3**
1990	643,843	643,843	1,287,686	479,771,700	**99.0**
1991	334,900	334,900	669,800	479,101,900	**98.9**
1992	334,900	334,900	669,800	478,432,100	**98.8**
1993	334,900	334,900	669,800	477,762,300	**98.6**
1994	334,900	334,900	669,800	477,092,500	**98.5**
1995	334,900	334,900	669,800	476,422,700	**98.4**
1996	421,994	421,994	843,988	475,578,712	**98.2**
1997	421,994	421,994	843,988	474,734,724	**98.0**
1998	421,994	421,994	843,988	473,890,736	**97.8**
1999	421,994	421,994	843,988	473,046,748	**97.7**
2000	397,550	397,550	795,100	472,251,648	**97.5**
2001	397,550	397,550	795,100	471,456,548	**97.3**
2002	397,550	397,550	795,100	470,661,448	**97.2**
2003	397,550	397,550	795,100	469,866,348	**97.0**

9.2.27. Item ii: Australian and Victorian population

The Australian and Victorian populations were included to calculate per capita values of GDP/GSP and the GPI. The Rest-of-Australia population was determined by subtracting Victoria's population from the Australian population.
Sources:

ABS, Catalogue No. 3101.0, 3105.0.65.001, and 3311.2.55.001.

9.2.28. Items jj, kk, and ll: Per Capita GPI(1), GPI(2), and GPI(3)

In the the case of Australia's per capita GPI(1), GPI(2), and GPI(3), all three were calculated by dividing the three Australian GPI estimates by the Australian population. The per capita GPI(1), GPI(2), and GPI(3) estimates of Victoria were calculated in the same fashion but using the Victorian population. The same also applied for the Rest-of-Australia.

9.2.29. Item mm: Per Capita GDP and GSP

The per capita GDP of Australia and the Rest-of-Australia were determined by dividing their respective GDP values by the Australian and Rest-of-Australian populations. The per capita GSP of Victoria is equal to Victoria's GSP divided by the Victorian population.

9.2.30. Items nn, oo, pp, and qq: Index Values of per Capita GPI(1), GPI(2), GPI(3), and per capita real GDP/GSP

The index values of per capita GPI(1), GPI(2), GPI(3), and per capita real GDP/GSP for Australia, Victoria, and the Rest-of-Australia were produced by setting the 1986 values at 100.0 and adjusting the values for each year thereafter accordingly.

9.2.31. Item rr: Investment in Producer Goods (Private and Public) (INV)

The values pertaining to the annual investment in producer goods (INV) — both by the private and public sector — were drawn directly from the ABS national and state accounts. The values are revealed in Tables 9.2 (Australia), 9.3 (Victoria), and 9.4 (Rest-of-Australia). The values for the Rest-of-Australia were determined by subtracting Victoria's investment expenditure from that of Australia.

Data sources:

ABS, Catalogue No. 5204.0.
ABS, Catalogue No. 5220.0.

9.2.32. Item ss: Investment in all Human-made Capital (INV*)

Investment in all human-made capital (INV*) was calculated by following equation (3.4).

9.2.33. Item tt: Consumption of Fixed Capital (DEP)

The values representing the consumption of fixed capital (DEP) were obtained from the national and state accounts produced by the ABS. The Australian, Victorian, and Rest-of-Australian values appear in Tables 9.2, 9.3, and 9.4 respectively.
  Data sources:

ABS, Catalogue No. 5204.0.
ABS, Catalogue No. 5220.0.

9.2.34. Item uu: Depreciation of All Human-made Capital (DEP*)

The depreciation of all human-made capital (DEP*) was calculated as per equation (3.5).

9.2.35. Item vv: Net Capital Investment (NCI)

Net capital investment (NCI) was calculated by adhering to equation (3.6).

9.2.36. Item ww: Ratio of NCI to Depreciation of Human-made Capital (NCI/DEP*)

The NCI/DEP* ratios for Australia, Victoria, and the Rest-of-Australia were calculated by dividing net capital investment (NCI) by the depreciation of all human-made capital (DEP*).

9.2.37. Item xx: Growth Rate of Economy

The growth rate of the Australian, Victorian, and Rest-of-Australian economies was determined by observing the change in the NCI/DEP* ratio and assessing them in terms of the growth categorisations outlined in sub-section 3.5.7.

EXECUTIVE SUMMARY

Gross Domestic Product (GDP) and Gross State Product (GSP) are widely used to indicate the well-being of a nation's or state's citizens. Unfortunately, GDP and GSP fail to account for a large number of economic, social, and environmental benefits and costs associated with a growing national or state economy. Indeed, both indicators perversely treat many social and environmental costs as if they contribute positively to human well-being.

To overcome the deficiencies associated with both GDP and GSP, a Genuine Progress Indicator (GPI) is calculated for Victoria, Australia, and the Rest-of-Australia (Australia minus Victoria). The GPI is a new indicator specifically designed to ascertain the impact of a growing economy on sustainable well-being. Comprised of nineteen individual benefit and cost items, the GPI succeeds where GDP and GSP flounder because it integrates the wide-ranging impacts of economic growth into a single monetary-based index.

Upon making the GPI calculations for Victoria, Australia, and the Rest-of-Australia, our results show that, for the period 1986 to 2003, the average Victorian was better off than the average person living elsewhere in Australia (see Figure ES1). However, like the Rest-of-Australia, sustainable well-being in Victoria rose only marginally over the study period ($18,839 per Victorian in 1986 compared to $22,951 per Victorian in 2003).* Furthermore, the per capita GDP of the Rest-of-Australia and the per capita GSP of Victoria considerably overstated the genuine progress made in both Victoria and the Rest-of-Australia (e.g., in 2003, Victoria had a per capita GPI of $22,951 but a per capita GSP of $39,067) (see Figure ES2).

Victoria's superior performance vis-a-vis the Rest-of-Australia was due largely to its attenuated rate of native vegetation clearance and land degradation; its lower rate of unemployment and, more recently, its reduced rate of underemployment and labour underutilisation; and its considerably lower reliance on non-renewable resource extraction as a source of state income.

From a policy perspective, the advanced position of Victoria can be credited to more stringent environmental regulations and land clearance controls and a greater commitment to value-added production and excellence in higher education. Nevertheless, in view of the much smaller rise over the study period in Victoria's per capita GPI compared to the rise in its per capita GSP (21.8% vis-a-vis 46.1%), there is considerable room for improvement.

---

* This assessment is based on GPI (3) as our preferred indicator of sustainable well-being. For more on the three variations of GPI, see Chapter 3.

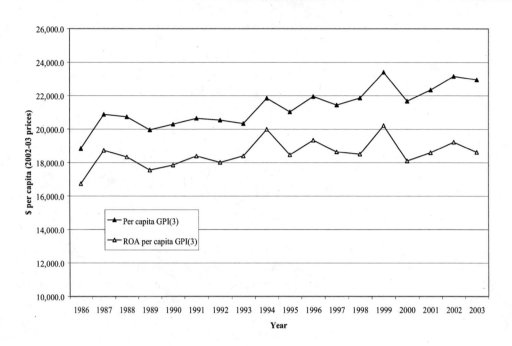

Figure ES1. Per capita GPI(3) of Victoria versus per capita GPI(3) of the Rest-of-Australia (ROA) (Australia minus Victoria), 1986-2003

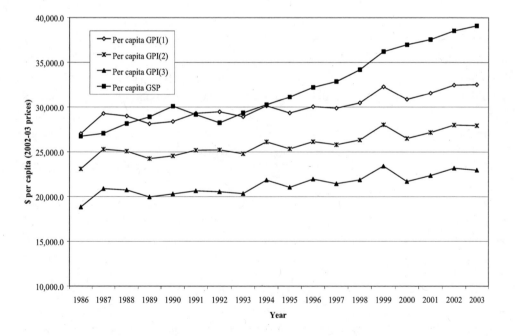

Figure ES2. Per capita Genuine Progress Indicator (GPI) (1), (2), and (3) and per capita Gross State Product (GSP): Victoria, 1986-2003

How can Victoria improve its overall performance? Major factors contributing to the stifled rise in Victoria's per capita GPI include a growing income disparity between the rich and poor during the 1990s; an unacceptable level of underemployment and long-term unemployment; a languishing welfare contribution from the state's publicly-provided service capital; a significant share of Australia's large overseas debt; a high cost of irrigation water use; and a bourgeoning long-term environmental cost caused by increased rates of per capita energy consumption. The cost of crime and family breakdown is another dampening factor that presumably reflects the continuing rich-poor disparity and a persistently large number of long-term unemployed citizens. More should therefore be done to:

- encourage resource use efficiency — in particular, energy efficiency;
- reduce air and urban waste-water pollution;
- limit Victoria's ecological footprint to one that is consistent with the regenerative and waste assimilative capacities of the state's natural capital;
- preserve and rehabilitate natural ecosystems and confine economic activities to areas where Victoria's natural environment has already been significantly modified;
- produce better quality rather than more goods (i.e., encourage production excellence);
- reduce the need to import goods by promoting import-replacement and not just export-augmentation initiatives;
- increase government investment in critical infrastructure to both augment the equitable share of welfare benefits enjoyed by all Victorians and stimulate private sector investment in high value-adding, resource-saving technologies;
- reduce the proportion of private sector investment being directed into non-productive, 'rent-seeking' ventures;
- increase public and private sector investment in human capital formation and minimise the mismatch between labour supply and demand that is currently leading to a shortage of skilled workers in some industry sectors;
- fight both observable and hidden unemployment head-on with an explicit commitment to a full employment objective.

The above listed developments can be facilitated by altering the mix of taxes, charges, and subsidies to: (a) reward 'welfare-increasing' business behaviour (e.g., activities that add greater value in production); (b) encourage the development and uptake of resource-saving technologies; and (c) penalise environmentally-destructive and 'welfare-harming' behaviour (e.g., high energy-intensive and polluting activities). Despite state government limitations, we believe the tax system can be creatively manipulated to induce behavioural and industrial process modifications that increase Victoria's GPI without having to rely so heavily — as is the current perception — on GSP growth. Moreover, this can be achieved without the need to increase the overall tax burden. In cases where environmental systems are clearly over-committed (e.g., the Murray-Darling Basin), it may be necessary for governments to introduce tradeable permit systems to reduce resource extractions. This, in turn, may require governments to purchase resource rights currently held by resource users.

Also required to improve Victoria's performance is a commitment on the part of governments to maintain Victoria's edge in higher education and a regulatory reform process that reduces compliance costs for Victorian businesses without forgoing the welfare benefits that regulations are designed to protect.

Industrial relations reform is also critical, however, it needs to involve the establishment of genuinely flexible labour markets that, rather than leading to greater casualisation of the workforce, provides workers with greater work-leisure-family options while simultaneously protecting full-time work entitlements. Industrial relations reform must also engender greater workplace trust and the establishment of well-defined internal career paths supported by a dual employer-employee commitment to on-going training and skills development.

ACKNOWLEDGMENTS

We are grateful for the research support provided by various members of the Victorian Department of Premier and Cabinet (DPC), especially Dr Marion Frere, Mark Burford, and Mark Lister, and from Catherine Andersson and Neil McLean on secondment to the DPC from the Australian Bureau of Statistics. We are also grateful to the support from Professors Peter Sheehan and Sardar Islam from the Centre for Strategic Economic Studies at Victoria University, and Professor Ralph Shlomowitz from the School of Business Economics at Flinders University.

REFERENCES

Abramowitz, M. (1979), 'Economic growth and its discontents', in M. Boskin (ed.), *Economics and Human Welfare*, New York, Academic Press.

Anielski, M. (2001), *The Alberta GPI Blueprint: The Genuine Progress Indicator (GPI) Sustainable Well-Being Accounting System*, Pembina Institute for Appropriate Development.

Arthur, W. (1989), 'Competing technologies, increasing returns, and lock-in by historical events', *The Economic Journal*, 99, pp. 116-131.

Asheim, G. (1994), 'Net national product as an indicator of sustainability', *Scandinavian Journal of Economics*, 96, pp. 257-265.

Asheim, G. (1996), 'Capital gains and net national product in open economies', *Journal of Public Economics*, 59, pp. 419-434.

Atkinson, A. (1970), 'On the measurement of inequality', *Journal of Economic Theory*, 2, pp. 244-263.

Atkinson, G. (1995), *Measuring sustainable economic welfare: A critique of the UK ISEW*, Working Paper GEC 95-08, Centre for Social and Economic Research on the Global Environment, Norwich and London.

Australian Bureau of Agricultural and Resource Economics (ABARE) (various), *Australian Forest and Wood Product Statistics*, AGPS, Canberra.

Australian Bureau of Statistics (ABS), Census of Population and Housing (various), AGPS, Canberra.

Australian Bureau of Statistics (ABS), Catalogue No. 1301.0 (various), *Yearbook Australia*, AGPS, Canberra.

Australian Bureau of Statistics (ABS), Catalogue No. 1301.2 (various), *Victorian Yearbook*, AGPS, Canberra.

Australian Bureau of Statistics (ABS) (2002), Catalogue No. 1370.0, *Measuring Australia's Progress: The Headline Indicators*, AGPS, Canberra.

Australian Bureau of Statistics (ABS), Catalogue No. 3101.0, *Australian Demographic Statistics*, AGPS, Canberra.

Australian Bureau of Statistics (ABS), Catalogue No. 3105.0.65.001, *Australian Historical Population Statistics*, AGPS, Canberra.

Australian Bureau of Statistics (ABS), Catalogue No. 3307.0.55.001, *Divorces, Australia*, AGPS, Canberra.

Australian Bureau of Statistics (ABS) (2002), Catalogue No. 3310.0, *Marriages and Divorces, Australia*, AGPS, Canberra.

Australian Bureau of Statistics (ABS), Catalogue No. 3311.2.55.001, *Demography, Victoria*, AGPS, Canberra.

Australian Bureau of Statistics (ABS) (2003), Catalogue No. 4102.0, *Australian Social Trends, 2003*, AGPS, Canberra.

Australian Bureau of Statistics (ABS) (1997), Catalogue No. 4326.0, *Mental Health and Well-being: Profile of Adults, Australia*, AGPS, Canberra.

Australian Bureau of Statistics (ABS) (1996), Catalogue No. 4441.0, *Voluntary Work, Australia, 1995*, AGPS, Canberra.

Australian Bureau of Statistics (ABS) (2001), Catalogue No. 4441.0, *Voluntary Work, Australia, 2000*, AGPS, Canberra.

Australian Bureau of Statistics (ABS) (2002), Catalogue No. 4509.0, *Crime and Safety*, AGPS, Canberra.

Australian Bureau of Statistics (ABS) (2004), Catalogue No. 4510.0, *Recorded Crime — Victims, Australia*, AGPS, Canberra.

Australian Bureau of Statistics (ABS), Catalogue No. 4603.0, *Cost of Environmental Protection, Australia: Selected Industries, 1991-92*, AGPS, Canberra.

Australian Bureau of Statistics (ABS), Catalogue No. 4604.0, *Energy and Greenhouse Gas Emissions Accounts, Australia*, AGPS, Canberra.

Australian Bureau of Statistics (ABS), Catalogue No. 4608.0 (various), *Mineral Account, Australia*, AGPS, Canberra.

Australian Bureau of Statistics (ABS) (2003), Catalogue No. 4613.0, *Australia's Environment: Issues and Trends*, AGPS, Canberra.

Australian Bureau of Statistics (ABS) (2003), Catalogue No. 4617.0, *Environment by Numbers*, AGPS, Canberra.

Australian Bureau of Statistics (ABS), Catalogue No. 5204.0 (various), *Australian System of National Accounts*, AGPS, Canberra.

Australian Bureau of Statistics (ABS) (2002), Catalogue No. 5206.0, *Australian National Accounts: National Income, Expenditure, and Product*, AGPS, Canberra.

Australian Bureau of Statistics (ABS), Catalogue No. 5220.0 (various), *Australian National Accounts: State Accounts*, AGPS, Canberra.

Australian Bureau of Statistics (ABS) (1994), Catalogue No. 5240.0, *Unpaid Work and the Australian Economy, 1992: Occasional Paper*, AGPS, Canberra.

Australian Bureau of Statistics (ABS) (2000), Catalogue No. 5240.0, *Unpaid Work and the Australian Economy, 1997: Occasional Paper*, AGPS, Canberra.

Australian Bureau of Statistics (ABS), Catalogue No. 5241.0, *National Balance Sheets for Australia: Issues and Experimental Estimates, 1989-1992*, AGPS, Canberra.

Australian Bureau of Statistics (ABS), Catalogue No. 5241.0.40.001, *Australian National Accounts: National Balance Sheet, 1999-2000*, AGPS, Canberra.

Australian Bureau of Statistics (ABS), Catalogue No. 5302.0, *Balance of Payments and International Investment Position, Australia*, AGPS, Canberra.

Australian Bureau of Statistics (ABS), Catalogue No. 6105.0, *Australian Labour Market Statistics*, AGPS, Canberra.

Australian Bureau of Statistics (ABS), Catalogue No. 6202.0, *Labour Force, Australia*, AGPS, Canberra.

Australian Bureau of Statistics (ABS), Catalogue No. 6202.2, *Labour Force, Victoria*, AGPS, Canberra.

Australian Bureau of Statistics (ABS), Catalogue No. 6203.0, *Labour Force, Australia*, AGPS, Canberra.

Australian Bureau of Statistics (ABS), Catalogue No. 6265.0, *Underemployed Workers, Australia*, AGPS, Canberra.

Australian Bureau of Statistics (ABS), Catalogue No. 6302.0, *Average Weekly Earnings, Australia*, AGPS, Canberra.

Australian Bureau of Statistics (ABS), Catalogue No. 6401.0, *Consumer Price Index, Australia*, AGPS, Canberra.

Australian Bureau of Statistics (ABS), Catalogue No. 7113.0, *Agriculture, Australia, 1999-2000*, AGPS, Canberra.

Australian Bureau of Statistics (ABS), Catalogue No. 8415, *Mining Operations, Australia*, AGPS, Canberra.

Australian Conservation Foundation-National Farmers' Federation (ACF-NFF) (2000), *Repairing the Country: A Five Point Plan*, An ACF and NFF Joint Vision.

Australian Institute of Criminology (2003), *Australian Crime: Facts and Figures, 2003*, AIC, Canberra.

ASSO (2004), *Obesity in Australian Adults: Prevalence Data* (www.asso.org.au).

Biodiversity Unit (1995), *Native Vegetation Clearance, Habitat Loss, and Biodiversity Decline: An Overview of Recent Native Vegetation Clearance in Australia and its Implications for Biodiversity*, Department of Environment, Sports, and Territories, Biodiversity Series Paper No. 6, AGPS, Canberra.

Bishop, R. (1993), 'Economic efficiency, sustainability, and biodiversity', *Ambio*, May 1993, pp. 69-73.

Blandy, R. and Brummitt, W. (1990), *Labour Productivity and Living Standards*, Allen & Unwin, Sydney.

Blinder, A. (1987), *Hard heads, Soft Hearts*, Addison-Wesley, New York.

Blum, H. (1962), *Times Arrow and Evolution*, Third Edition, Harper Torchbook, Princeton.

Breakspear C. and Hamilton, C. (2004), *Getting a Life: Understanding the Downshifting Phenomenon in Australia*, Australia Institute Discussion Paper, Number 62.

Brown, R. (2005), 'Reserve Bank buys into infrastructure debate', *Local Government Focus* (http://loc-gov-focus.aus.net/editions/2005/march/resbank.html)

Bureau of Resource Sciences (1998), *Australia's State of the Forests Report: 2003*, AGPS, Canberra.

Bureau of Resource Sciences (2003), *Australia's State of the Forests Report: 2003*, AGPS, Canberra.

Cameron, A., Welborn, T., Zimmit, P., Dunstan, D., Owen, N. and Salmon, J. (2003), Overweight and Obesity in Australia: The 1999-2000 Australian Diabetes, Obesity, and Lifestyle Study (AusDiab), *Medical Journal of Australia*, 178(9), pp.427-432.

Capra, F. (1982), *The Turning Point*, Fontana, London.

Castaneda, B. (1999), 'An index of sustainable economic welfare (ISEW) for Chile', *Ecological Economics*, 28 (2), pp. 231-244.

Clarke, M. and Islam, S. (2004), *Economics Growth and Social Welfare: Operationalising Normative Social Choice Theory*, North-Holland, Amsterdam.

CLMI (CofFEE) (2004), *An Alternative View of the Labour Market*, May 2004 (http://e1.newcastle.edu.au/coffee).

Commonwealth Bank of Australia (CBA) (2004), *HIA-Commonwealth Bank Affordability Report*, September Quarter 2004.

Connolly, S. and Munro, A. (1999), *Economics of the Public Sector*, Prentice Hall, Essex.

Costanza, R., Daly, H., and Bartholomew, J. (1991), 'Goals, agenda, and policy recommendations for ecological economics', in R. Costanza (ed.), *Ecological Economics: The Science and Management of Sustainability*, Columbia University Press, New York, pp. 1-20.

Costanza, R., Erickson, J., Fligger, K., Adams, A., Adams, C., Altschuler, B., balter, S., Fisher, B., Hike, J., Kelly, J., Kerr, T., McCauley, M., Montone, K., Rauch, M., Schmiedeskamp, K., Saxton, D., Sparacino, L., Tusinski, W. and Williams, L. (2004), 'Estimates of the Genuine Progress Indicator (GPI) for Vermont, Chittendon County, and Burlington from 1950 to 2000', *Ecological Economics*, 51, pp. 139-155.

Cowling, S., Mitchell, W. and Watts, M. (2003), 'The right to work versus the right to income', *Centre of Full Employment and Equity Working Paper* 03-08, July 2003.

Daly, H. (1979), 'Entropy, growth, and the political economy of scarcity', in V. K. Smith (ed.), *Scarcity and Growth Reconsidered*, John Hopkins University Press, Baltimore, pp. 67-94.

Daly, H. (1991), *Steady-State Economics*, Second edition, Washington DC, Island Press.

Daly, H. (1996), *Beyond Growth: The Economics of Sustainable Development*, Beacon Press, Boston.

Daly, H. and Cobb, J. (1989), *For the Common Good: Redirecting the Economy Toward Community, the Environment, and a Sustainable Future*, Beacon Press, Boston.

David, P. (1985), 'Clio and the economics of QWERTY', *American Economic Review*, 75 (2), pp. 332-337.

Department of Budget and Management (1984), *Victoria: The Next Step*, DBM, Melbourne.

Department of Environment, Sport, and Tourism (DEST) (1996), *Subsidies to the Use of Natural Resources*, Environmental Economics Research Paper No. 2, AGPS, Canberra.

Department of Sustainability and Environment (DSE) (2004), *Melbourne 2030 Implementation Reference Group Reports: Priority Implementation Issues Report*, Department of Sustainability and Environment, Victorian State Government, Melbourne.

Diefenbacher, H. (1994), 'The index of sustainable economic welfare in Germany', in C. Cobb and J. Cobb (eds.), *The Green National Product*, University Press of America, New York.

Dornbusch, R. and Fischer, S. (1990), *Macroeconomics*, 5th Edition, McGraw-Hill, New York.

Dosi, G. and Metcalfe, J. (1991), 'On some notions of irreversibility in economics', in P. Saviotti and J. Metcalfe (eds.), *Evolutionary Theories of Economic and Technological Change*, Harwood Academic Publishers, Reading.

Easterlin, R. (1974), 'Does economic growth improve the human lot? some empirical evidence', in P. David and R. Weber (eds.), *Nations and Households in Economic Growth*, Academic Press, New York.

El Serafy, S. (1989), 'The proper calculation of income from depletable natural resources', in Y. Ahmad, S. El Serafy, and E. Lutz, E. (eds.), *Environmental Accounting for Sustainable Development*, World Bank, Washington DC, pp. 10-18.

El Serafy, S. (1996), 'Weak and strong sustainability: natural resources and national accounting — part I', *Environmental Taxation and Accounting*, 1(1), pp. 27-48.

Fisher, I. (1906), *Nature of Capital and Income*, A. M. Kelly, New York.

Folke, C., Hammer, M., Costanza, R. and Jansson, A. (1994), 'Investing in natural capital — why, what, and how', in A. Jansson, M. Hammer, C. Folke, and R. Costanza (eds.), *Investing in Natural Capital*, Island Press, Washington DC, pp. 1-20.

Foster, R. (1996), *Australian Economic Statistics: 1949-50 to 1994-95*, Reserve Bank of Australia Occasional Paper No. 8.

George, S. (1988), *A Fate Worse than Debt*, New York, Grove.

Graetz, R., Wilson, M. and Campbell, S. (1995), *Landcover Disturbance Over the Australian Continent: A Contemporary Assessment*, Department of Environment, Sports, and Territories, Biodiversity Series Paper No. 7.

Guenno, G. and Tiezzi, S. (1998), *An Index of Sustainable Economic Welfare for Italy*, Working Paper 5/98, Fondazione Eni Enrico Mattei, Milan.

Hamilton, C. (1999), 'The genuine progress indicator: methodological developments and results from Australia', *Ecological Economics*, 30, pp. 13-28.

Hamilton, C. (2003), *Growth Fetish*, Allen and Unwin, Australia.

Hamilton, C., Hundloe, T. and Quiggin, J. (1997), *Ecological Tax Reform in Australia*, Australia Institute Discussion Paper, Number 10.

Hamilton, C. and Saddler, H. (1997), *The Genuine Progress Indicator: A new index of changes in well-being in Australia*, Australia Institute Discussion Paper, Number 14.

Hamilton, C. and Denniss, R. (2000), *Tracking Well-being in Australia: The Genuine Progress Indicator 2000*, Australia Institute Discussion Paper, Number 35.

Hamilton, K. (1994), 'Green adjustments to GDP', *Resources Policy*, 20 (3), pp. 155-168.

Hamilton, K. (1996), 'Pollution and pollution abatement in the national accounts', *Review of Income and Wealth*, 42, pp. 291-304.

Hicks, J. (1946), *Value and Capital*, Second Edition, Clarendon, London.

Howarth, R. and Norgaard, R. (1990), 'Intergenerational resource rights, efficiency, and social optimality', *Land Economics*, 66 (1), pp. 1-11.

Infochoice Banking (Ratewatch) (www.infochoice.com.au/banking/ratewatch/historical.asp) (accessed January 13, 2005)

Intergovernmental Panel on Climate Change (IPCC) (2001a), *Climate Change 2001: The Scientific Basis*, UNEP, Washington DC.

Intergovernmental Panel on Climate Change (IPCC) (2001b), *Climate Change 2001: Impacts, Adaptation, and Vulnerability*, UNEP, Washington DC.

Jackson, T. and Stymne, S. (1996), *Sustainable Economic Welfare in Sweden: A Pilot Index 1950-1992*, Stockholm Environment Institute, The New Economics Foundation.

Jackson, T., Laing, F., MacGillivray, A. Marks, N., Ralls, J. and Styme, S. (1997), *An Index of Sustainable Economic Welfare for the UK, 1950-1996*, University of Surrey Centre for Environmental Strategy, Guildford.

Lawn, P. (1998), 'In defence of the strong sustainability approach to national income accounting', *Environmental Taxation and Accounting*, 3 (1), pp. 29-47.

Lawn, P. (1999), 'On Georgescu-Roegen's contribution to ecological economics', *Ecological Economics*, 29 (1), pp. 5-8.

Lawn, P. (2000a), *Toward Sustainable Development: An Ecological Economics Approach*, CRC Press, Boca Raton.

Lawn, P. (2000b), 'Ecological tax reform: Many know why but few know how', *Environment, Development, and Sustainability*, 2, pp. 143-164.

Lawn, P. (2003), 'A theoretical foundation to support the Index of Sustainable Economic Welfare (ISEW), Genuine Progress Indicator (GPI), and other related measures', *Ecological Economics*, 44, pp. 105-118.

Lawn, P. (2004a), 'Reconciling the policy goals of full employment and ecological sustainability', *International Journal of Environment, Workplace, and Employment*, 1(1), pp. 62-81.

Lawn, P. (2004b), 'How well are resource prices likely to serve as indicators of natural resource scarcity?', *International Journal of Sustainable Development*, 7(4).

Lawn, P. (2004c), 'How important is natural capital in sustaining real output? Revisiting the natural capital/human-made capital substitutability debate', *International Journal of Global Environmental Issues*, 3(4), pp. 418-435.

Lawn, P. (2005), 'An assessment of the valuation methods used to calculate the Index of Sustainable Economic Welfare (ISEW), Genuine Progress Indicator (GPI), and Sustainable Net Benefit Index (SNBI)', *Environment, Development, and Sustainability*, 7, pp. 185-208.

Lawn, P. and Sanders, R. (1999), "Has Australia surpassed its optimal macroeconomic scale? Finding out with the aid of benefit and cost accounts and a sustainable net benefit index", *Ecological Economics*, 28 (2), pp. 213-229.

Lebergott, S. (1993), *Pursuing Happiness: American Consumers in the Twentieth Century*, Princeton University Press, Princeton.

Maler, K. (1991), 'National accounts and environmental resources', *Environmental and Resource Economics*, 1, pp. 1-15.

Max-Neef, M. (1995), 'Economic growth and quality of life', *Ecological Economics*, 15, pp. 115-118.

Mayhew, P. (2003), 'Counting the costs of crime in Australia', *Australian Institute of Criminology: Trends and Issues*, No. 247, AIC, Canberra.

Meadows, D. H., Meadows, D. L., Randers, J., and Behrens, W. III. (eds.) (1972), *The Limits to Growth*, Universe Books, New York.

Mitchell, W. and Carlson, E. (2002), 'Labour underutilisation in Australia and inflation', *Centre of Full Employment and Equity Working Paper* 02-10, September 2002.

Mitchell, W., Cowling, S. and Watts, M. (2003), *A Community Development Job Guarantee: A new Paradigm in Economic Policy*, Report by the Centre of Full Employment and Equity, University of Newcastle.

Mitchell, W. and Mosler, W. (2001), 'Fiscal policy and the Job Guarantee', *Centre of Full Employment and Equity Working Paper* 01-09, August 2001.

Mitchell, W. and Muysken, J. (2002), 'The Phillips Curve, the NAIRU, and unemployment asymmetries', *Centre of Full Employment and Equity Working Paper* 02-05, June 2002.

Mitchell, W. and Watts, M. (1997), 'The path to full employment', *Australian Economic Review*, 30, pp. 436-444.

Mitchell, W. and Watts, M. (2001), 'Addressing demand deficient unemployment: The Job Guarantee', *Centre of Full Employment and Equity Working Paper* 01-05, June 2001.

Modigliani, F. (2000), 'Europe's Economic Problems', *Carpe Oeconomiam Papers in Economics*, Third Monetary and Finance Lecture, Freiburg, April 6.

Moffat, I. and Wilson, M. (1994), 'An index of sustainable economic welfare for Scotland, 1980-1991', *International Journal of Sustainable Development and World Ecology*, 1, pp. 264-291.

Moulton, B. (2001), *The Expanding Role of Hedonic Methods in the Official Statistics of the United States*, Bureau of Economic Analysis Working Paper, June 2001.

Murray-Darling Basin Commission (M-DBC) (1989), *Basis for Economic Analysis Using the Murray-Darling Basin Commission's Computer Models*, M-DBC Technical Report, 89/6.

Murray-Darling Basin Commission (M-DBC) (various), *Water Audit Monitoring Report*, M-DBC.

National Coalition Against Poverty (NCAP) (2003), *Poverty Scorecard for Australia: 2003*.

Neumayer, E. (1999), 'The ISEW — Not an index of sustainable economic welfare', *Social Indicators Research*, 48, pp. 77-101.

Neumayer, E. (2000), 'On the methodology of the ISEW, GPI, and related measures: Some constructive suggestions and some doubt on the threshold hypothesis', *Ecological Economics*, 34, pp. 347-361.

Norgaard, R. (1988), 'Sustainable development: a co-evolutionary view', *Futures*, December 1988, pp. 606-620.

Norgaard, R. (1990), 'Economic indicators of resource scarcity: a critical essay', *Journal of Environmental Economics and Management*, 19, pp. 19-25.

Norris, K.(1989), *The Economics of Australian Labour Markets*, Longman Cheshire, Melbourne.

O'Riordan, T. (ed.) (1997), *Ecotaxation*, Earthscan, London.

Pearce, D., Markandya, A. and Barbier, E. (1989), *Blueprint for a Green Economy*, Earthscan, London.

Pearce, D. and Turner, R. (1990), *Economics of Natural Resources and the Environment*, Harvester Wheatsheaf, London.

Pezzey, J. (1993), *The Optimal Sustainable Depletion of Non-renewable Resources*, University College, London.

Pezzey, J. and Wiltage, C. (1998), 'The rise, fall, and sustainability of capital-resource economies', *Scandinavian Journal of Economics*, 100, pp. 513-527.

Premier's Round Table on Sustainability (2004), *Three, Four, Five: 3 Challenges, 4 Principles, 5 Actions for a Sustainable Future*, Report to the Government of South Australia on implementing the State Strategic Plan, 2004.

Redefining Progress (1995), 'Gross production vs genuine progress', Excerpt from the *Genuine Progress Indicator: Summary of Data and Methodology*, San Francisco, Redefining Progress.

Report of the House of Representatives Standing Committee on Legal and Constitutional Affairs (1998), *To Have and to Hold: Strategies to Strengthen Marriage and Relationships*, Commonwealth of Australia, Canberra.

Reserve Bank of Australia (RBA) (2004), *Quarterly Statistical Release*, October 2004 update (www.rba.gov.au/Statistics/measures_of_cpi.html)

Reserve Bank of Australia (RBA) (2005), *Opening Statement to the House of Representatives Standing Committee on Economics, Finance, and Public Administration*, 18 February, www.rba.gov.au/Speeches/2005.

Roodman, D. (1998), *The Natural Wealth of Nations: Harnessing the Market for the Environment*, Worldwatch Institute, Washington DC.

Rosenberg, K. and Oegema, T. (1995), *A Pilot ISEW for The Netherlands 1950-1992*, Instituut Voor Milieu — En Systeemanalyse, Amsterdam.

Salvation Army (2003), *Poverty in Australia: Fact Sheet*, The Salvation Army of Australia.

Sen (1997), 'Inequality, unemployment, and contemporary Europe', *International Labour Review*, 136(2), pp. 155-171.

Senate Community Affairs Reference Committee (2004), *A Hand Up not a Hand Out: Renewing the Fight Against Poverty*, Commonwealth of Australia, Canberra.

Stockhammer, E. and Hochreiter, H., Obermayr, B. and Steiner, K. (1997), 'The index of sustainable economic welfare (ISEW) as an alternative to GDP in measuring economic welfare: The results of the Australian (revised) ISEW calculation 1955-1992', *Ecological Economics*, 21, pp. 19-34.

Tiffen, R. and Gittins, R. (2004), *How Australia Compares*, Cambridge University Press, Sydney.

United Nations Statistical Division (1993), *Integrated Environmental and Economic Accounting*, Handbook of National Accounting, Series F, No.61, New York.

Victorian Department of Premier and Cabinet (VDPC) (2004), *Victoria: Leading the Way*, Economic Statement, April 2004.

Wackernagel, M., Onisto, L., Bello, P., Callejas Linares, A., Susana Lopez Falfan, S., Mendez Garcia, J., Suarez Guerrero, A. I., and Suarez Guerrero, Ma. G. (1999), 'National natural capital accounting with the ecological footprint concept', *Ecological Economics*, 29, pp. 375-390.

Walker, J. (1992), 'Estimates of the cost of crime in Australia in 1988', *Australian Institute of Criminology: Trends and Issues*, No. 39, AIC, Canberra.

Walker, J. (1997), 'Estimates of the cost of crime in Australia in 1996', *Australian Institute of Criminology: Trends and Issues*, No. 72, AIC, Canberra.

Williams, R. and Van Dyke, N. (2004), *The International Standing of Australian Universities*, Melbourne Institute of Applied Economic and Social Research, University of Melbourne.

Wilson, E. O. (1992), *The Diversity of Life*, Harvard University Press, Cambridge MA.

Zolotas, X. (1981), *Economic Growth and Declining Social Welfare*, New York University Press, New York.

INDEX

S

T